S0-ASI-370

15.90

DOG'S & EYE DEAD HORSE

THE COMPLETE GUIDE TO
Australian rhyming slang

GRAHAM SEAL

ABC
Books

The ABC 'Wave' device is a trademark of the
Australian Broadcasting Corporation and is used
under licence by HarperCollins*Publishers*Australia.

First published in Australia in 2009
by HarperCollins*Publishers*Australia Pty Limited
ABN 36 009 913 517
www.harpercollins.com.au

Copyright © Graham Seal 2009

The right of Graham Seal to be identified as the author of this work
has been asserted by him in accordance with the *Copyright
Amendment (Moral Rights) Act 2000.*

This work is copyright. Apart from any use as permitted under the
Copyright Act 1968, no part may be reproduced, copied, scanned,
stored in a retrieval system, recorded, or transmitted, in any form
or by any means, without the prior written permission of the publisher.

HarperCollins*Publishers*
25 Ryde Road, Pymble, Sydney, NSW 2073, Australia
31 View Road, Glenfield, Auckland 0627, New Zealand
A 53, Sector 57, Noida, UP, India
77–85 Fulham Palace Road, London W6 8JB, United Kingdom
2 Bloor Street East, 20th floor, Toronto, Ontario M4W 1A8, Canada
10 East 53rd Street, New York NY 10022, USA

National Library of Australia Cataloguing-in-Publication data:

Seal, Graham, 1950-
   Dog's eye and dead horse / Graham Seal.
   ISBN: 978 0 7333 2589 2 (pbk.)
   Australianisms.
   English language–Slang–Dictionaries.
   English language–Australia–Slang.
   English language–Australia–Terms and phrases.
427.994

Cover design and illustration by Matt Stanton
Internal design and layout by Agave Creative Group
Typeset in 10.5/12pt Garamond Premier Pro
Printed and bound in Australia by Griffin Press
70gsm Classic used by HarperCollins*Publishers* is a natural, recyclable product
made from wood grown in sustainable forests. The manufacturing processes conform to the
environmental regulations in the country of origin, New Zealand.

5 4 3 2 1   09 10 11 12 13

CONTENTS

How to Use this Book

The dictionary entries are arranged alphabetically according to the rhyming slang term, followed by the word with which it rhymes. Figures in parentheses (1, etc.) are given where terms have more than one rhyme. Any necessary translations or explanations are given, as is any information regarding origins, usage, provenance, etc. Dates are usually the earliest known or assumed Australian appearance of the term, although reference is often made to dates and usage in other countries. The term 'obsolete' is used sparingly, often with a question mark, to indicate the strong likelihood that a term is no longer current. This is speculative, as rhyming slangs can persist among older speakers and are occasionally revived from the usage of previous generations. Finally, 'see also' references to related rhyming slangs elsewhere in the dictionary are given where appropriate.

The Thematic Categories section arranges rhyming slang terms according to their subject reference/s. These are arranged alphabetically within each section and sub-section. Readers may find this a useful way to access the dictionary. Occasionally, a rhyming slang appears in more than one category.

INTRODUCTION:
Roast Pork the Bill Lang

I think I had better tell you the *grim and gory* right
from the *horse and cart*. When I saw you off on the
thunder and rain at Weenia, I was feeling pretty lonely
being left on my *Pat Malone*. So I rambled over to the
rubbity dub and had a pint of *oh my dear*. In fact I had
several and finished up in the dead house, broke to the
wide. But they left me my *Willy Wag* and gave me a bit
of tucker.

FROM 'DUKE' TRITTON'S RHYMING SLANG LETTER

Australian rhyming slang was first noticed in the speech of Sydney and
Melbourne larrikins in the late 19th century, although it was probably on
at least some lips during the 1880s, and perhaps much earlier. Larrikins
were flashily dressed, pipe-smoking and often antisocial youths who
operated in all-male gangs known as 'pushes'. They were noted users of
slang, for which they had quick ears and ready tongues.

The earliest known example of Australian rhyming slang is the term
Jimmy Grant for 'immigrant'. It was noted in Australia in 1859, and
more than a decade earlier in New Zealand. The term does not appear
in British rhyming slang. There is then a puzzling 30-or-so year gap
before anyone mentions Australians talking this way. In 1900, a writer
for the Sydney *Truth* observed that 'Cockney slang is quickly displacing
the old push lingo in Sydney.' The examples given in the article were
Cockney rhyming slang:

I 'ad a brown *I'm afloat*, a green *Jacky Lancashire* in me
left 'andsky and tan *daisy roots*. When I meets the *cheese
and kisses* and pratted orf down the *frog and toad*, I tell
you I was a bit orl right.

By way of translation, this resplendent dresser wants us to know that he
was wearing a brown coat, a green handkerchief (probably around his

neck in the style of the time) and tan boots. When he met his missus and they walked down the road together, he (no reference to her, a characteristically larrikin omission) thought he looked very impressive.

As well as making use of what seems like a good supply of Cockney rhymes, it was around this time that Australians began to develop their own variety of this colourful form of streetspeak.

What Is Rhyming Slang?

Rhyming slang is a sometimes-complex form of language play that rhymes the names of everyday objects, places and experiences with (usually) two words to form a brief, sometimes odd or colourful couplet. Some common examples are *frog and toad* for road, *dog's eye* for pie and *dead horse* for sauce.

Once a particular rhyming slang has been established among its speakers, it may often be shortened, or 'clipped'. So *trouble and strife* becomes simply *the trouble*; *old China plate* becomes just *China*; and *thief and robber* simply *thief*. This shortening is the preferred mode of conversation between competent rhyming slangsters.

A further elaboration is to use the shortened form to refer to something quite different. An *Aristotle*, for example, is a bottle; usually abbreviated to just *Aris*. This is close enough to 'arse' for Aris to be used as a playful term for that part of the body. It is also possible for an accomplished user to rhyme on the shortened slang form of the original, as in the World War II example of *ocean liner* for mate — a rhyme on *China*, the short form of *China plate*.

Where It Came from and Where It Went

One of the mysteries surrounding rhyming slang is exactly when it originated. Rhyming slang was first recorded as common parlance among Londoners — not only Cockneys — in the late 1850s, although it is thought to have been spoken in the 1840s or perhaps a little earlier. Certainly there is only passing mention of it by observers of everyday life and language such as Charles Dickens and Henry Mayhew in the first half of the 19th century. The apparently sudden appearance of this poetic playspeech in the mouths of Cockneys and costermongers inspired various theories about its origins. Some thought that it was the clandestine language of street ballad-sellers, or *paper-fakers*. Others suggested it was a secret criminal code, or was perhaps adapted from the street speech of beggars.

Whatever its exact origins — and none of these suggestions needs to be mutually exclusive — rhyming slang has been a vital part of London's linguistic life. It was certainly popular and widely known by the 1890s, when the writer 'Doss Chidderdoss' (A. R. Marshall) wrote entire poems in rhyming slang for sporting periodicals. Rhyming slang was also used in the now mostly obsolete British racecourse sign language of *tic tac*, and it appears in slightly adapted form in the venerable gambling game known as 'Bingo', or in its earlier form of 'Housey-housey' or just 'Housey'. In Bingo, the number sixty-six is usually rhymed — almost — on *clicketty-click*; two may be called as *me and you*; five may be called *man alive* or *Jack's alive*; and *dirty Gertie* is often thirty, among many other variations.

The criminal connections of a few rhyming slang terms have led some to conclude that the Australian version originated in the 'flash', or 'kiddy', language of the transportation era. This is not so. Rhyming slang was, and is, used in specialised forms by criminals and those with ambivalent relationships to the law, such as patterers and other vagabonding entrepreneurs. However, it did not originate as a secret criminal language but more likely as a playful form of linguistic sparring within London's Cockney and itinerant communities, quite possibly with some stimulation from the many Irish navvies who lived and worked in England in the 18th and 19th centuries.

Rhyming slang appears to be originally an English rather than a British phenomenon. Apparently it did not exist previously in Scots or Welsh varieties of English though, having been exported — it is thought — to Irish English and possibly to Irish Gaelic and some dialect forms of speech. It is reportedly spoken in Scotland and Northern Ireland.

As well as spreading to various parts of Britain, rhyming slang migrated to other primarily English-speaking nations, including Ireland, New Zealand, Canada, South Africa and the USA. While these parts of the world have greater or lesser repertoires of rhyming slang, it is probably true to say that Australia has been the place outside England where rhyming slang is most broadly spoken. As well as borrowing and adapting many British rhymes, Australians have developed a large stock of local rhyming slang.

Early Years

There is some evidence that rhyming slang was in Australian streetspeak at least as early as the 1880s, and perhaps before. The single *Jimmy Grant* (immigrant) example from 1859, recorded here around the same time as British collectors were first documenting London rhyming slang, does raise the slight possibility that the form existed in Australia from as early as it seems to have appeared in England. But if so, it seems that no one bothered to make a note of it.

It has been suggested that Cockney rhyming slang became popular in Australia through the influence of touring British theatrical entertainments. Some of these shows featured this then-fashionable form of street speech, which also became popular in British music hall songs. The larrikin ear for linguistic novelty, colour and vulgarity would certainly have been attuned to its cheeky rhymes, rhythms and occasional alliterations. While there is probably some truth in this view, the continual arrival of British migrants throughout the 19th and early 20th century is the most likely explanation for the presence of rhyming slang in Australian speech. The street life of Sydney was still noticeably Cockney in the 1820s and probably for some time after. The author of *A Walk Through Sydney*, published in 1829, noted of the street sellers calling their wares that, 'The cries of Sydney are all genuine Cockney.' Australia, despite its growing sense of national identity, was still a strongly British — predominantly English — culture in which imported speech forms were widely spoken. Much late 19th-century Australian rhyming slang drew heavily on that spoken in England. *Pen and ink* for stink; *trouble and strife* for wife; *cheese and kisses* for missus are just a few examples of rhyming slang terms common to Britain and Australia.

But as well as these borrowed items, Australians fairly quickly developed a range of terms with a salty local flavour, increasingly spicing the vernacular of the period with home-grown flights of miniature rhyming fantasy. A relatively early piece of evidence for the general provenance of rhyming slang is a novelty letter written by the traditional singer, yarnspinner and autobiographer 'Duke' Tritton, allegedly in 1905, although probably composed about a decade later. The letter includes the Cockneyisms *China plate* for mate and *frog and toad* for road, among others. But it also uses some distinctively Australian specimens, such as *steak and kidney* for the city of Sydney, *Joe Blakes* for snakes and *thief and robber* for cobber.

World War I

Although there are doubts about the accuracy of the early date of Tritton's letter, it seems reasonable to assume that British and Australian rhyming slang developed along their separate ways from around the early 20th century. Certainly, the form was well established among Australian troops by World War I, when such terms as *pork and cheese* for Portuguese and *disaster* for piastre, *mad mick* (a pick), *plink plonk* (vin blanc) and *Henry Tate* (RE8, a two-seater reconnaissance plane, used by the Australian Flying Corps) were recorded among Australian troops.

By way of comparison, a rhyming slang letter written by a British soldier in 1917 included none of the Australian terms that by then were being bandied about by Diggers. But it did contain a number of the Cockney items that have also been heard in Australian rhyming slang, including *old pot-and-pan* for old man (father), *pig's ear* for beer, *nanny-goats* for throats and *you-and-me* for tea. While it is unlikely that this letter was ever posted, its appearance in a trench journal, or soldier newspaper, provides a rare earful of rhyming slang in the British trenches of the Great War. According to the editorial comment, rhyming slang was an often-heard feature of trench talk.

From this evidence it is reasonable to suggest that the British and Australian (and New Zealand) forms of rhyming slang came into contact through military cooperation, as well as during the leave periods of Australian troops in 'Blighty'.

Between the Wars

Little definite is known of rhyming slang during the interwar years, 1919–39. But the names of personalities from the early cinema and of sports celebrities used for rhymes, as well as the rhymes on other Australian vernacular terms, suggest that the form was alive and well.

Rhymes on common slang terms for currency, such as *Riverina* for 'deaner' (one shilling), *horse and dray* for 'trey' (threepence) and *Jill and Jack* for 'zac' (sixpence) were numerous. These words had been around for a long time. 'Deaner' had been in use at least as early as 1882, while 'trey' and 'zac' were recorded in the 1890s. Given the frequent application of rhyming to general slang terms for currency (for money terms, see Part 2: Thematic Categories), it would be unusual for these words not to rapidly attract rhymes.

The period between the wars also generated items such as *macaroni* for baloney (from the Americanism for nonsense or lies), *Mary Lou* for blue (credit) and *Willy Lees* for fleas, as well as perpetuating already well-established items from the late 19th and early 20th centuries.

World War II

World War II (1939–45) produced another burst of rhyming among Australian soldiers. War correspondent Gavin Long heard it frequently and wrote down many examples. So common was rhyming slang at this time that it featured in the *Bluey and Curley* comic strip carried by the *Sydney Mirror* in 1942:

> **Struth, a *bag of coke* comes into the *Sydney Harbour* for a *dig in the grave*, and finds the *pitch and toss* has gone down th' *field of wheat*. Blimey no *Mark Foy* is going to give me a *dig in the grave*. You might take me *Port Melbourne Pier* off.**

Explanation: a bloke comes into the barber's shop for a shave only to find that the boss has gone down the street. The bloke exclaims that no boy — as in the barber's apprentice — is going to give him a shave as he might cut his ear off.

The compilers of the *Instructions for American Servicemen in Australia 1942* thought it important to provide some examples of rhyming slang to unsuspecting American service personnel. These were *trouble and strife* (wife), *rubbadedub* (pub), *Joe Blakes* (snakes), *Oscar Asche* (cash), *plates of meat* (feet) and *John* (for a cop, or police officer, from the rhyming slang *Johnhop*). They could have added *fiddly-did* for quid (or pound sterling), *ginger beer* for an engineer (later, the term was used to mean a queer, or homosexual), *Dorothy Gish* for a dish of food, *Betty Grable* for a table, and *Gregory Peck* for neck, to mention but a few in circulation at this time.

Another Mystery

In 1944, the American lexicographer David Maurer set out to discover why some criminals in his country, especially in gaols, used rhyming slang. Intriguingly, these criminals held a strong belief that this lingo had been brought to America by wayfaring Australian criminals and sometimes the Americans called it 'Australian slang'.

Using the pan-American network of criminal informants he had developed over many years, together with the assistance of the Australian lexicographer Sidney Baker, Maurer came up with some interesting findings. While there may well have been more than a few Australian con men, thieves and forgers disgracing American shores, attracted in part by the California gold rushes of the 1840s, there was a statistical anomaly. Of the 352 rhyming slang terms collected from American *hooks* (crooks), only three per cent — 12 terms — could be traced to Australia, and almost half of the rest came from Britain. Even though the US crims thought of rhyming slang as Australian, it did not seem to be an accurate depiction.

Maurer wrote that American criminal rhyming slang 'appears to be Australian only in a trivial degree; it is infinitely more English (or Cockney) and still more is it indigenously American'. The Australian-only terms used in America included *Captain Cook* for look, *Hawkesbury Rivers* for the shivers and *Mad Mick* for a pick(axe). Another Australian-influenced usage was *Pat Malone* for being alone.

Neat and tidy though this all appears, there are still some mysteries. One American rhyming slang term sounds to be of unmistakeably Australian origin. *Cockies clip* is a *dip* (a pickpocket) in American rhyming slang. A *cocky* is an Australian term for a small farmer, and not known in America. *Clip* refers to the wool harvest, also an Australianism. However, *cockies clip*, while not unknown here was, and is, rare in Australian colloquial speech, criminal or otherwise. A similar perplexing example was *Cobar shower*. Cobar is a small town in outback New South Wales and the term is used in Australian vernacular to denote a dust storm. However, the term exists as Australian speech rhyming slang for a flower, which is also its American criminal usage.

Maurer and Baker compared their respective collections, did some calculations and arrived at a number of reasonable conclusions. It seemed clear that the clandestine travel routes of the internationally mobile criminal connected Britain, Australia and America into a powerful linguistic communication channel. Maurer had found that the majority of rhyming slang was concentrated on the West Coast, the most convenient point of entry and departure for Australians. Although weaker in the east, rhyming slang was still spoken there, and Maurer found that its internal migration followed the usual criminal tracks across the country. A lot of rhyming slang was used in prisons and it was a general criminal form of expression rather than one associated with particular specialisations, such as safe crackers (*jug heavies*) or pick pockets (*whizzers*), and so on.

After the War

In the post-World War II era, rhyming slang continued to be spoken by many Australians, if not perhaps as widely as during the war years themselves. Rhyming slang may have retreated to its lodging in certain forms of occupational speech. Judging by the number of rhyming slang terms with sporting connotations (a persistent connection from the earliest years of rhyming slang's popularity), the form almost certainly continued to be used by followers of, and commentators on, popular sports. These were cricket, Rugby League, Australian Rules football and horseracing, in which fields rhyming slang is still heard today.

The many rhyming slang terms based on the names of film stars and sports personalities of the 1940s and '50s strongly suggests that the form continued to be a firm element of colloquial speech throughout those decades. The male generation that came to maturity in that period and who served in the armed forces, where rhyming slang had been pervasive, ensured its peacetime persistence in Australian colloquial speech.

Rhyming slang seems to have also been a common form of discourse among wharfies or stevedores and to have had some purchase among theatricals, musicians and what is now known as the hospitality industry. Baker provides an example of a Sydney social club steward, quite possibly a football club, communicating a table order to the barman in the kind of impenetrable code that could be heard in football and RSL clubs during the 1960s and '70s:

> **Three lilies, new; Paterson Laing, old; a oncer, rogans the Kembla.**

This translates as: 'Three schooners of new beer, two schooners of old beer, one pound received for payment and give me the change in shillings', all clipped from *Lily of Laguna*; *Paterson, Laing and Bruce* (a deuce, or two); *rogans* (for shillings); and *Kembla Grange*. ('Oncer' was general slang for one pound rather than rhyming slang.)

The 1970s

The advent of cheaper airfares from the 1970s allowed a greater number of Australians to travel more frequently than previously. The 'grand tour' became a rite of passage for youthful adventurers, the majority of whom spent most, or at least a good part of their trips, in Britain.

Here, like their World War I forebears, they were confronted with a culture towards which they often felt the need to project a distinctive national identity. As did the Diggers of World War I, they made a fetish of Australian folk speech, creating the image of the beer-sodden and foul-mouthed Aussie.

This remarkable cultural moment was, perhaps unfortunately, captured to some extent in the Australian film genre known as the 'ocker movies'. In these films, bizarre colonial creations like 'Bazza' Mackenzie, played by Barry Crocker (himself the subject of a rhyming slang), wielded uncouth Australianisms, including rhyming slang, against the unsuspecting 'poms'. Creator of the Bazza character, Barry Humphries, also played to the ocker stereotype in many of his stage creations, such as the especially repellent Sir Les Patterson. In these circumstances, rhyming slang provided the perfect vehicle for testing the always edgy love–hate relationship between Britain and Australia — a linguistic equivalent of the rivalries involved in cricket and rugby football. A good deal of rhyming slang originates in the 1960s and '70s, as suggested by the many terms from this era included in the dictionary.

Today

It is possible to argue that rhyming slang is a form of language play that features in the folk speech of intermittent generations. Its first serious Australian appearance is in the late 19th century, then around twenty years later in World War I, again in World War II and, if the popularity of the 'ocker' films and image of the 1970s is any guide, once more in that era. We might expect, then, to hear it again from around the beginning of the present century. If the more recent examples found in this book are any guide, the form has certainly not died out and is being renewed with rhymes on contemporary figures such as *Stuart Diver* (a survivor), *Mal Meninga* (finger) and *David Boon* (spoon). While we are not in the midst of a rhyming slang mania, the form is far from obsolete, even if many of its older and more obscure manifestations are rarely heard. Australian rhyming slang has its periods of greater or lesser popularity, but it never fades entirely away. Like most forms of folklore it hibernates beneath the surface of everyday life, kept alive mostly in the mouths of in-groups and the memories of older speakers, always available to be summoned back to linguistic duty when times demand. And while they may not use it themselves, many individuals will be aware of at least the more common terms and, when questioned, recall relations or colleagues who have spoken it.

The worldwide web and email mean that rhyming slang that was once restricted to certain regions or countries may now be rapidly spread and subsequently adopted in different countries. This is evident in the use of terms like *Britney Spears* for 'beers' in Britain as well as in Australia, and quite possibly elsewhere. This trend is likely to continue the traditions of rhyming on the names of celebrities, of which the current era seems heavily supplied. Rhyming slang may well become more frequently created, more quickly diffused but also more rapidly dated as users move on to the next fad, a feature also apparent in relation to other forms of modern slang. Whatever the future of rhyming slang might be, it has played a significant role in Australia's history and culture.

National Identity

The distinctive and colourful folk speech form of rhyming slang has been prevalent at a number of important moments in our history, particularly up to the time of Federation in 1901 and during both world wars. While rhyming slang is probably no longer as frequently employed as it was during those periods, it is still an important element of the greater Australian lingo. As it often did in the past, rhyming slang continues to have a relationship to popular notions of national identity as expressed and projected through colloquial speech.

This enduring aspect of our folk culture is a characteristically Australian response to the perceived need to articulate nationality, not only within Australia but also beyond, particularly in situations where we are confronted or challenged by the presence of 'others' in large numbers, whether at home or abroad. This was especially the case in World War I and again, with the addition of a large American presence, in World War II. Subsequent generations' travel encounters with 'others' since the 1970s have also produced a revival of the colourful possibilities of rhyming slang.

Australian colloquial speech often forms the basis for distinctively Australian rhymes. Examples include *willy wag* for a swag; *knock me silly* for a billy(can); *billy lids* for kids; *cattle dog* for catalogue. The rhymes *chocolate frogs* and *hollow logs* both refer to the derogatory term 'wogs', applied originally to migrants from southern Europe in the post-World War II period, although now often used more broadly. The same applies to *Dapto dog* (usually just a *Dapto*), a New South Welshism after the famous dog races, the Dapto Dogs. The famous comic strip character *Ginger Meggs* provides an irresistible rhyme for legs, and there are many other home-grown varieties in the following pages.

Gender

Rhyming slang is also a significant speech form in relation to gender. Most observers of the form have noted its almost totally masculine appeal and usage. Women may use the occasional term but they rarely converse in extended rhyming slang. While this is true of the form in Britain and America, it is especially so in Australia. Here, our strongly masculine history and persistent culture of mateship have made rhyming slang the preserve of the *bag of coke* since its beginnings. The terms chosen for rhyming slang purposes are powerfully male in orientation and subject, including a variety of terms for women and their sexual attributes.

The male-dominated culture of the urban larrikin seems to have been the incubator for our form of rhyming slang. It received another major boost from 1914, when the largest single assemblage of Australians ever created was the almost totally male grouping of the First AIF. And once again, between 1939 and 1945, rhyming slang blossomed within the Australian military forces — mainly, it seems, among foot soldiers rather than the navy or the fledgling air force, probably because these were smaller professional bodies with their own traditions of argot and jargon (which include the odd example of rhyming slang). While the number of Australian males involved in fighting the war in Vietnam was relatively small, this era did produce another brief blooming of rhyming slang, with terms like *septic tank* for 'Yank' becoming established.

Rhyming slang is also used a great deal by sporting practitioners, their followers and their chroniclers, the sports journalists. Yet again, these are mostly sports played by males, although the horseracing industry — these days slightly less gender-restricted — also makes extensive use of the form. The sporting connection has been a constant element of Australian rhyming slang, with terms like *Adrian Quist* (tennis), *Edgar Britt* (horseracing) among earlier examples and more recent entries such as *Frank Hyde* (Rugby League) and *George Moore* (horseracing). Rhymes formed on the names of football celebrities are particularly regional, given the variable popularity of the various codes in different states. Interestingly, there seem to be few rhymes formed on the names of noted players of other sports, apart from tennis. These sports all have, or had, close connections with popular conceptions of national identity.

A specialised form of rhyming slang retains a firm hold within prisons. A few valuable collections of prison slang have been made by amateur convict lexicographers and these, together with the informants of other researchers, confirm the broad use of rhyming slang among male criminals, past and present. Other largely male collectivities in which rhyming slang has been noted include wharf labourers, folk and jazz musicians and a sprinkling in the speech of sailors.

A further reflection of this masculinism is revealed in the thematic grouping of rhyming slang terms. There are no female terms for males, while there are a considerable number of mostly vulgar male terms for women. Some recorded examples of rhyming slang highlight the connection between the form and male sexual interests, with its use in phrases such as, 'Look at the *Vatican cities* on that *three wheeler*.' Similarly, with another major category of rhyming slang, the naming of clothes, most of the items refer to male rather than female apparel.

Cultural Influences

Australian rhyming slang accurately reflects the main cultural, political and economic realities of our past and present. A significant proportion of the repertoire is borrowed or derived from English usage, probably of London, including *Bristol/Manchester Cities, trouble and strife, pen and ink*, etc. Another significant sector shows the influence of America, especially American popular culture, with many of the proper names used as rhymes being those of Hollywood stars or other celebrities. Some examples are *Clark Gable* (table), *Betty Grable* (table), *Bob Hope* (soap) and even going back as far as *Lillian Gish* (dish/fish) and *Mae West* (breast), both personalities from the very early days of cinema. As our history and culture have, to date, been strongly influenced by these countries it is not surprising to find that we have based some of our distinctive rhyming slang on prominent names from elsewhere, as we have with other forms of folk speech.

Irish influence in Australian rhyming slang can be clearly heard in items such as *Rory O'Moore* (floor) and *Dublin Fair* (hair), and rhymes on Irish names like Maguire and Malone. Even eponymous heroines of sentimental songs, such as *Kathleen Mavourneen* for 'morning', appear — although this seems to be an Australian original. Solid though these contributions are, given the preponderance of Irish in the Australian

19th-century population and since, these items are relatively few in number.

Despite these multicultural influences, Australian rhyming slang contains numerous derogatory terms for those who originated many of its forms. 'Pom' and 'Yank' are terms used as mild banter by most Australians, although they can be offensive to those against whom they are directed — who do not necessarily share the angular sense of humour practised by many Australians. Try explaining to American visitors why they need not be offended at being cheerily referred to as *septic tanks* and *seppos*.

Characteristics

Most rhyming slang takes the form of a couplet on a single term. There are very few rhyming slang terms that are longer than two words and few shorter. It is arguable that words rhymed on one monosyllabic word — such as *sprouse* for grouse — are not true rhyming slang anyway. They certainly lack the rhythmic impact of the 'X + X' formula which, when properly used, invokes not only the rhyme but broader, sometimes whimsical, sometimes ironic connotations, as in *Harold Holt*, to bolt, the *red hots* for the trots (diarrhoea), *trick cyclists* for psychiatrists and *mystery bags* for snags, or sausages.

Another rhyming slang characteristic is its convenient capacity for euphemism. Rhymes like *brown bread*, *garden shed* and *kangaroo Ted* humorously avoid the reality of death. The threat of cancer is euphemised in a great many terms, including *Johnny Dancer*, *candy dancer* and *Mario Lanza*. The numerous rhymes for a variety of vulgarisms, including swear words, body parts and functions, as well as sexual acts, perform a similar role.

Rhyming slang is also useful as double entendre insofar as the often-vulgar reference of the full term can be disguised by using only (usually) the first part of the rhyme, as in *sheep* (*shanker*) for wanker, or masturbator, and *Wellington* (*boot*), or just *Wello*, for root, where the meaning is sexual intercourse.

An obvious and appealing characteristic of rhyming slang is its colourful and generally visual nature. Terms such as *dog's eye* (pie), *Noah's Ark* (shark), *kid blister* (sister) involve metaphorical juggling that conjures up humorous images. This feature is amplified when a number of rhyming slang terms are run together in combinations such as, 'Give me a *dog's eye* and *dead horse*' or 'Take a *butcher's hook* at the *Ballarat* on that *artichoke*' (Take a look at the hat on that bloke). Even the more banal forms can be made to sparkle when used in a sustained sequence of speech, such as that given in the *Bulletin* of 18 January 1902:

> *Me mother's away*, as I was *swiftly flowing up the field of wheat* in the *bread-and-jam*, *a heavenly plan* with a big *charming mottle* of *O-my-dear* sticking out of his *sky rocket fancy-sashed* the *girl-abductor* on his *bundle-of-socks* with it 'cos he wouldn't let him have a *virgin bride* for nothing.

This translates as: 'The other day, as I was going up the street in a tram, a man with a big bottle of beer sticking out of his pocket bashed the conductor over the 'think-box' (head) with it (that is, the bottle) because he wouldn't let him have a ride for nothing.'

While many rhyming slangs are fairly pedestrian and predictable, the repertoire contains some startlingly colourful, whimsical and apt items. Some examples include *dodge and shirk* for work, *sudden death* for bad breath, *Mallee root* for a prostitute, *heavenly plan* for man, *tiddlywink* for a drink — incorporating the folk term for being mildly drunk — *Moreton Bay bugs* for drugs and the Freudian *strangle and smother* for mother.

It is this characteristic of rhyming slang, together with its rhythmic and often-alliterative qualities, that makes it appealing to children. As June Factor demonstrates in *Kidspeak*, her dictionary of Australian children's folk speech, terms such as *horse and cart* (fart), *pickle and pork* (walk), *Germaine Greer* (beer), *frog and toad* (road) or *hollow log* (dog, meaning one who breaks the rules of a game) are part of children's language play. Children have a strong tendency to adapt adult lore to their own needs. The rhyming slang *Jimmy Britt* for shit has come, through the linguistic trick of reversal, to mean something deemed particularly good in children's folk speech, much as 'wicked' and 'sick' came to mean 'good' in adolescent folk speech from the late 20th century.

Sources and Subjects
Names of prominent and even not-so-prominent people have always proved fertile sources of Australian rhyming slang, such as *Bass and Flinders* for windows (pronounced winders), and *Captain Cook* for look, as in *Take a Captain Cook* at that, also used in Cockney rhyming slang.

Relatively recent examples include *Germaine Greer* for a beer or ear; *Kerry Packered* for knackered; and *Reg Grundies* (usually abbreviated to *Reginalds*) for male underpants. Rhyming slang in use among a group of thirty-somethings in Melbourne in 2006 included plays on the names of a number of figures currently or relatively recently prominent in the media, including *David Gower* for a shower, *Billy Guyatt* for diet, *Mark Boucher* for a voucher, and *Stuart Diver* for a survivor.

This last term nicely demonstrates the ability of rhyming slang to capitalise on a topic of the day, in this case the near-miraculous survival of a man buried under snow for sixty-five hours in 1997, as well as its ability to encapsulate the essence of its meaning in the rhyme term. In 2007, the visit of the Dalai Lama to Australia in controversial circumstances produced the new rhyming slang *Dalai Lamas* for dramas, as in the idiom, 'No dramas' — meaning everything is all right — rendered as 'No Dalai Lamas.' Whether this opportunistic coinage will persist much beyond its beginnings is unknown, but even if it does not it provides a useful example of the process by which new rhyming slang can arise.

The tendency of a large segment of this form of speech to rhyme on the names of prominent people is as pronounced today as it was in the past. While most of these recent rhymes are innocuous, a few might cause embarrassment or offence to those still living. These have not been included.

Fictional or mythic characters present no such problems. From many sources, they have also provided an important basis for Australian rhyming slang. An example is Steele Rudd's famous characters *Dad and Dave* (shave). Although most people are not aware of it, *Chunderloo* (spew), derives from a Norman Lindsay cartoon character, now immortalised in abbreviated form as *chunder*. Those we have imported from elsewhere are, like most Australian slang, happily incorporated into the local lingo. From America, *Mickey Mouse* is grouse (good), after the evergreen Disney character, although the term 'Mickey Mouse' is also used in non-rhyming slang form as a description of someone or something considered unreliable or faulty. Another American cartoon-inspired rhyme is *Bugs Bunny* for money. From Britain we get *Andy Capp* for crap and *Wallace and Gromit* for vomit, among others. Overall, names of individuals, real or not, are the largest single source of Australian rhyming slangs.

Similarly, the names of places have contributed their share to the formation of our rhyming slang, often adding a local touch. A *Barossa Pearl* is a girl. Some further examples include *Bulli Pass* (sometimes simply *Bulli* or *Pass*) for arse (compare with the English *Khyber Pass*, or *Khyber*, which have also been heard in Australia); *Coffs Harbour* for barber; *Hawkesbury Rivers* for shivers (usually abbreviated to *Hawkesburies*); *Tennant Creek* and *Werris Creek* for a 'Greek'; and *Williamstown Piers* for ears.

Examples of restricted or special usage can be found in cities and states, with regionalism being a definite and mostly overlooked feature of the form. *Lewis and W(h)itties* is a Melbournism for titties; *Onkaparingas* are fingers, after the South Australian town of that name; while an arm is a *Warwick Farm* in New South Wales. A *Dr Bevan* is — or was, as it is now probably obsolete — a seven only in Melbourne. Other rhymes on well-known places, though, are heard around the country, including *Sydney Harbour* for a barber, *Kembla Grange* for small change and *Melbourne Piers* for ears. *Kirk's Bazaar* for a car is a Melbournism, after a well-known annual event in that city, while the penis, or 'cock', may be a *Victoria Dock* in Melbourne but a *Mort's Dock* in Sydney. A distinctively Western Australian example is *jarrah blocks* for socks.

Does this mean that banana-benders, Territorians, Croweaters and Taswegians do not rhyme their slang? No. The mainstream forms of rhyming slang are spoken in all these places, and further research will no doubt eventually turn up regional and local variations. These will probably be based on the names of local places or even individuals, as in the case of a New England town where a prominent local's surname rhymed with schooner, the largest NSW measure of beer. For some years since the early 2000s, locals have been ordering their schooners at local pubs simply by asking for 'an Eris', the now immortalised identity's first name, a classic rhyming slang routine.

British lexicographer John Ayto remarks in his *Oxford Dictionary of Rhyming Slang* (2002) that in Australian rhyming slang 'inventions abound in terms relating to cleanliness and personal grooming'. This is an interesting observation that reflects one of our longstanding cultural sensitivities in relation to Britain. The broader Australian folk speech includes the comparison 'dryer than a Pommie's towel' as well as jokes about the British hiding their money underneath the soap. One of the imputed points of difference — and superiority — between Australians and the British is the ethnic slur that 'they' are not as clean as 'us'. Despite the difference in climates, the Australian partiality for showering may appear excessive from some vantage points.

The major focus of rhyming slang involves playfully naming/re-naming aspects of everyday life. The largest single category refers to the human body, its parts and functions, from the *lump of lead* (head) to the *buttons and bows* (toes). This is closely followed by sex, clothes and various forms of drug taking, notably of the alcoholic variety. The thematic section of this book reveals these major areas of rhyming slang.

Organisation of the Book

The organisation of the material of this book is designed to present Australian rhyming slang as comprehensively and usefully as possible. Part 1 is an A–Z dictionary, including notes on origins, provenance, usage and meaning/s, with cross-references and variant forms. It features every example of rhyming slang in this book.

Part 2 sets out the main topical, or thematic, groupings into which Australian rhyming slang seems to fall. There are 23 topics, which may be further broken down into categories. For instance, the topic Drugs has three categories: Alcohol, Tobacco and Other Drugs.

In Part 3, which is titled, 'Don't forget Hers', the full texts of the rhyming slang letters mentioned in the Introduction are provided.

The book concludes with a list of the sources for the collection and a brief selection of references relevant to the story of rhyming slang, particularly in its Australian form.

While a book on any aspect of colloquial language can never be fully comprehensive or final, I hope this collection will usefully extend our understanding of this neglected aspect of Australian English.

A final word of caution: rhyming slang belongs firmly at the vulgar end of the language spectrum and so some readers may find the colourful crudities of the common tongue offensive.

Acknowledgements

My thanks to the following people and organisations who contributed to the gathering of rhyming slang and related information for the writing of this book: Rob Willis, Bruce Cameron, Phyl Lobl, Maureen Seal, Jane Roxby, Kylie Seal, Jenna and Kristian Dawson, Pat Billing, Warren Fahey, Bruce Moore of the Australian National Dictionary Centre at the Australian National University, ABC Regional Radio, editorial staff at ABC Books/HarperCollins, and Pete and Frank at Mother's Cellar Restaurant a very long time ago — and to all the speakers and keepers of Australian English.

PART 1

Dictionary –
Acker Bilk to Zubrick

A

Acker Bilk — milk
After the English jazz clarinettist. Said to be used mainly when referring to the alcoholic beverage of rum and milk. Used in UK from *c.* 1960s. Rare in Australia. Obsolete? See also *soft as silk*.

Acker Bilk (2) — rum and milk
After the English jazz clarinettist. Used in UK from *c.* 1960s. Rare in Australia. Obsolete?

Adrian Knox — pox, meaning sexually transmissible infection, usually syphilis
After Sir Adrian Knox (1863–1932), former Chief Justice of the High Court and chairman of the Australian Jockey Club. Probably used only in horseracing circles. See also *boots and sox, Jack-in-the-box*.

Adrian Quist — pissed, meaning drunk
Often abbreviated to *Adrian* or *Adrians*. Adrian Quist (1913–91) was a well-known Australian tennis player from the 1930s to the '50s. Current. See also *Brahms and Liszt, Franz Liszt, Mozart and Liszt, Oliver Twist* (1), *Schindler's List, sisters apart*.

Adrians — see *Adrian Quist*

African nigger (1) — cigger (short for cigarette)
Obsolete.

African nigger (2) — jigger, a wooden rest for a billiard cue
Obsolete?

after darks — sharks
See also *Cutty Sark* (2), *Joan of Arc/s, Joe Marks, Jonah, Luna Park, Marcus Clark(e), Noah's Ark* (6).

AIF — deaf
AIF stands for Australian Imperial Force, a term used from 1915. See also *Mutt and Jeff*.

air raid warning — morning
Probably World War II. Obsolete. See also *Gypsy's warning*.

airs and graces — races (horseracing)
Usually said to mean 'braces'. Cockney term. **See also** *braces, fireman's braces, trot and paces.*

airy Jane — aeroplane
From around the mid-20th century. **See also** *King of Spain* (1).

Al Capone — phone, telephone
After the notorious American gangster Alphonse Capone (1899–1947). Apparently originating in Australia rather than the USA. In use since the 1930s. **See also** *Darby and Joan* (2), *dog and bone, eau de Cologne* (1), *ozone.*

All Quiet on the Western Front — cunt, as in female genitalia
Usually abbreviated to *All quiet*. Probably used only in horseracing circles. **See also** *Ballina Punt, Berkshire Hunt, Billy Hunt, drop kick and punt, grumble and grunt, Joe Hunt, mumble and grunt, Stockton Punt.*

all stations — Alsatian (dog)

Alma Grey — trey, meaning a threepenny coin (pre-decimal currency)
'Trey' has been Australian slang for threepence (pre-decimal currency), usually in the form of a 'thruppeny bit', since at least the 1890s. Obsolete since the introduction of decimal currency in 1966. **See also** *Dolly Gray, Dora Gray, horse and dray.*

almond rocks — socks
Sometimes abbreviated to *rocks*. Probably of World War I vintage. Still in use among convicts in 1950. **See also** *bobby rocks, curly locks, Goldilocks, Jarrah blocks, Joe Rocks, keys and locks, ton o' my rocks.*

Alsatian dog — wog, meaning a person of southern European/Mediterranean origin or, more generally, anyone considered 'foreign'
See also *chocolate frog/s* (2), *Dapto dog, Freddo Frog, hollow log* (3), *spotty dog, woolly dog.*

Amos and Andy — brandy
Amos 'n Andy was a popular American radio series from the 1920s until it was last broadcast in 1960, with three years of television versions in the early '50s. In use since the '20s. The term is rarely heard today.

Amster — see Amsterdam

Amsterdam (1) — ram, meaning a criminal's accomplice
Usually abbreviated to *amster*. Also used in American west coast crimespeak during the 1920s and '30s.

Amsterdam (2) — ram, meaning a sideshow tout, or 'spieler'
Usually abbreviated to *amster*. Also used in American west coast crimespeak during the 1920s and '30s.

Andy Capp — crap, as in defecate, faeces
A famous British newspaper cartoon character created by Reg Smythe, Andy Capp began to appear in British newspapers in the late 1950s and was also popular in Australia from *c.* '60s.

Andy Devine — wine
Mid-20th century. Melbourne? See also *Lindsay Kline, Randall Vines, Tilly Devine.*

Andy Mac — zac, meaning a sixpenny coin (pre-decimal currency)
World War II and probably earlier as the term 'zac' was in use from at least the 1890s. Obsolete. See also *Brodie Mack, hammer and tack* (5), *I'll be back, Jill and Jack, tin tack* (3).

Andy Maguire — fire (conflagration)
Australian invention from World War II. See also *Anna Maria, Barney Maguire, Bob Dyer, Molly Maguire.*

angel's kiss — piss, as in urinate, urine
20th-century Australian original. See also *cat's hiss, Gypsy's kiss, hit and/ or miss, horse's hiss, Johnny Bliss, Les Kiss, Shirley Bliss, snake's hiss, swing and a miss.*

Angus and Coote — root, as in sexual intercourse
After the Sydney jewellers of the same name and probably restricted to that city and possibly NSW. Obsolete? Related to the now obsolete expression for obtaining female sexual favours — to 'get a downtown jeweller'. See also *gumboot, Herby de Groote, juicy fruit, silly galoot, tin flute, Wellington boot.*

Angus Murray — curry
From the name of a Melbourne murderer and associate of the notorious 'Squizzy' Taylor (1888–1927). World War II. Obsolete. See also *Arthur Murray, River Murray.*

Anna Maria — fire (conflagration)
See also *Andy Maguire, Barney Maguire, Bob Dyer, Molly Maguire*.

Annalise — crack, back and sac, meaning hair removal from male bottom and torso
After Annalise Braakensiek (born 1972), an Australian model whose surname is pronounced 'Brak-en-sak'. Early 21st century.

Annie (Anna) Louise — cheese
Since at least World War II. **See also** *cough and sneeze, piper's knees, stand at ease*.

apple Charlotte — harlot
Obsolete.

apple fritter — bitter, meaning beer
Obsolete.

apple sauce — horse
World War II. **See also** *condiments and sauces, Ella May Morse, tomato sauce/s* (2).

apple tart — fart, as in break wind
Australian in origin. **See also** *bacon and egg tart, bottle mart, cupcake, Dicky Bart, fairy dart, horse and cart (1), jam tart (2), raspberry tart, Stevey Hart*.

apples and pears — stairs
One of the earliest rhyming slangs to be recorded in London during the 1850s. **See also** *Doctor Kildare/s*.

apples and rice — nice
This term and its variant *apples and spice* are the origin of the Australian phrase 'She's apples.' Long used instead of the full form. First noted in 1943 but almost certainly older. **See also** *apples and spice, sugar and spice*.

apples and spice — nice
Australian original. First noted in 1943 but almost certainly older. See *apples and rice, sugar and spice*.

April fool — tool, as in penis
Originally a Cockneyism for working tools.

Archie Moore — **poor**
Often abbreviated to *Archie*. After an American heavyweight boxer, Archie Moore (1813/16–1898). **See also** *on the floor*.

Aris — **arse, meaning bottom**
A shortened form of *Aristotle*, in which the primary rhyme of 'bottle' invokes another rhyming slang: bottle and glass for 'arse'. **See also** *Bulli Pass, bottle and glass, Coke and sars(parilla), Herb Alpert, Khyber Pass, lemonade and sars(parilla)* (1), *Mark Ella, Reg Gasnier*.

Aristotle — **bottle**
Usually abbreviated to *Aris*, in which form it usually means 'arse'. After the third-century BC Greek philosopher. From at least 1897. **See also** *charming mottle, Horace Tottle*.

armour float — **coat, overcoat**
From World War II. **See also** *Collier and Moat, I'm afloat, motorboat*.

Army and Navy — **gravy**
Obsolete.

army tank — **Yank, meaning American**
Used by Australian prisoners-of-war to refer to American military personnel, 1942–45. **See also** *ham shank, iron tank* (2), *Jodrell Bank, mutton shanks, septic tank/s* (1), *ship's tank, tin tank* (2).

arsehole of the goanna — **Varsovienna (a dance)**
See also *arse-over-Anna, arse-over-header, heart and soul of the goanna, Var Susy Anne*.

arse-over-Anna — **Varsovienna (a dance)**
See also *arsehole of the goanna, arse-over-header, heart and soul of the goanna, Var Susy Anne*.

arse-over-header — **Varsovienna (a dance)**
Current from at least the 1950s? **See also** *arsehole of the goanna, arse-over-Anna, heart and soul of the goanna, Var Susy Anne*.

Arthur Ashe — **cash**
After American tennis player Arthur Ashe (1943–93), who was men's single champion at Wimbledon in 1975. Obsolete. **See also** *Charlie Ash, Christopher Ash, J. Carroll Nash, Oscar Asche, sausage and mash, smash, splash*.

Arthur Murray — curry
After the dancing teacher Arthur Murray (1895–1991). Obsolete. **See also** *Angus Murray, River Murray*.

artichoke — bloke, meaning man
Mid-20th century. Melbourne? **See also** *bag of coke, Davey Cloak*.

Arty Rolla — (shirt) collar
Australian. In use during late 1890s. Male only?

Ashley Mallett — pallet
After Ashley Mallett (born 1945), Australian cricketer. From *c.* 1960s–70s. Possibly restricted to Melbourne wharfies?

ask for more — thirty-four (Bingo)

asteroids — haemorrhoids
See also *Bea Miles, Chalfont St Giles, Farmer Giles, laughs and smiles, metric miles*.

Atilla the Hun — sun
After the fourth-century leader of the Huns. Obsolete. **See also** *currant bun* (2), *hot cross bun, Peter Gunn*.

atomic bomb — pom, pommie, meaning a person from Britain
Mid-20th century. Melbourne? **See also** *to and from*.

Aunt Ella — umbrella
See also *Aunt Molly, Irish Folly, Lake's Folly*.

Aunt Molly — brolly (short for umbrella)
See also *Aunt Ella, Irish Folly, Lake's Folly*.

Aunt Nelly — belly, meaning stomach
See also *Darby Kelly, Ned Kelly* (1), *Nelly Kelly*

auntie — silly
From a play on Uncle Willy, meaning 'silly'. Used in the form of 'Don't be *auntie*.' Obsolete. **See also** *dilly, Kirribilli, Wollondilly, Uncle Willy*.

Auntie Meg — keg (usually of beer)
Apparently an Australian original. **See also** *Jersey Flegg*.

B

baa lamb — tram
See also *bread and jam*.

babbler — see *babbling brook* (1)

babbling brook (1) — cook
Often occurs as *babbler*. First noted as *babbler* in print in 1904 and used widely by troops in World War I and World War II to refer to army cooks. According to Baker, derived from English usage. Also criminal slang. Used in New Zealand.

babbling brook (2) — crook, meaning unwell
Also used in this sense in the USA during the 1920s. Current in Australia 1920s–c. '60s. See also *butcher's hook* (1).

babbling brook (3) — crook, meaning criminal
Said to have been in use in this sense between the 1920s and '60s. Obsolete? See also *second look*.

baby blue — true

bacon and egg tart — fart, as in break wind
Usually abbreviated to *bacon and egg*. Recorded in children's folk speech, often as eggy, as in 'He's just done an eggy!' See also *apple tart, bottle mart, Dicky Bart, fairy dart, cupcake, horse and cart* (1), *jam tart* (2), *raspberry tart, Stevey Hart*.

bacon and eggs — legs
From at least the 1940s. Used in American as well as Australian criminal speech. See also *clothes pegs, Dutch pegs, fried eggs, Ginger Meggs, Gregory pegs, ham and eggs, Neville Beggs, nine gallon kegs, Scotch pegs*.

bacon and liver — river
See also *bullock's liver, shake and shiver*.

Baden Powell — towel
After English Boer War hero Robert (later Lord) Baden Powell (1857–1941), who founded the Scouting movement in 1907. From at least the early 20th century and still current. See also *Bob Powell, Dick Powell, dog's growl*.

bag of coke — **bloke**
From earlier English form *bushel of coke*. Coke here refers to solid fuel once widely used for domestic heating. In use since at least World War II. **See also** *artichoke, Davey Cloak.*

bag of fruit — **suit**
Also occurs as *bagga*. Cockney, but in use in Australia since at least the early 1920s, during World War II and after. Male only. **See also** *bowl of fruit, whistle and flute, whistle and toot.*

bag of yeast — **priest**

baked bean — **queen, meaning male homosexual**
See also *haricot bean, in-between, pork and bean, submarine.*

baked dinner — **winner (horseracing)**

baker's bun — **sixty-one (Bingo)**

baker's dozen — **cousin**

ball and bat — **hat**
See also *Ballarat* (1), *barrel of fat, bowl of fat, this and that* (2), *thises and thats, tit for tat* (1).

ball of twine — **railway line**
Australian origin. 20th century.

Ballarat (1) — **hat**
Current early 21st century. **See also** *ball and bat, barrel of fat, bowl of fat, this and that* (2), *thises and thats, tit for tat* (1).

Ballarat (2) — **cat**

Ballarat (3) — **fat, meaning an erection**
See also *larrikin's hat, State election, Yasser Arafat.*

ballet dancer — **cancer**
See also *Bengal lancer, candy dancer, Charlie Dancer, civil answer, Jack the dancer, Jimmy Dancer, Johnny Dancer, Mario Lanza, Spanish dancer.*

Ballina Punt — **cunt, as in female genitalia**
Ballina is in northern NSW. **See also** *All Quiet on the Western Front, Berkshire Hunt, Billy Hunt, drop kick and punt, grumble and grunt, Joe Hunt, mumble and grunt, Stockton Punt.*

Band of Hope — soap

Often occurs as *bander*. Apparently from the late 19th-century temperance organisation known as the 'Band of Hope'. **See also** *Bob Hope* (1), *Cape of Good Hope*, *Joe Hope*.

bander — see Band of Hope

bang on the drum — seventy-one (Bingo)

barmaid's blush (1) — flush (a hand in the card game of poker)
World War II.

barmaid's blush (2) — flush, meaning the drink rum and raspberry
World War II.

Barnet Fair — hair

Barnet Fair was a popular London entertainment. Recorded in one of the earliest English rhyming slang sources in the late 1850s. In use in Australia during the 1930s and also in the USA in the '20s. If heard at all in Australia, it is only in the abbreviated Cockney form of Barnet. **See also** *Dublin Fair*, *Fred Astaire* (2), *here and there*, *over there*, *preference share*, *table and chair*.

Barney Maguire — fire (conflagration)

Australianism from at least the early 20th century. See also *Andy Maguire*, *Anna Maria*, *Bob Dyer*, *Molly Maguire*.

Barney Rubble — trouble

From a character in *The Flintstones* television cartoon series since the 1960s. **See also** *froth and bubble* (2).

Barossa — see Barossa Pearl

Barossa Pearl — girl

Often abbreviated to *Barossa*. From the name of a cheap white sparkling wine that was a popular drink in the 1960s and early '70s. **See also** *mother of pearl*, *twist/s and twirl/s*.

barrel of fat — hat

Australianism from at least the early 20th century. Current in World War II. **See also** *ball and bat*, *Ballarat* (1), *bowl of fat*, *this and that* (2), *thises and thats*, *tit for tat* (1).

Barrier Reef — teeth
Mid-20th century. Melbourne? **See also** *Barry Beath, cricket bats, Hampstead Heath, Ted Heath*.

Barry Beath — teeth
After the 1970s Rugby League footballer. Current early 21st century. **See also** *Barrier Reef, cricket bats, Hampstead Heath, Ted Heath*.

Barry Crocker — shocker, as in something bad
Often abbreviated to *Barry*. After Barry Crocker (born 1935), the well-known entertainer and star of the 'Bazza' McKenzie movies of the 1970s. Still current. **See also** *Joe Cocker*.

Barry Fitzgerald — Sydney Morning Herald (newspaper)
Probably after the stage name of a Hollywood actor of Irish birth, William Shields (1888–1961), rather than the Australian Rules footballer (born 1938). A Sydneyism. **See also** *Jim Gerald*.

bart — tart, meaning a girl
20th century. Obsolete.

basin crop — haircut
While this is not, apparently, a rhyming slang, it might be if the rhyme inferred were 'chop'.

Basin Street blues — shoes
After the song of this title composed in 1928. **See also** *Ben Blues, canoes, kangaroo/s* (2), *ones and twos, Peggy Sue, Pete Kelly's blues, Saint Louis blues, splash throughs, ten to twos*.

Bass and Flinders — windows (pronounced 'winders')
After the English navigators who circumnavigated Tasmania in 1798–99, proving that it was indeed an island.

bat and ball (1) **— stall, as in stall one's car**
Current 2007.

bat and ball (2) **— wall**
World War II. **See also** *Duncan Hall, Queenie Paul*.

bath bun — son
See also *buttered bun, sixteen ton*.

Bea Miles — piles, meaning haemorrhoids
Bea Miles (1902–73) was an eccentric Sydney streetwoman, well-known in the 1950s and '60s. **See also** *asteroids, Chalfont St Giles, Farmer Giles, laughs and smiles, metric miles.*

Beecham pill — bill (for goods and services, as at a restaurant)
See also *Jack and Jill* (1).

Beecham's — see *Beecham's Pill/s*

Beecham's Pill/s — dill, meaning a foolish or naive person
Usually abbreviated to *Beecham's*. Derived from the famous pills developed and marketed by Thomas Beecham from 1850. From around the mid-1920s. Also used in criminal speech from at least 1950. **See also** *Burke and Wills, Jack and Jill* (2).

beehive — five
See also *eat 'em alive, Jack's alive, man alive.*

bees and honey — money
See also *Bugs Bunny, Gene Tunney* (1), *sugar and honey.*

bell ringer — finger
An imperfect rhyme. More common in Britain than Australia. **See also** *Mal Meninga/s, Manly-Warringahs, Onkaparingas.*

Ben Blues — shoes
Current *c.* mid–late 20th century. **See also** *Basin Street blues, canoes, kangaroo/s (2), ones and twos, Peggy Sue, Pete Kelly's blues, Saint Louis blues, splash throughs, ten to twos.*

Bengal lancer — cancer
See also *ballet dancer, candy dancer, Charlie Dancer, civil answer, Jack the dancer, Jimmy Dancer, Johnny Dancer, Mario Lanza, Spanish dancer.*

Berkshire Hunt — cunt, as in a despicable person
Origin of the general insult 'a berk'. Rarely used in Australia. **See also** *All Quiet on the Western Front, Ballina Punt, Billy Hunt, drop kick and punt, grumble and grunt, Joe Hunt, mumble and grunt, Stockton Punt.*

Bernie Purcell — tell
After a Rugby League footballer and coach of the 1950s and '60s.

Betty Grable — table
Betty Grable (1916–73) — known as 'the girl with the million dollar legs' — was the favoured American pin-up girl and film actress of the era, so the rhyme would have been irresistible. Current from World War II. **See also** *Cain and Abel, Clark Gable* (1).

between the sticks — eighty-six (Bingo)

bib — see *Bib and Bub* (2)

Bib and Bub (1) — pub
Bib and Bub were characters created by children's writer May Gibbs (1877–1969) in 1924. **See also** *rubbidy dub.*

Bib and Bub (2) — (bath)tub
As in 'take a *bib*', meaning 'have a bath'.

big and bulky — sulky (horse-drawn vehicle)
From at least the late 19th century. Obsolete.

Big Ben — ten
See also *clucky hen, cock and hen, Tony's Den.*

big hit — shit, as in defecate
Invented in Australia in the 1920s and current into the '60s. **See also** *brace and bit, Dinny Hayes-er, Eartha Kitt, Edgar Britt, gravel pit, hard hit, Jimmy Britt (1), king hit, Mickey Fritt, Oscar Britt, Tom tit.*

Bill and Ted — bed
See also *God strike me dead, needle and thread, Rocky Ned, roses red, Uncle Ned* (1), *white and red.*

Bill Buck (1) — truck
See also *Donald Duck* (2), *Frank Buck, goose and duck, Joe Buck* (2), *Mickey Duck* (2).

Bill Buck (2) — fuck, as in sexual intercourse
See also *Donald Duck* (1), *Friar Tuck, Joe Buck* (1), *Mickey Duck* (1).

Bill Lang — slang
From the professional name of the Victorian footballer and heavyweight-boxing champion of the early 20th century, William Langfrachini. Current in World War II, but probably much older. **See also** *Jack Lang.*

Bill Peach — speech
After the ABC journalist and TV presenter.

Bill Picken — chicken
After a Sydney trotting champion. **See also** *Charles Dickens*.

billy (bong) — bong, meaning apparatus for smoking marijuana
Perhaps not a true rhyming slang. Unlikely to be earlier than the 1970s.

Billy Dunk — spunk, meaning a fit and attractive male
After the Australian golfer (born 1938). A rare example of a female-oriented rhyming slang. Used during the 1960s and '70s. **See also** *New York junk*.

billy goat (1) — throat
Current WA, 2007. **See also** *nanny goat* (1).

billy goat (2) — tote, totalisator (horseracing)
See also *canal boat, giddy goat, nanny goat* (2).

Billy Guyatt — diet
Billy Guyatt was a well-known elite Victorian cyclist between the two world wars. Melbourne 2006.

Billy Hunt — cunt, as in female genitalia
After an Australian cricketer of the 1930s. **See also** *All Quiet on the Western Front, Ballina Punt, Berkshire Hunt, drop kick and punt, grumble and grunt, Joe Hunt, mumble and grunt, Stockton Punt*.

billy lid/s — kid/s, meaning child(ren)
See also *Captain, God-forbids, saucepan lids, tin lid/s* (1).

Billy the Kid — yid, meaning a Jewish person
After the American badman whose real name was Henry McCarty (1859?–81).

Bing and swing — wing
Presumably derived from the singer and Hollywood star Bing Crosby (1903–77).

bird's lime (1) — time (of day)
One of the earliest English rhyming slang terms to be recorded in the late 1850s, as bird-lime, from which form the English 'bird' for a prison sentence is derived. **See also** *Harry Lime*.

bird's lime (2) — time, meaning prison sentence
One of the earliest English rhyming slang terms to be recorded in the late 1850s, as bird-lime, from which form the English 'bird' for a prison sentence is derived. **See also** *Harry Lime.*

biscuits and cheese — knees
See also *bugs and fleas, bumblebees, gum tree/s, Gypsy Rose Lee/s, Syngman Ree(s).*

bit on the cuff — rough, meaning excessive or over-the-top
As in 'That's a *bit on the cuff.'* 1930s.

bladder and lard — card
See also *Carole Lombard.*

blister — see blood blister

blood and blister — see blood blister

blood blister — sister
Sometimes abbreviated to *blister*, as in 'How's your big *blister*?' Variations are *blood and blister* and *big toe blister*. World War II. **See also** *kid blister, skin and blister.*

blue moon — hoon, meaning a prostitute's pimp in this usage
Since at least the 1970s, in general Australian slang the term 'hoon' has come to mean a (usually) young man who drives his car recklessly and noisily, as in a noisy lout. **See also** *silver spoon* (1), *silvery moon.*

Bluey and Curly — early
From the characters in a famous comic strip from 1939. The term was current on Melbourne wharves from *c.* 1940s.

Blundstone — see Blundstone boot

Blundstone boot — ute (short for utility wagon)
Usually abbreviated to *Blundstone*. After the name of a famous brand of Australian boots established in 1870. Current in the first decade of the 21st century. **See also** *you beaut.*

boat — see boat race

boat race — face
Usually abbreviated to *boat*. Also English from *c.* mid-20th century.

Current in Australia 2007. **See also** *Chevvy Chase, Epsom Races, first base, first place, Martin Place, Melrose Place, Princess Grace, smile place.*

Bob Dyer — fire (conflagration)
After the recording, radio and TV celebrity Robert Neal Dyer (1909–84). **See also** *Andy Maguire, Anna Maria, Barney Maguire, Molly Maguire.*

Bob Hope (1) — soap
From the American comedian and actor Bob Hope (1903–2003). Current in Sydney's Long Bay Gaol and probably other prisons during the 1960s and also in general use. **See also** *Band of Hope, Cape of Good Hope, Joe Hope.*

Bob Hope (2) — dope, meaning drugs

Bob Powell — towel
Australian invention of unknown derivation. **See also** *Baden Powell, Dick Powell, dog's growl.*

Bobby Martin — carton (of goods, often beer)

Bobby rocks — socks
Probably 1950s. **See also** *almond rocks, curly locks, Goldilocks, jarrah blocks, Joe Rocks, keys and locks, ton o' my rocks.*

bona fide — terrified

Bondi Junction — function (social event)
Sydneyism.

bones and rags — fags
See also *old nags.*

boots and sox — pox, meaning sexually transmissible infection, usually syphilis
World War II. **See also** *Adrian Knox, Jack-in-the-box.*

bo-peep — sleep
Criminal speech from at least the 1940s. Still current in Sydney's Long Bay Gaol during the '60s. From British rhyming slang of at least the 1880s. **See also** *hit the deep, rolling deep.*

boracic — see boracic lint

boracic lint — skint, meaning without funds
Usually abbreviated to *boracic*. Boracic lint was a 19th-century medical dressing impregnated with boracic acid and glycerine; still sometimes used today. Cockneyism. First recorded in the UK in the late 1950s but also used sometimes in Australia.

Boris Becker — pecker, meaning penis
After the German tennis star Boris Becker (born 1967).

Botany — see *Botany Bay*

Botany Bay — run away
As in to 'do a *Botany*'. From the 1940s. Also used in America as a rhyme for 'hit the hay', meaning 'go to sleep'.

bottle and glass — arse, as in bottom
See also *Aris, Bulli Pass, Coke and sars(parilla), Herb Alpert, Khyber Pass, lemonade and sars(parilla)* (1), *Mark Ella, Reg Gasnier*.

bottle and stopper — copper, meaning police officer
See also *bottle stopper, grasshopper, greasy mop, hot scone, John Cleese, Johnhop/s, Johnhopper*.

bottle mart — fart, as in break wind
See also *apple tart, bacon and egg tart, cupcake, Dicky Bart, fairy dart, horse and cart* (1), *jam tart* (2), *raspberry tart, Stevey Hart*.

bottle of booze — news
From the late 20th century. See also *nails and screws*.

bottle of Scotch — (wrist)watch
See also *Gordon and Gotch* (1).

bottle stopper — copper, meaning police officer
Mid-20th century. Melbourne? See also *bottle and stopper, grasshopper, greasy mop, hot scone, John Cleese, Johnhop/s, Johnhopper*.

bow and arrow — sparrow

bowl of fat — hat
Since at least the 1940s. See also *ball and bat, Ballarat* (1), *barrel of fat, this and that* (2), *thises and thats, tit for tat* (1).

bowl of fruit — suit
See also *bag of fruit, whistle and flute, whistle and toot*.

bowsers — see *petrol bowsers*

box of toys — noise
See also *Johnny Moyes*.

brace and bit — shit, as in defecate
See also *big hit, Dinny Hayes-er, Eartha Kitt, Edgar Britt, gravel pit, hard hit, Jimmy Britt (1), king hit, Mickey Fritt, Oscar Britt, Tom tit.*

brace and bits — tits, meaning female breasts
Sometimes abbreviated to *braces*. From the name of a form of hand drill. Also in British and American usage. See also *Eartha Kitts, tracy-bit/s, trey bits* (2), *Vita Brits*.

braces — races (horse or dog)
Current in Sydney's Long Bay Gaol during the 1960s. See also *airs and graces, fireman's braces, trot and braces*.

Brahms — see *Brahms and Liszt*

Brahms and Liszt — pissed, meaning drunk
Sometimes abbreviated to *Brahms*. See also *Adrian Quist, Franz Liszt, Mozart and Liszt, Oliver Twist (1), Schindler's List, sisters apart*.

brass bands — hands
See also *Brighton le Sands, Dave Sands, German band/s, Ray Millands*.

brass tacks — facts
Originally English but has now become so commonplace as an idiom that its rhyming slang origins have been all but forgotten.

brave and bold — cold
Since at least the early 20th century. Current in World War II. See also *Cheltenham bold, soldiers bold, young and old*.

bread and jam — tram
Also in British and American rhyming slang and from at least 1902 in Australia, where it was still current in prisons around 1950. See also *baa lamb*.

breadcrumb — hum, meaning someone who is down and out
Australian variant of the American 'bum'. Since at least 1915. Still current in first decade of the 21st century.

breeze(y?) — **easy**
From 'It's a breeze.' From World War II. Perhaps not rhyming slang.

Brett Parker — **afterdarker, meaning a dinner suit**
Often abbreviated to a *Brett*. Possibly after a footballer of this name.

Brighton le Sands — **hands**
After a southern Sydney suburb. **See also** *brass bands, Dave Sands, German band/s, Ray Millands.*

Brighton line — **fifty-nine (Bingo)**

Bristol Cities — **titties, meaning female breasts**
Usually abbreviated to *Bristols.* Also Cockney. Current 2007. **See also** *cats and kitties, Denver Cities, Elsie Whitty/ies, Lewis and W(h)itties, Manchester City/ies, Salt Lake Cities, Vatican City/ies.*

Bristols — **see** *Bristol Cities*

Britney Spears — **beers**
Sometimes abbreviated to *Brittos.* After the American pop singer Britney Spears (born 1982). Current early 21st century on the worldwide web and in speech. **See also** *cherry cheer, Crimea, Germaine Greer/s* (1), *oh my dear, Perc Galea, pig's ear, Port Melbourne Pier* (2), *pot of good cheer, Ray Stehr, Terry Dear.*

Brittos — **see** *Britney Spears*

Brodie Mack — **zac, meaning a sixpenny coin (pre-decimal currency)**
See also *Andy Mac, hammer and tack* (5), *I'll be back, Jill and Jack, tin tack* (3).

broken mug — **hug**

Brooklyn Bridge — **fridge, refrigerator**
See also *ridgy didge.*

broom handle — **candle**
See also *Harry Randle, Ron Randle.*

brown bread — **dead**
Recorded in British use in 1973 and still popular there. Current in Australia 2007. **See also** *garden shed, kangaroo Ted, lump of lead* (2), *wombat.*

brown Joe — know, in the know; meaning to be informed, to understand
From at least World War II in Australia; perhaps derived from mid-19th century English slang, where the term was used to mean 'no'.

Bruce Reed — feed, as in to 'have a feed', meaning eat a meal
Current 2008.

Brussels sprout — boy scout
1960s and probably earlier in Australia and perhaps from *c.* 1910 in England. **See also** *giddy gout*.

bubble and squeak (1) — Greek
Bubble and squeak is an English dish made of leftovers. **See also** *Merri Creek, ox cheek, Tennant Creek, Werris Creek* (1).

bubble and squeak (2) — leak, as in urinate
From *c.* mid-20th century. **See also** *Jacob's Creek, Werris Creek* (2).

buckle my shoe — thirty-two (Bingo)

Buckley and Nunn — none
From the name of a Melbourne company. Better known in the general slang form 'Buckley's chance', or just 'Buckley's'. In use from at least the 1890s.

buckshee — free
Perhaps a coincidental rhyme rather than rhyming slang. Probably derived during World War I from Arabic.

bugs and fleas — knees
See also *biscuits and cheese, bumblebees, gum tree/s, Gypsy Rose Lee/s, Syngman Ree(s)*.

Bugs Bunny — money
Often abbreviated to *Bugs*. From the name of the Warner Brothers cartoon character which began to appear from the early 1940s. **See also** *bees and honey, Gene Tunney* (1), *sugar and honey*.

bull and cow — row, meaning an argument

bull ants — pants
Since at least World War II in Australia and in the form *bull's aunts* in America in the 1930s, thought to be derived from the Australian original. **See also** *fleas and ants, Saint Vitus' Dance*.

Bulli Pass — arse, as in bottom
Sometimes abbreviated to *Bulli* or *Pass*. From a once-notoriously steep
road hill near Wollongong (NSW). **See also** *Aris, bottle and glass, Coke
and sars(parilla), Herb Alpert, Khyber Pass, lemonade and sars(parilla)*
(1), *Mark Ella, Reg Gasnier.*

**Bullock('s) horn — pawn, as in being 'in pawn' or having 'to
pawn'; meaning to use possessions as security for a cash loan**
One of the earliest rhyming slang terms to be recorded in England in
1859. From at least World War II in Australia. **See also** *ram's horn.*

bullock's kidney — Sydney
See also *steak and kidney.*

bullock's liver — river
Although it appears in 'Duke' Tritton's rhyming slang letter dated 1905
(see Appendix), Australian troops probably picked up the term from
British troops. Since the late 19th century in England; popular there
and abroad in World War I. Obsolete? **See also** *bacon and liver, shake
and shiver.*

bumblebees — knees
See also *biscuits and cheese, bugs and fleas, gum tree/s, Gypsy Rose Lee/s,
Syngman Ree(s).*

bundle of socks (1) **— rocks**

bundle of socks (2) **— think-box, meaning the head**
Recorded 1902.

Bunkey Naylor — tailor
See also *Sinbad the Sailor.*

**Bunsen burner — turner, meaning a cricket pitch that takes the
spin from the ball**

Burke and Wills — dills, meaning foolish or naive people
After the names of the famously tragic explorers Robert O'Hara Burke
(1821–61) and William John Wills (1834–61), who perished near
Cooper's Creek. **See also** *Beecham's Pill/s, Jack and Jill* (2).

bushel and peck — neck
See also *Gregory Peck* (3).

***butcher's hook* (1) — crook, meaning unwell, sick**
Sometimes abbreviated to *butchers*. In this meaning since the 1960s.
See also *babbling brook* (2).

***butcher's hook* (2) — crook, as in go crook, meaning to express anger**
Recorded in 1898. Common in World War I and beyond.

***butcher's hook* (3) — look**
As in 'Have a *butcher's* at that.' **See also** *Captain Cook, cook, squiz.*

***butchers* — see *butcher's hook* (3)**

***buttered bun* — son**
See also *bath bun, sixteen ton.*

***button my shoe* — two**
See also *Peggy Lou.*

***buttons and bows* — toes**
Originating in Australia, possibly from the 1940s. **See also** *GPOs, Matt Monroes, Old Black Joe/s, these and those* (2), *Uncle Joes.*

***by the light* (of the silvery moon) — spoon**
From the popular song of the same name. **See also** *David Boon, Marjorie Moon, Ruby Moon.*

C

***cabbage tree* — flee**

***cabbage tree hat* — rat, meaning an informer**
After a popular form of colonial Australian hat wear. In the form *cabbage hat* used in American criminal rhyming slang with the same meaning in the 1930s and '40s. **See also** *tit for tat* (2).

***Cain and Abel* — table**
After the biblical brothers of the same names in Genesis. In use since at least the early 20th century in Australia and probably long before, as this term was recorded in London in the late 1850s. **See also** *Betty Grable, Clark Gable* (1).

***camel's hump* — pump**

Canadian caper — newspaper
See also *Johnny Raper*.

canal boat — tote, totalisator (horseracing)
Probably an English-derived term from inland waterways craft. See also *billy goat* (2), *giddy goat*, *nanny goat* (2).

candy dancer — cancer
See also *ballet dancer, Bengal lancer, Charlie Dancer, civil answer, Jack the dancer, Jimmy Dancer, Johnny Dancer, Mario Lanza, Spanish dancer*.

candy store — seventy-four (Bingo)

canoes — shoes
Current in World War II and since in childspeak. See also *Basin Street blues, Ben Blues, kangaroo(s)* (2), *ones and twos, Peggy Sue, Pete Kelly's blues, Saint Louis blues, splash throughs, ten to twos*.

Cape of Good Hope — soap
From at least the early 20th century. See also *Band of Hope, Bob Hope* (1), *Joe Hope*.

Captain — kid, meaning child
From 'Captain Kidd', the notorious and much-romanticised pirate. World War II. Not a true rhyming slang? See also *billy lid/s, God-forbids, saucepan lid, tin lid/s* (1).

Captain Blood's — spuds, meaning potatoes
May come from Rafael Sabatini's fictional pirate character in the novel first published in 1922 and played in the movie of the same name by Errol Flynn in 1935. Or possibly from the nickname of the much later Australian Rules footballer Jack Dyer. Australian original. See also *Steele Rudds*.

Captain Cook — look
As in 'Take a *Captain Cook* at that'; often abbreviated, as in 'Take a *captain's*.' After the navigator James Cook (1728–79), who claimed what we now call Australia in the name of Britain in 1770. First noted in Australia during the 1930s. Also used in Cockney rhyming slang. See also *butcher's hook* (3), *cook, squiz*.

Captain scratches — matches (firelighters)
See also *Darryl Patch, fleas and scratches, itch and scratch*.

captain's — see *Captain Cook*

carburettor — **letter**
Since World War II. **See also** *don't forget her* (2), *never better/s*.

Carole Lombard — **card**
After the stage name of American film actress Jane Alice Peters (1908–42). **See also** *bladder and lard*.

cash and carry — **marry**

cast a net — **bet, meaning to lay a wager**

cat cuff — **bluff, meaning a feint in boxing**
Since at least World War II.

cat's hiss — **piss, as in urinate**
See also *angel's kiss, Gypsy's kiss, hit and/or miss, horse's hiss, Johnny Bliss, Les Kiss, Shirley Bliss, snake's hiss, swing and a miss*.

cats and kitties — **titties, meaning female breasts**
See also *Bristol Cities, Denver Cities, Elsie Whitty/ies, Lewis and W(h)itties, Manchester City/ies, Salt Lake Cities, Vatican Cities*.

cats and mice — **dice**
From World War II. **See also** *fried rice* (2).

cattle bruisers — **battle cruisers**
A Royal Australian Navy term. A perhaps unique example of a rhyming spoonerism?

cattle dog — **catalogue**
A rhyming wordplay, similar to *trick cyclist*. Australian original.

cattle tic — **catholic**
From World War II, and perhaps earlier.

Chalfont St Giles — **piles, meaning haemorrhoids**
Usually abbreviated to *Chalfonts*. English origin. Current WA 2007. **See also** *asteroids, Bea Miles, Farmer Giles, laughs and smiles, metric miles*.

Chalfonts — see *Chalfont St Giles*

chalk farms — **arms**
See also *Warwick Farm/s*

Charles Dickens — chickens
After the famous English writer Charles Dickens (1812–70). **See also** *Bill Picken*.

(the) Charlie — see Charlie Chase

Charlie or Charley (1) — lesbian
Shortened from *Charlie Wheeler*. Since at least World War II. **See also** *Charlie Wheeler*.

Charlie (2) — prostitute
In underworld usage from at least 1950. **See also** *Charlie Wheeler*.

Charlie Ash — cash
See also *Arthur Ashe, Christopher Ash, J. Carroll Nash, Oscar Asche, sausage and mash, smash, splash.*

Charlie Britt — fit, as in to 'take a fit' (of anger or frustration)
20th century.

Charlie Chase — race
As in 'not in the *Charlie*', meaning 'not in the race', which means being without a chance of success. After the American comedian of the silent film era Charlie Chase (1893–1961). Recorded in World War II, though probably older. Obsolete?

Charlie Dancer — cancer
See also *ballet dancer, Bengal lancer, candy dancer, civil answer, Jack the dancer, Jimmy Dancer, Johnny Dancer, Mario Lanza, Spanish dancer.*

Charlie Howard — coward
See also *Leslie Howard.*

Charlie Mason — basin

Charlie Prescott — waistcoat (pronounced 'wescot')
Late 1890s and probably earlier as this term appears in the first English rhyming slang collection of the late 1850s.

Charlie Wheeler — sheila, meaning a girl or woman
From Irish Gaelic. Usually abbreviated to *Charlie*. Originally from the name of artist Charles Wheeler (1881–1977), a noted painter of nudes. In use since the 1940s. **See also** *Charlie* (1), *Charlie* (2), *potato peeler, rock-wheeler, two wheeler.*

Charlie's coat — **Carley float (nautical item)**
Used in Royal Australian Navy in World War II.

charming mottle — **bottle**
Also abbreviated to *mottle*. Recorded 1902 in Australia in the form of 'a *mottle* of *O-my-dear*', a bottle of beer. Of 19th-century English origin. Obsolete. **See also** *Aristotle*, *Horace Tottle*.

charming wife — **knife**

cheap and nasty — **pasty, as in a pastry with a savoury filling**
Depends on the Australian pronunciation for the rhyme. 20th-century original. Obsolete?

cheese and kisses — **missus, meaning wife**
Since at least the 1890s. Although from English rhyming slang, Franklyn claims it is more commonly heard in Australia than in England. **See also** *cows and kisses*, *hugs and kisses*.

cheesy kiss — **miss, as in to miss catching a ball, mainly in cricket**
20th century.

Cheltenham bold — **cold**
Of English origin and rare in Australia. **See also** *brave and bold*, *soldiers bold*, *young and old*.

cherry — **see *cherry plum***

cherry cheer — **beer**
See also *Britney Spears*, *Crimea*, *Germaine Greer/s* (1), *oh my dear*, *Perc Galea*, *pig's ear*, *Port Melbourne Pier* (2), *pot of good cheer*, *Ray Stehr*, *Terry Dear*.

cherry plum — **mum, meaning mother**
Recorded in the shortened form of *cherry*. Current 2008.

cherry ripe — **pipe (smoking)**
Since at least the early 20th century and probably much earlier as the term was in use in London during the late 1850s and before. It also turns up in American 'thief talk' of the early to mid-19th century, with the additional meaning of 'full-grown woman'.

Chevvy Chase — **face**
In the abbreviated form *chiv* can mean 'face' or 'chin'. Originating in

19th-century English usage. Obsolete. **See also** *boat race, Epsom Races, first base, first place, Martin Place, Melrose Place, Princess Grace, smile place.*

China — see China plate

China plate — mate, meaning friend; likely to be male
Usually abbreviated to *China.* Also Cockney. **See also** *five-eight* (2), *ocean liner* (2), *old China plate, Royal Doulton.*

chiv — see Chevvy Chase

choc and log — dog (animal)
Also used to mean a dingo in World War II. Possibly from a 'chock and log fence'.

chock-a-block up 'er — supper
See also *Tommy Tucker.*

chocolate frog (1) — dog, meaning an informer
Underworld slang. 1970s.

chocolate frog/s (2) — wog/s, meaning person/s of southern European/Mediterranean origin
Recorded as *choc* in children's folk speech. **See also** *Alsatian dog, Dapto dog, Freddo Frog, hollow log* (3), *spotty dog, woolly dog.*

chocolate frog (3) — wog, meaning a virus such as influenza

choof — puff
Recorded in children's speech in the context of smoking marijuana. Possibly from otherwise unrecorded rhyming slang of chuff for puff.

chow — cow (an insult)
20th century. Obsolete.

Christmas cake — thirty-eight (Bingo)
An imperfect rhyme.

Christmas card (1) — guard on a train

Christmas card (2) — guard, meaning prison warder
Convict slang.

Christmas crackers — knackers, meaning testicles
In use during the 1970s. **See also** *Jatz crackers, Kerry Packers.*

Christopher Ash — cash
Usually abbreviated to *C. Ash*. See also *Arthur Ashe, Charlie Ash, Oscar Asche, J. Carroll Nash, sausage and mash, smash, splash*.

Chuck Berry — ferry
After American rock and roll pioneer Charles Edward 'Chuck' Berry (born 1926).

chuck me in the gutter — butter
See also *Dark Town strutter, Johnny Rutter, kerb and gutter, lisp and stutter, mumble and stutter, mutter and stutter, roll me in the gutter, stammer and stutter*.

Chunderloo — spew, meaning to vomit
Usually abbreviated to *chunder*. Thought to derive from the cartoon character 'Chunder Loo of Akim Foo' created by Norman Lindsay (1879–1969). Also used in Cobra shoe polish advertisements 1909–20. 'Chunder' is still current and has been in continual use, most famously perhaps in the Men at Work song 'Land Down Under' (1981): 'I've just come back from the land down under, Where women glow and men chunder.' Obsolete in the full form. See also *Dan McGrew* (1), *Danny La Rue* (2), *Harvey Drew, Spiro Agnew, up and under*.

chunk of beef (1) — chief, meaning the leader, or boss
Also occurs as *chunka*. Australian from World War II.

chunk of beef (2) — thief
20th century. See also *tea leaf, tea leafing*.

chunka — see chunk of beef (1)

church bazaar — car
See also *Hedy Lamarr, jam jar, Kirk's Bazaar, lah de dah* (1), *Malvern Star, Marie La Var, Mars Bar, near and far* (2).

citronella — quinella (a horseracing bet)
World War II.

civil answer — cancer
See also *ballet dancer, Bengal lancer, candy dancer, Charlie Dancer, Jack the dancer, Jimmy Dancer, Johnny Dancer, Mario Lanza, Spanish dancer*.

Clark Gable (1) — table
After the Hollywood actor (1901–60). World War II. **See also** *Betty Grable, Cain and Abel*.

Clark Gable (2) — cable

clerk of the course — sauce
From horseracing. **See also** *dead horse, racehorse, rocking horse, Tommy farter*.

clicketty-click (1) — stick
Probably onomatopoeic. **See also** *Rickety Dick* (2).

clicketty-click (2) — sixty-six (Bingo)
Recorded during World War I. Probably older.

clothes pegs — legs
See also *bacon and eggs, Dutch pegs, fried eggs, Ginger Meggs, Gregory pegs, ham and eggs, Neville Beggs, nine gallon kegs, Scotch pegs*.

cloven hoofter — poofter, meaning a male homosexual
Also occurs as *cloven hoof*. **See also** *cow's hoof, horse's hoof, willy woofter, woolly boof, woolly woofter*.

clucky hen — ten
See also *Big Ben, cock and hen, Tony's den*.

coalbox — chorus of a song
A very imperfect rhyme reported by Meredith but unrecorded elsewhere.

Cobar shower/s — flower/s
Apparently first recorded in Australia in 1959 but known in American criminal speech since perhaps the 1920s. **See also** *David Gower/s* (1), *half an hour* (2), *ivory towers*.

cobblers — see cobblers' awls

cobblers' awls — balls (as in testicles): used to express disbelief, disagreement
Usually abbreviated to *cobblers*. More common in Britain than in Australia, except among those of English origin. **See also** *Niagara Falls, orchestra stalls, Queenie Pauls, town halls, Wentworth Falls*.

Coca Cola — bowler (in cricket)
World War II.

cock and hen — ten
See also *Big Ben, clucky hen, Tony's den*.

cock sparra — Yarra, meaning insane
Probably derived from the mental hospital at Yarra Bend on Melbourne's famous River Yarra. In use since the 1960s.

cocky's clip (1) — dip, meaning a pickpocket
Used in this sense in the USA. 1920s.

cocky's clip (2) — dip, meaning swim, as in to 'take a dip' or possibly 'sheep dip'
1920s?

cocky's joy — boy
See also *Mark Foy, mother's joy/s, pride and joy*.

Coffs Harbour — barber
World War II and after the NSW coastal town. **See also** *Sydney Harbour*.

Coke and sars(parilla) — arse, as in bottom
See also *Aris, bottle and glass, Bulli Pass, Herb Alpert, Khyber Pass, lemonade and sars(parilla)* (1), *Mark Ella, Reg Gasnier*.

Cole Porter — water
After the American songwriter (1891–1964). **See also** *fisherman's daughter, LKS Mackinnon Stakes, mother and daughter, squatter's daughter*.

Collier and Moat — coat
See also *armour float, I'm afloat, motorboat*.

comic cuts — guts, meaning intestines
Australian original from World War II, although thought to be after an Australian children's publication of that name which first appeared in 1890. **See also** *Fred Strutt*.

Conan Doyle — boil, meaning a skin abscess
After the creator of Sherlock Holmes, Sir Arthur Conan Doyle (1859–1930). **See also** *Theatre Royal*.

condiments and sauces — horses
See also *apple sauce, Ella May Morse, tomato sauce/s* (2).

constant screamer — concertina
Since the 19th century in England, at which time the concertina was a popular instrument. Still in use among Australian concertina players.

cook — look
Probably a shortened form of *Captain Cook*. From the 1940s. **See also** *butcher's hook* (3), *Captain Cook*, *squiz*.

corroboree — spree, or drunken spree
According to Julian Franklyn this term, derived from a southeastern Aboriginal language, was used by Australian soldiers in London during World War I. It reappeared in World War II.

cotton wool — pull, as in male masturbation
See also *John Bull* (2), *Roy Bull* (1).

cough and sneeze — cheese
See also *Annie (Anna) Louise*, *piper's knees*, *stand at ease*.

council houses — trousers
Of British derivation. **See also** *dead wowsers*, *petrol bowsers*, *rammy rousers*, *round the houses*, *terrace houses*.

country cousin — dozen (usually bottles or cans of beer)

cow's hoof — poof, poofter, meaning a male homosexual
World War II. **See also** *cloven hoofter*, *horse's hoof*, *willy woofter*, *woolly boof*, *woolly woofter*.

cows and kisses — missus, meaning wife
See also *cheese and kisses*, *hugs and kisses*.

cricket bats — tatts, meaning teeth
World War II. Recorded in Royal Australian Navy speech. **See also** *Barrier Reef*, *Barry Beath*, *Hampstead Heath*, *Ted Heath*.

cries and screeches — leeches
From at least the early 20th century.

Crimea — beer
See also *Britney Spears*, *cherry cheer*, *Germaine Greer/s* (1), *oh my dear*, *Perc Galea*, *pig's ear*, *Port Melbourne Pier* (2), *pot of good cheer*, *Ray Stehr*, *Terry Dear*.

cry and laugh — scarf
World War II. **See also** *scrum half*.

cucumber — number
20th century.

cuff link — drink
World War II. **See also** *kitchen sink, pen and ink, Silver Link* (1), *tiddlywink*.

cupcake — fart, as in break wind
Possibly from cupcake rhyming with *break* wind. Recorded in children's speech. Possibly related to the practice of cupping one's hand to 'catch' a fart and then pushing it into the face of another child. **See also** *apple tart, bacon and egg tart, bottle mart, Dicky Bart, fairy dart, horse and cart* (1), *jam tart* (2), *raspberry tart, Stevey Hart*.

curly locks — socks
Australian. 20th century. **See also** *almond rocks, Bobby rocks, Goldilocks, Jarrah blocks, Joe Rocks, keys and locks, ton o' my rocks*.

currant bun (1) — Hun, meaning German
Obsolete.

currant bun (2) — sun
Cockney but also heard in Australia. **See also** *Atilla the Hun, hot cross bun, Peter Gunn*.

currant bun (3) — nun
See also *you're the one*.

currant cake — awake

curried mince — prince
See also *pear and quince*.

curry and rice — price
Australian from World War II. **See also** *fried rice* (1).

custard and jelly — telly (short for television)
Current early 2000s, though first recorded in England in the 1960s. **See also** *Ned Kelly* (2).

cut lunch — punch

***Cutty Sark* (1) — nark, meaning an informer?**
After the famous clipper ship. **See also** *dog and bark, Noah's Ark* (5).

***Cutty Sark* (2) — shark**
See also *after darks, Joan of Arc/s, Joe Marks, Jonah, Luna Park, Marcus Clark(e), Noah's Ark* (6).

D

***Dad and Dave* — shave**
After the characters created by Steele Rudd (Arthur Hoey Davis, 1868–1935), which first appeared in print in the late 19th century to great acclaim and then became even more famous on stage and in the early cinema. From the 1930s, the stories were serialised on radio, from which time the rhyming slang is thought to have originated. It was still current throughout World War II. Dad and Dave yarns — often of a risqué nature — are still quite widely told. **See also** *dig a grave, digging in a grave, misbehave.*

***dad and mum* (1) — rum**
From at least World War II. **See also** *deaf and dumb* (2), *finger and thumb, poofter's bum, Tom Thumb* (1).

***dad and mum* (2) — Bonox and rum**
From at least World War II.

***daisy roots* — boots**
English, South African and American. Recorded in Australia 1900 (and in the USA by at least the 1850s) but almost certainly in use here long before. **See also** *fiddles and flutes, silly galoots.*

***Dalai Lamas* — dramas, as in 'No dramas'**
The Dalai Lama visited Australia in mid-2007 amidst some controversy. Internet 2007.

***dancing queen* — seventeen (Bingo)**

***Dan McGrew* (1) — spew, meaning vomit**
Current WA 2007. **See also** *Chunderloo, Danny La Rue* (2), *Harvey Drew, Spiro Agnew.*

***Dan McGrew* (2) — 'flu, influenza**

Dan Milecki's — eckies, meaning Esctasy tablets
Dan Milecki is a Melbourne racecaller. Current WA 2007.

Dan Quayle — bail, meaning flee; as in, to 'bail out on' someone

Danny La Rue (1) — fifty-two (Bingo)
After the stage name of a famous female impersonator, Daniel Carroll (1927–2009).

Danny La Rue (2) — spew, meaning vomit
See also *Chunderloo*, *Dan McGrew* (1), *Harvey Drew*, *Spiro Agnew*.

Dapto — dog
Seems to fall outside the definition of rhyming slang. See also *Dapto dog*.

Dapto dog — wog, meaning a person of southern European/ Mediterranean origin
Usually abbreviated to *Dapto*, from the famous NSW dog races, the Dapto Dogs. NSW only? From at least the 1980s. See also *Alsatian dog*, *chocolate frog/s* (2), *Freddo Frog*, *hollow log* (3), *spotty dog*, *woolly dog*.

Darby and Joan (1) — loan
After the codgerly old couple of popular sentiment since the 18th century. From the 1940s. See also *Jack Jones*, *on your own*, *Vic Damone*.

Darby and Joan (2) — phone, telephone
See also *Al Capone*, *dog and bone*, *eau de Cologne* (1), *ozone*.

Darby Kel — see *Darby Kelly*

Darby Kelly — belly, meaning stomach
Also in the shortened form *Darby Kel*, probably from the late 19th century? See also *Aunt Nelly*, *Ned Kelly* (1), *Nelly Kelly*.

dark and dim — swim
See also *Jungle Jim*, *Tiger Tim*.

dark felt — belt (clothing)
Australian from World War II. See also *paddy melt*, *South African veldt*.

Dark Town strutter — butter
Presumably after the jazz standard 'Darktown Strutter's Ball' composed around World War I. See also *chuck me in the gutter*, *Johnny Rutter*, *kerb*

and gutter, lisp and stutter, mumble and stutter, mutter and stutter, roll me in the gutter, stammer and stutter.

darling it hurts — Darlinghurst
Not quite a rhyme, but perhaps an appropriate evocation of the once-rough inner Sydney suburb of Darlinghurst, or 'Darlo' as it has long been known, as well as 'Razorhurst' during the 1920s and '30s. Recently used ironically in an early '90s song of the same title by Paul Kelly and Steve Connelly.

Darryl Patch — match
Often abbreviated to *Darryl*. **See also** *Captain scratches, fleas and scratches, itch and scratch.*

date — see *date and plum*

date and plum — bum, as in bottom; anus
Often abbreviated to *date*. From early 20th century; also in the UK and NZ. **See also** *deaf and dumb* (3), *fife and drum.*

Dave Prince — quince, probably meaning a male homosexual
From the name of a Melbourne bookmaker. World War II.

Dave Sands — hands
After the boxing champion Dave Sands (1926–52). **See also** *brass bands, Brighton le Sands, German band/s, Ray Millands.*

Davey Cloak — person, man
Recorded in children's folk speech. From *Davey Cloak* for bloke. Possibly after a Victorian AFL footballer of that name, spelled 'Cloke'. Reported on the worldwide web 2008. **See also** *artichoke, bag of coke.*

Davey Crockett (1) — socket (for lightbulb)
After the American frontiersman, soldier, wit and politician Colonel David Crockett (1786–1836). This probably dates from the 1950s film and Top 40 hit song based, allegedly, on his life and legend.

Davey Crockett (2) — pocket
See also *locket, Lucy Locket, sky rocket.*

David Boon — spoon
After the legendary Tasmanian cricketer David Boon (born 1960), widely known as 'Boony'. Current Melbourne 2006. **See also** *by the light, Marjorie Moon, Ruby Moon.*

David Gower/s (1) — flower/s
See also *Cobar shower/s, half an hour* (2), *ivory towers.*

David Gower (2) — shower (bath)
After the English cricketer David Gower (born 1957). Current Melbourne 2006. See also *fairy bower, lazy hour, now is the hour, Tyrone Power.*

Dawn Fraser — razor
After the well-known champion Olympic swimmer and public figure Dawn Fraser (born 1937).

Deacon Skinner — dinner
Since at least World War II. See also *Derby winner.*

dead horse — sauce
Invariably tomato, as in 'a *dog's eye* and a *dead horse*'. See also *clerk of the course, dog's eye* (1), *flies and dead horse, lies and dead horse, racehorse, rocking horse, Tommy Farter.*

dead spotted ling — dead ring, as in 'dead ringer', meaning identical
Ling is a species of fish. From early 20th century.

dead wowsers — trousers
Wowser, meaning someone of excessively and repressively puritanical temperament, was coined in the 1870s, though at that time meant someone who complained excessively. Noted in World War II, but probably older. See also *council houses, petrol bowsers, rammy rousers, round the houses, terrace houses.*

deaf adder — ladder
Perhaps derived from the 19th-century term for the snake often known as a 'death adder', a 'deaf adder'. Mid-20th century. Melbourne.

deaf and dumb (1) — drum, meaning the truth and/or the full information about someone or something.
As in 'Give us the drum.' See also *Tom Thumb* (2).

deaf and dumb (2) — rum
World War II. See also *dad and mum* (1), *finger and thumb, poofter's bum, Tom Thumb* (1).

deaf and dumb (3) — bum, as in bottom
See also *date and plum, fife and drum.*

decky dirt — shirt
See also *Dicky dirt, dinky dirt, dirty Bert, Ernie and Bert,Uncle Bert, Val Quirk.*

Dennis Lillee — chilly
After the West Australian cricketer Dennis Lillee (born 1949). Mid-20th century. See also *Piccadilly.*

Denver Cities — titties, meaning female breasts
Usually abbreviated to *Denvers.* See also *Bristol Cities, cats and kitties, Elsie Whitty/ies, Lewis and W(h)itties, Manchester City/ies, Salt Lake Cities, Vatican Cities.*

Denvers — see *Denver Cities*

Derby winner — dinner
20th century. See also *Deacon Skinner.*

Diana Dors — forty-four (Bingo)

dibs and dabs — crabs, meaning body lice (sexually transmissible infection)
Since at least the 1950s. Current in WA 2007. See also *dribs and drabs, Sandy McNabs, smash and grabs.*

Dick Powell — towel
See also *Baden Powell, Bob Powell, dog's growl.*

dickory dock — clock
See also *Eva Bartok, hickery dickery dock, tick tock.*

Dicky Bart — fart, as in break wind
A character in a 1940s radio serial titled *Mrs 'Obbs.* See also *apple tart, bacon and egg tart, bottle mart, cupcake, fairy dart, horse and cart* (1), *jam tart* (2), *raspberry tart, Stevey Hart.*

dicky bird — word, meaning a chat
As in 'Can I have a *dicky bird*?' Cockney origin.

Dicky dirt — shirt
Since at least the early 20th century. See also *decky dirt, dinky dirt, dirty Bert, Ernie and Bert, Uncle Bert, Val Quirk.*

***Dicky Lee* (1)** — **pee, as in urinate**
See also *lolly, Nancy Lee, one hundred and three, Robert E. Lee, wasp and bee* (2), *you and me* (2).

***Dicky Lee* (2)** — **tea**
See also *Gypsy Lee, Jack Shay* (1), *Jenny Lee, Jimmy Lee, Mother Machree, Rosie Lee, wasp and bee* (1), *you and me* (3).

didn't ought — **port (fortified wine)**
See also *Goldsborough Mort*.

dig a grave — **shave**
See also *Dad and Dave, digging in a grave, misbehave*.

Digger's nest — **chest (human)**
World War II. See also *Digger's vest, east and west* (1).

Digger's vest — **chest**
See also *Digger's nest, east and west* (1).

digging in a grave — **having a shave**
Variations are *dig in the grave, dig the grave*. Australian original from at least the early 20th century. Widespread in World War I among British and Australian troops. See also *Dad and Dave, dig a grave, misbehave*.

dilly — **silly**
Possibly an abbreviation of *dillypot* or *Wollondilly*, or possibly not rhyming slang. See also *auntie, Kirribilli, Uncle Willy, Wollondilly*.

dillypot — **twat, meaning vagina; also used as an insult, meaning an unpleasant person**
Another variation is *dillpot*. This rhyme depends on the pronunciation of 'twat' to rhyme with 'pot', although the word is also pronounced to rhyme with 'hat'. Given as 20th-century Australian by Franklyn. See also *dollypot*.

dimple and blotch — **scotch, the alcoholic drink**
See also *Gordon and Gotch* (2).

dingaling — **king**
Recorded in World War II.

dink — **Chink, meaning a Chinese or other Asian person**
20th century.

dinky dirt — shirt
See also *decky dirt, Dicky dirt, dirty Bert, Ernie and Bert, Uncle Bert, Val Quirk*.

Dinny Hayes-er — shit, as in defecate
Said to be after a boxer of the same name. This term arises because *Dinny Hayser* is general slang for 'a king hit', a term that is also, along with *big hit* and *hard hit*, used as rhyming slang for 'shit'. See also *big hit, brace and bit, Eartha Kitt, Edgar Britt, gravel pit, hard hit, Jimmy Britt* (1), *king hit, Mickey Fritt, Oscar Britt, Tom tit*.

dip and chuck it — bucket
See also *dip and duck it*.

dip and duck it — bucket
World War II. See also *dip and chuck it*.

dipstick — prick, as in penis
See also *drop kick* (1), *mad Mick* (2), *Pogo stick* (2), *Rickety Dick* (1), *Uncle Dick, zubrick*.

dirt, grime and dust — crust (on a pie)
See also *dog's eye* (1).

dirty Bert — shirt
See also *decky dirt, dinky dirt, dicky dirt, Ernie and Bert, Uncle Bert, Val Quirk*.

dirty dish — a fish
20th century. See also *Lillian Gish* (2).

dirty Gertie — thirty (Bingo)

disaster — piastre (Egyptian currency)
World War I and revived for use in World War II.

dish ran away with the spoon — hoon, meaning a noisy lout
Derived from the well-known nursery rhyme. Thought to be the longest item of rhyming slang, See also *egg and spoon* (1), *Terry Toon* (1).

do as you like — bike, bicycle
See also *Jimmy Pike*.

do me good — (fire)wood
From at least the late 19th century.

docker's hook — book, meaning a bookmaker's list of odds
After a grappling tool used by wharfies. Australian 20th-century original. **See also** *Tommy Rook*.

Doctor Bevan — seven
After a Melbourne doctor. World War II. Obsolete.

Doctor Kildare/s — stairs
After the character in the 1960s television medical series of the same name. **See also** *apples and pears*.

dodge and shirk — work
Australian original from at least the early 20th century. **See also** *terrible Turk*.

(the) dog — see *dog and bone*

dog and bark — nark, meaning a criminal informer
In criminal and police speech, a 'dog' is an informant. **See also** *Cutty Sark* (1), *Noah's Ark* (5).

dog and bone — phone, telephone
Usually abbreviated to *dog*. **See also** *Al Capone*, *Darby and Joan* (2), *eau de Cologne* (1), *ozone*.

dog's date — eight
See also *garden gate*.

dog's dinner (1) — deaner, meaning one shilling (pre-decimal currency)
In Australia 'deaner' was/is usually pronounced to rhyme with 'meaner' rather than with 'dinner'. Obsolete. **See also** *Riverina*.

dog's dinner (2) — skinner, meaning when the house wins the bets in the gambling game of two-up
World War II.

dog's dinner (3) — spinner, meaning the person who tosses the coins in the gambling game of two-up
World War II.

dog's eye (1) — pie
Australian invention. From the 1960s at least. **See also** *dead horse* (with which this term is frequently joined), *Nazi spy* (1), *Nelly Bligh* (3), *pig's eye* (1), *stock and die* (2), *2KY* (3).

dog's eye (2) — (neck)tie
See also *Fourth of July*, *lamb's fry*, *mud in your eye*, *Nazi spy* (2), *Nellie Bligh* (5), *Russian spy*, *stock and die* (1), *2KY* (1).

dog's growl — towel
See also *Baden Powell*, *Bob Powell*, *Dick Powell*.

Dolly Gray — trey, meaning a threepenny coin (pre-decimal currency), or a three in cards
Obsolete. See also *Alma Grey*, *Dora Gray*, *horse and dray*.

dollypot — twat, as in vagina
Derived from the goldmining apparatus of the same name and so, presumably, originating in the 19th century, possibly from the WA goldrushes of the 1890s. Rhyme depends on the Australian pronunciation of 'twat'. Obsolete. See also *dillypot*.

Don Doak — smoke, meaning cigarette
See also *laugh and joke*; *Sentimental Bloke*; *wood, coal and coke* (2).

Donald Duck (1) — fuck, as in sexual intercourse
As in to 'have a *Donald Duck*'. After the well-known Disney cartoon character and dating from the 1960s. See also *Bill Buck* (2), *Friar Tuck*, *Joe Buck* (1), *Mickey Duck* (1).

Donald Duck (2) — truck (motor vehicle)
Usually abbreviated to *Donald*. After the Walt Disney cartoon character and current from the 1960s. See also *Bill Buck* (1), *Frank Buck*, *goose and duck*, *Joe Buck* (2), *Mickey Duck* (2).

don't be funny — dunny, meaning toilet
20th century. See also *Gene Tunney* (2), *jam and honey*.

don't forget her (1) — French letter, meaning a condom
don't forget her (2) — letter (correspondence)
Used in this sense in 'Duke' Tritton's rhyming slang letter, dated 1905. See also *carburettor*, *never better/s*.

Dora — see Dora Gray

Dora Gray — trey, meaning a threepenny coin (pre-decimal currency)
Often abbreviated to *Dora*. Obsolete. See also *Alma Grey*, *Dolly Gray*, *horse and dray*.

Doris Day — gay, meaning homosexual

Often abbreviated to *Doris*. After the American film star and singer Doris Day (born 1924), who is widely celebrated in the gay community. Probably since the 1960s or '70s.

Dorothy — see *Dorothy Dix*

Dorothy Dix — six (cricket)

Dorothy Dixer is a common variation; sometimes abbreviated to *Dorothy*. After the American journalist Dorothy Dix (1870–1951), who ran a famous question and answer column that was syndicated to newspapers throughout the world, including Australia. Australian in origin. The Australian slang term 'a *Dorothy Dixer*' for a 'tame' question asked in parliament was first recorded in the 1960s, but is certainly older — and still current. From the '70s, *Dorothy Dix* became cricketing rhyming slang. **See also** *Richard Dix, Tom Mix.*

Dorothy Gish — dish

After Dorothy Gish (1898–1968), Hollywood actress of the early silent cinema and sister to actress Lillian Gish, who also features in Australian rhyming slang. **See also** *Lillian Gish* (1).

dot — wine drinker

Derived from the rhyming slang *wine dot* for a sot, or drunkard. **See also** *plonk dot, wine dot.*

down and up — cup

World War II. **See also** *Fox terrier pup.*

down on your knees — forty-three (Bingo)

Bingo callers often call the end of a number in its plural form.

dribs and drabs — crabs, meaning body lice (sexually transmissible infection)

World War II. **See also** *dibs and dabs, Sandy McNabs, smash and grabs.*

droopy drawers — forty-four (Bingo)

Bingo callers will often call the end of a number in its plural form.

drop kick (1) — prick, meaning penis

See also *dipstick, mad Mick* (2), *Pogo stick* (2), *Rickety Dick* (1), *Uncle Dick, zubrick.*

***drop kick* (2) — thick, meaning stupid**
An insult in children's folk speech.

***drop kick and punt* — cunt, as in female genitalia**
Usually abbreviated to *drop kick*. See also *All Quiet on the Western Front*, *Ballina Punt*, *Berkshire Hunt*, *Billy Hunt*, *grumble and grunt*, *Joe Hunt*, *mumble and grunt*, *Stockton Punt*.

***drum and fife* — wife**
See also *trouble and strife*.

***dry rots* — trots, meaning diarrhoea**
See also *red hots* (1).

***Dublin Fair* — hair**
Australian–Irish variation of *Barnet Fair* since at least the early 20th century. See also *Barnet Fair*, *Fred Astaire* (2), *here and there*, *over there*, *preference share*, *table and chair*.

***duck and dive* — twenty-five (Bingo)**

***duck's neck* — cheque**
World War II. See also *goose's neck*, *Gregory Peck* (1), *nervous wreck*, *total wreck*.

***ducks and drakes* — shakes (the DTs, or delirium tremens)**
World War II; still current. See also *Joe Blake/s* (1), *Sexton Blakes* (1).

***ducks and geese* — police**
World War II; still heard among older Australians in 2007.

***Duke of Kent* — rent**
From at least 1950 and widely used in English rhyming slang.

***Duke of York* (1) — fork**
***Duke of York* (2) — walk**
See also *pickle and pork*, *stick of chalk*.

***Duncan Hall* — wall**
See also *bat and ball* (2), *Queenie Paul*.

***dunny door* — Commodore (make of car)**
Current WA 2007.

Dutch pegs — legs
Since at least the early 20th century in Australia and from the earlier English *Scotch pegs*. Appears in 'Duke' Tritton's rhyming slang letter dated 1905. See also *bacon and eggs, clothes pegs, fried eggs, Ginger Meggs, Gregory Pegs, ham and eggs, Neville Beggs, nine gallon kegs, Scotch pegs.*

E

each way bet — set, meaning pair of female breasts

eagle — bar, meaning two under par in golf
Possibly not rhyming slang?

early morn — horn, meaning an erection
See also *Sarah Vaughan, Somerset Maugham.*

Eartha Kitt — shit, as in defecate
Eartha Kitt (born 1927), is a well-known American singer noted for sensual renditions of torch songs. See also *big hit, brace and bit, Dinny Hayes-er, Edgar Britt, gravel pit, hard hi, Jimmy Britt* (1), *king hit, Mickey Fritt, Oscar Britt, Tom tit.*

Eartha Kitts — tits, meaning female breasts
Current among English-background speakers WA 2007. See also *brace and bits, tracy bits, trey bits* (2), *Vita Brits.*

east and west (1) — chest
Also in English usage. See also *Digger's nest, Digger's vest.*

east and west (2) — vest
World War II. See also *hairy chest.*

East Melbourne Piers — see *Melbourne Piers*

east o' Sydneys — kidneys
Melbourne from *c.* early 20th century. See also *North Sydney, South Sydney.*

eat 'em alive — five
World War II. See also *beehive, Jack's alive, man alive.*

eau de Cologne (1) — phone, the telephone
World War II. See also *Al Capone, Darby and Joan* (2), *dog and bone, ozone.*

eau de Cologne (2) — alone
See also *Jack Malone, Pat Malone, Tod Sloane*.

Edgar Britt — shit, as in defecate
After the Australian jockey Edgar Britt (born 1913), who retired in 1959. Surprisingly, this term seems to date only from the 1960s. **See also** *big hit, brace and bit, Dinny Hayes-er, Eartha Kitt, gravel pit, hard hit, Jimmy Britt* (1), *king hit, Mickey Fritt, Oscar Britt, Tom tit*.

Edgar Britts — (the) shits, meaning to be irritated
As in 'He is giving me the *Edgars*.' **See also** *Jimmy Britts* (1), *Tom tits, trey bits* (1), *trizzy bits*.

Edna May — way
Usually as in to lose one's way.

egg and spoon (1) — hoon, meaning a noisy lout
An earlier use of the term 'hoon', which is now more widely used to mean a nuisance automobile driver. **See also** *dish ran away with the spoon, Terry Toon* (1).

egg and spoon (2) — goon, meaning a person acting in a stupid and/or inconsiderate manner
Dates from the 1970s.

egg and spoon (3) — coon, meaning a coloured person
See also *Terry Toon* (2).

egg flip — a tip, meaning horseracing
Since World War II. **See also** *egg flipper*.

egg flipper — tipper, meaning one who tips on horse races
See also *egg flip*.

Eiffel Tower — a shower (of rain)
After the Paris icon built 1887–89. 20th century. **See also** *happy hour*.

eight-day clock — cock, meaning penis
See also *Mort's Dock, Rock Around the Clock, Victoria Dock*.

eighteen pence (1) — fence (structure)
World War II.

eighteen pence (2) — fence, meaning a receiver of stolen goods

elephant's — see *elephant's trunk*

elephant's herd — turd, as in faeces
See also *George the Third, Henry the Third, King George the Third, King Henry the Third, King Richard the Third, mocking bird, Richard the Third* (2), *William the Third.*

elephant's tool — stool (furniture)

elephant's trunk — drunk
Often abbreviated to *elephant's*. Recorded in England during the 1850s and in Australia from the 1890s. Current in underworld parlance during 1950s and still heard occasionally today. **See also** *Molly/Mollo the Monk, Molly Monk.*

Ella May Morse — horse
American singer of the 1940s and '50s (born 1924). She had a hit with 'Cow-Cow Boogy' in 1942. **See also** *apple sauce, condiments and horses, tomato sauce/s* (2).

Elmer — dud, meaning ineffectual
See also *Elmer Fudd, Kevin Rudd, potato and spud.*

Elmer Fudd — dud, meaning ineffectual
After the comic character created by Ted Avery in the late 1930s and subsequently popularised in film and television by Warner Brothers. Probably from the 1940–50s. **See also** *Elmer, Kevin Rudd, potato and spud.*

Elsie Whitty/ies — titty/ies, meaning female breasts
See also *Bristol Cities, cats and kitties, Denver Cities, Lewis and W(h)itties, Manchester City/ies, Salt Lake Cities, Vatican Cities.*

Enoch Arden — garden
After a poem of the same name by Alfred Lord Tennyson first published in 1864, although it is the film version of the story of a returned sailor believed drowned (1911) that is the more likely origin of the rhyme. Used by Japanese prisoners-of-war from 1940. Obsolete.

Epsom Races — faces
See also *boat race, Chevvy Chase, first base, first place, Martin Place, Melrose Place, Princess Grace, smile place.*

Eric Baume — home
After New Zealand-born radio and TV personality Eric Baume (1900–67).

Ernie and Bert — shirt
Possibly after the characters of the same name in the American television children's show *Sesame Street*, first broadcast in 1969. **See also** *decky dirt, Dicky dirt, dinky dirt, dirty Bert, Uncle Bert, Val Quirk.*

Errol Flynn — chin
After Tasmanian-born adventurer and Hollywood star Errol Flynn (1909–59). **See also** *thick and thin* (1), *Vera Lynn* (1).

Ethel Merman — German
Stage name of American singer and actress Ethel Zimmerman (1908–84), noted for her powerful voice and broad range. Mid-20th century.

Eva Bartok — clock
Eva Bartok was the stage name of Hollywood actress Eva Ivanova Szöke (1927–98). **See also** *dickory dock, hickery dickery dock, tick tock.*

F

fairy bower — shower (as in bathing)
World War II, though perhaps considerably older. **See also** *David Gower* (2), *happy hour, lazy hour, now is the hour, Tyrone Power.*

fairy dart — fart, as in break wind
See also *apple tart, bacon and egg tart, bottle mart, cupcake, Dicky Bart, horse and cart* (1), *jam tart* (2), *raspberry tart, Stevey Hart.*

fancy sash — bash, as in beat someone up
Also as *fancy sashed*. Recorded in 1902.

Farmer Giles — piles, meaning haemorrhoids
World War II; still current. **See also** *asteroids, Bea Miles, Chalfont St Giles, laughs and smiles, metric miles.*

fiddle(s) and flutes — boots
World War II. **See also** *daisy roots, silly galoots.*

fiddly — see fiddly-did

fiddly-did — quid, meaning one pound (pre-decimal currency)
Usually abbreviated to a *fiddly*. From World War II, perhaps earlier. Obsolete. **See also** *tin lid* (3), *yid.*

field of wheat — street
Recorded 1902.

fife and drum — bum, as in bottom
See also *date and plum*, *deaf and dumb* (3).

fine and dandy — brandy

finger and thumb — rum
See also *dad and mum* (1), *deaf and dumb* (2), *poofter's bum*, *Tom Thumb* (1).

fireman's braces — races (horseracing)
See also *airs and graces*, *braces*, *trot and paces*.

first base — face
See also *boat race*, *Chevvy Chase*, *Epsom Races*, *first place*, *Martin Place*, *Melrose Place*, *Princess Grace*, *smile place*.

first place — face
See also *boat race*, *Chevvy Chase*, *Epsom Races*, *first base*, *Martin Place*, *Melrose Place*, *Princess Grace*, *smile place*.

fisherman's daughter — water
See also *Cole Porter*, *LKS Mackinnon Stakes*, *mother and daughter*, *squatter's daughter*.

five b' two — Jew
Often occurs as *five-ter*. See also *five to two*, *four b' two* (1).

five to two — Jew
Current in prison speech around 1950. See also *five b' two*, *four b' two* (1).

five-eight (1) — plate
See also *Harry Tait*, *Michael Pate*, *Reg Date*.

five-eight (2) — mate, meaning friend; likely to be male
See also *China plate*, *ocean liner*, *old China plate*, *Royal Doulton*.

fleas and ants — pants
See also *bull ants*, *Saint Vitus' Dance*.

fleas and itches — pictures (pronounced 'pichers'), meaning cinema

Australian. Dates from at least the 1950s; probably the '30s, when fleas at the cinema were a possibility.

fleas and louse — **house**
See also *Mickey Mouse* (2), *Minnie Mouse*.

fleas and scratches — **matches (firelighters)**
See also *Captain Scratches*, *Darryl Patch*, *itch and scratch*.

Flemington Races — **braces**
World War II. See also *airs and graces*, *Randwick Races*.

flick pass — **arse, as in lose one's job**
As in to 'get the arse'. Probably obsolete, except in the variation, 'get the flick', meaning to be dismissed from a job or brushed off.

flies and dead horse — **pies and sauce**
See also *dead horse*, *lies and dead horse*.

flowers and frolics — **bollocks**
See also *hydraulics*, *Jackson Pollocks*.

flowery dell — **cell (prison)**
Also used in Britain since at least the 19th century, and may be derived from 19th-century peddler's slang for a room in a lodging house.

football pools — **jewels**

forgive and forget — **cigarette**
20th century, Australian origin. See also *African nigger*, *you-can-bets*.

forward pass/es — **glass/es (drinking)**
See also *pig's arse*.

found a nail — **round the tail**
From sheep shearing.

four b' two (1) — **Jew**
Usually abbreviated to *fourby*. See also *five b' two*, *five to two*.

four b' two (2) — **screw, meaning a prison warder**
Current in NSW gaols. See also *kangaroo* (1).

Fourth of July — **(neck)tie**
See also *dog's eye* (2), *lamb's fry*, *mud in your eye*, *Nazi spy* (2), *Nellie Bligh* (5), *Russian spy*, *stock and die* (1), *2KY* (1).

Fox terrier pup — cup
See also *down and up*.

France and Spain — rain
See also *Frankie Laine* (2), *Geoffrey Lane* (2), *King of Spain* (2).

Frank Buck — truck
See also *Bill Buck* (1), *Donald Duck* (2), *goose and duck*, *Joe Buck* (2), *Mickey Duck* (2).

Frank Hyde — wide (cricket), as in when a ball is delivered 'wide of the mark'
Frank Hyde (1916 or 1917–2007) was a prominent NSW Rugby League footballer, coach and broadcaster.

Frank Thring — ring (jewellery)
Well-known Australian actor and entertainer Frank Thring (1926–94) was famous for his flamboyant style of dress and gesture. From the 1970s. See also *gin sling*, *tingaling*.

Frankie Laine (1) — brain
After the stage name of actor and singer Francesco Paolo LoVecchio (1913–2007), who was well-known as the singer of the *Rawhide* TV series theme in the 1960s and since. See also *trams and trains* (1).

Frankie Laine (2) — rain
See also *France and Spain*, *Geoffrey Lane* (1), *King of Spain* (2).

Frankie Laine (3) — train
See also *Geoffrey Lane* (2), *hail and rain*, *King of Spain* (3), *Lois Lane*, *pouring rain*, *roaring rain*, *shower of rain*, *thunder and rain*, *wind and rain*.

Franz Liszt — pissed, meaning drunk
After the Hungarian-born composer Franz Liszt (1811–86). Current WA 2007. See also *Adrian Quist*, *Brahms and Liszt*, *Mozart and Liszt*, *Oliver Twist* (1), *Schindler's List*, *sisters apart*.

Fred — see *Fred Astaire* (2)

Fred Astaire (1) — chair
After the American dancer and actor Fred Astaire (1899–1987). Australian original from around World War II.

Fred Astaire (2) — hair, meaning a single hair

Sometimes abbreviated to a *Fred*. Fred Astaire was always impeccably coiffured. **See also** *Barnet Fair, Dublin Fair, here and there, over there, preference share, table and chair.*

Fred Astaire (3) — lair, as in a man given to flashy dress and behaviour
Fred Astaire was an especially debonaire personality. **See also** *teddy bear.*

Fred Nile — mile (pre-decimal unit of length)
After the NSW conservative politician Fred Nile (born 1934).

Fred Strutt — gut, meaning stomach
See also *comic cuts.*

Freddo — see Freddo Frog

Freddo Frog — wog, meaning a person of southern European/Mediterranean origin
A rhyming play on another rhyme for 'wog', *chocolate frog* (2). Usually abbreviated to *Freddo*. Freddo Frogs are a well-known chocolate confection, probably first invented in Australia by MacRobertsons in 1930. From *c.* 1980s. **See also** *Alsatian dog, chocolate frog* (2), *Dapto dog, hollow log* (3), *spotty dog, woolly dog.*

Freddo Frogs — togs, meaning trousers; also swimming costumes
Recorded in children's folk speech as *Freddos*, meaning swimming costumes. After the name of a popular chocolate confection.

Friar Tuck — fuck, as in sexual intercourse
After Robin Hood's portly monk companion. **See also** *Bill Buck* (2), *Donald Duck* (1), *Joe Buck* (1), *Mickey Duck* (1).

fried eggs — legs
Australian rhyme current since the 1930s. **See also** *bacon and eggs, clothes pegs, Dutch pegs, Ginger Meggs, Gregory Pegs, ham and eggs, Neville Beggs, nine gallon kegs, Scotch pegs.*

fried rice (1) — price
20th century. **See also** *curry and rice.*

fried rice (2) — dice
See also *cats and mice.*

frog and toad — road
Cockneyism since at least the 1850s; first recorded in Australia in 1900 but almost certainly in use earlier. **See also** *Rosewall and Hoad*.

Frog skin — sovereign (pronounced 'sov-rin'), meaning a pound coin (pre-decimal currency)
Late 19th century. Obsolete.

froth and bubble (1) — double, a kind of bet (horseracing)
World War II.

froth and bubble (2) — trouble
Said to be prison slang in 1955. **See also** *Barney Rubble*.

fuck shop — tuck shop; school canteen
Children's folk speech.

G

garden gate — eight (Bingo)
See also *dog's date*.

garden shed — dead
Current WA 2007. **See also** *brown bread, kangaroo Ted, lump of lead (2), wombat*.

Gary Ablett — tablet
After Victorian Australian Rules footballer Gary Ablett (born 1961). Australian from the 1980s.

gay and frisky — whisky
Was British rhyming slang. Current from the late 19th century. **See also** *young and frisky*.

gay and hearty — party
Australian. Obsolete? **See also** *Moriarty*.

Gene Tunney (1) — money
After the American boxer Gene Tunney (1898–1978). Recorded in New Zealand from the 1960s but likely to be much older. **See also** *bees and honey, Bugs Bunny, sugar and honey*.

Gene Tunney (2) — dunny, meaning toilet
See also *don't be funny, jam and honey*.

Geoffrey Lane (1) — rain
Geoffrey Lane is a champion jockey and trainer. Mid-20th century. Melbourne? **See also** *France and Spain, Frankie Laine* (2), *King of Spain* (2).

Geoffrey Lane (2) — train
Mid-20th century. Melbourne? **See also** *Frankie Laine* (3), *hail and rain, King of Spain* (3), *Lois Lane, pouring rain, roaring rain, shower of rain, thunder and rain, wind and rain*.

George Alfred Black — back
Usually abbreviated to *George Alfred*. **See also** *hammer and tack* (6), *Johnny Mack* (1), *Melbourne, tin tack* (1).

George Moore (1) — four (cricket)
George Moore (1923–2008) was a leading jockey who retired in 1971. Possibly from the 1960s.

George Moore (2) — sure

George the Third — turd, as in faeces; usually a dog's
After the British monarch (1738–1820) known for his madness and as the king who lost the American colonies. **See also** *elephant's herd, Henry the Third, King George the Third, King Henry the Third, King Richard the Third, mocking bird, Richard the Third* (2), *William the Third*.

Georgie Moore — door
Possibly also after jockey George Moore (1923-2008).

gerbera — Yarborough (term used in the card game of Bridge)
World War II. **See also** *lubra*.

Germaine Greer/s (1) — beer/s
After the feminist Germaine Greer (born 1939). Australian; from the 1980s. **See also** *Britney Spears, cherry cheer, Crimea, oh my dear, Perc Galea, pig's ear, Port Melbourne Pier* (2), *pot of good cheer, Ray Stehr, Terry Dear*.

Germaine Greer/s (2) — ear/s
See also *ginger beer/s* (2), *lager beers, Melbourne Piers, Perc Galeas, Port Melbourne Pier/s* (1), *Terry Dears, Williamstown Piers*.

German band/s — hand/s
Late 19th and early 20th century. Also current from *c.* late 1970s? **See also** *brass bands, Brighton le Sands, Dave Sands, Ray Millands*.

Gerry Riddle — piddle, as in urinate
Australian. **See also** *hey diddle diddle* (2), *hi diddle diddle* (2), *Jimmy Riddle*, *Nelson Riddle*, *Shannon*.

Gertie Gitana — banana
Gertie Gitana (1888–1957) was a music hall entertainer who had a hit with the song 'Let's All Go Down the Strand', which featured the refrain 'have a banana', often changed by audiences to 'Gertie Gitana'. First or second decade of the 20th century. Obsolete.

get up and run — thirty-one (Bingo)

giddy goat — tote, totalisator (horseracing)
World War II. **See also** *billy goat* (2), *canal boat*, *nanny goat* (2).

giddy gout — boy scout
Usually abbreviated to *giddy*. Thought to derive from the children's rhyme 'Giddy giddy gout with your shirt hanging out.' From *c*. World War I. **See also** *Brussels sprout*.

gin and water — mile and a quarter
Horseracing term.

ginger ale (1) — bail, meaning a bond

ginger ale (2) — tail, meaning bottom, as in 'The police are on my tail.'
1960s.

ginger beer (1) — engineer, usually on ships
British Merchant Navy usage, according to Franklyn, who also notes that the term was applied specifically in Australia to the (Military) Corps of Engineers. From World War II.

ginger beer/s (2) — ear/s
World War II. **See also** *Germaine Greer/s* (2), *lager beers*, *Melbourne Piers*, *Perc Galeas*, *Port Melbourne Pier/s* (1), *Terry Dears*, *Williamstown Piers*.

ginger beer (3) — queer, meaning a male homosexual

Ginger Meggs — legs
Ginger Meggs was a popular comic strip character from the 1920s, the creation of James Charles Bancks. **See also** *bacon and eggs*, *clothes pegs*, *Dutch pegs*, *fried eggs*, *Gregory Pegs*, *ham and eggs*, *Neville Beggs*, *nine gallon kegs*, *Scotch pegs*.

girl abductor — **conductor (of a tram)**
Recorded 1902. Obsolete.

gin sling — **ring (jewellery)**
Current 2007. **See also** *Frank Thring, tingaling.*

goanna — **piano (pronounced 'pianner')**
Recorded in 1918. Possibly rhyming slang on rhyming slang, as *Joanna* is also used for piano; or 'pee-anna', also in 1918. In Australia (although from at least 1846 in Britain). **See also** *Joanna.*

God strike me dead — **bed**
See also *Bill and Ted, needle and thread, Rocky Ned, roses red, Uncle Ned* (1), *white and red.*

God-forbids — **kids, meaning children**
English but also used in Australia and the USA. **See also** *billy lid/s, Captain, saucepan lids, tin lid/s* (1).

Golden Slipper — **ripper, meaning excellent**
Horseracing term and the name of a famous horse race.

Goldilocks — **socks**
See also *almond rocks, Bobby rocks, curly locks, Jarrah blocks, Joe Rocks, keys and locks, ton o' my rocks.*

Goldsborough Mort — **port (fortified wine)**
After the Australian company founded in 1843. **See also** *didn't ought.*

gone and forgotten — **rotten**
20th century.

gone or here — **gonorrhoea**

goodbye teens — **nineteen (Bingo)**
Possibly a coincidental near-rhyme.

goose and duck — **truck**
See also *Bill Buck* (1), *Donald Duck* (2), *Frank Buck, Joe Buck* (2), *Mickey Duck* (2).

goose's neck — cheque
See also *duck's neck, Gregory Peck* (1), *nervous wreck, total wreck.*

Gordon and Gotch (1) — (wrist)watch

After the name of a well-known newsagents' distributor in Australia. The rhyme is also used in English folk speech, where Gordon and Gotch operates as a firm of book and magazine importers. World War II. **See also** *bottle of Scotch*.

Gordon and Gotch (2) — Scotch (whisky)

Often abbreviated to *G. and G.* **See also** *dimple and blotch*.

Gordon and ten — Scotch (whisky) and water

This horseracing term combines two abbreviated rhyming slangs — the first part from *Gordon and Gotch* for Scotch and the second from *ten furlongs*, a distance of a mile and a quarter, from which is derived 'water'. **See also** *Gordon and Gotch* (2), *ten furlongs*.

Gough — cough

Possibly from the 1970s, after then Prime Minister Gough Whitlam (born 1916).

GPOs — toes

From General Post Office. **See also** *buttons and bows*, *Matt Monroes*, *Old Black Joe/s*, *these and those* (2), *Uncle Joes*.

Graham Eadie — seedy

After the Australian Rugby League player Graham Eadie (born 1953).

grasshopper — copper, meaning a police officer

See also *bottle and stopper*, *bottle stopper*, *greasy mop*, *hot scone*, *John Cleese*, *Johnhop/s*, *Johnhopper*.

gravel pit — shit, as in defecate

See also *big hit*, *brace and bit*, *Dinny Hayes-er*, *Eartha Kitt*, *Edgar Britt*, *hard hit*, *Jimmy Britt* (1), *king hit*, *Mickey Fritt*, *Oscar Britt*, *Tom tit*.

greasy — see *greasy mop*

greasy mop — cop, meaning police officer; can also mean a detective

Often abbreviated to *greasy*. **See also** *bottle and stopper*, *bottle stopper*, *grasshopper*, *hot scone*, *John Cleese*, *Johnhop/s*, *Johnhopper*.

Great Australian Bight — light (for a cigarette)

Great Barrier Reef — The Sheaf, a hotel in Double Bay.

A very local rhyming slang.

greengages — **wages**
World War II. **See also** *rock of ages*.

Gregory Peck (1) — **cheque**
Often abbreviated to the *Gregory*. After the well-known Hollywood star Gregory Peck (born 1916). **See also** *duck's neck, goose's neck, nervous wreck, total wreck*.

Gregory Peck (2) — **deck**
Possibly peculiar to Melbourne wharfies. Mid-20th century.

Gregory Peck (3) — **neck**
World War II. **See also** *bushel and peck*.

Gregory Pecks — **specs, spectacles**
1950s.

Gregory Pegs — **legs**
Thought to be mangled from *Gregory Peck*. **See also** *bacon and eggs, clothes pegs, Dutch pegs, fried eggs, Ginger Meggs, ham and eggs, Neville Beggs, nine gallon kegs, Scotch pegs*.

grey nurse — **purse**

grim and gory — **story**
From at least early 20th century. **See also** *John Dory*.

grocer's cart — **heart**
Since at least the early 20th century. **See also** *jam tart* (1).

grumble and grunt — **cunt, as in female genitalia; in this usage can also mean sexual intercourse**
See also *All Quiet on the Western Front, Ballina Punt, Berkshire Hunt, Billy Hunt, drop kick and punt, Joe Hunt, mumble and grunt, Stockton Punt*.

gumboot — **root, as in sexual intercourse**
Recorded in the form *gumby* in children's folk speech. **See also** *Angus and Coote, Herby de Groote, juicy fruit, silly galoot, tin flute, Wellington boot*.

gumby — **see gumboot**

gum tree/s — **knee/s**
World War II. **See also** *biscuits and cheese, bugs and fleas, bumblebees, Gypsy Rose Lee/s, Syngman Ree(s)*.

Gunga Din — gin
Often occurs in the combination '*Gunga Din* and *squatter's daughter*', meaning 'gin and water'. After the famous colonialist poem of the same name by Rudyard Kipling, published in 1892. 20th century. Obsolete. **See also** *Huckleberry Finn*, *mortal sin*, *thick and thin* (2), *Vera Lynn* (2).

Gypsy Lee — tea
Sometimes occurs as *Gypsy Rose Lee*. After the American burlesque artist Gypsy Rose Lee (1940–70). Australian original, first noted in the 1930s, and current through World War II. **See also** *Dicky Lee* (2), *Jack Shay* (1), *Jenny Lee*, *Jimmy Lee*, *Mother Machree*, *Rosie Lee*, *wasp and bee* (1), *you and me* (3).

Gypsy Rose Lee/s — knee/s
See also *biscuits and cheese*, *bugs and fleas*, *bumblebees*, *gum tree/s*, *Syngman Ree(s)*.

Gypsy's kiss — piss, as in urinate, urine
Used in English rhyming slang and current in WA in 2007, although certainly much older. **See also** *angel's kiss*, *cat's hiss*, *hit and/or miss*, *horse's hiss*, *Johnny Bliss*, *Les Kiss*, *Shirley Bliss*, *snake's hiss*, *swing and a miss*.

Gypsy's warning — morning
See also *air raid warning*.

H

had the dick — see had the Richard

had the Richard — exhausted, worn out, functionless
Also abbreviated to *had the dick*, using the shortened form of Richard. A general slang term derived from *Richard the Third*, meaning to have or get 'the bird', meaning the sack or a request to otherwise absent oneself. In use since the 1960s. **See also** *Richard the Third*.

hail and rain — train
See also *Frankie Laine* (3), *Geoffrey Lane* (2), *King of Spain* (3), *Lois Lane*, *pouring rain*, *roaring rain*, *shower of rain*, *thunder and rain*, *wind and rain*.

hairy chest — vest
See also *east and west* (2).

half a neddy — reddie, meaning a ten shilling note (pre-decimal currency)
World War II.

half an hour (1) — flour
Australian original from the 1940s, or earlier.

half an hour (2) — flower
Late 19th century–1930s. **See also** *Cobar shower, David Gower/s* (1), *ivory towers*.

half inch — pinch, meaning to steal

half mast — past, meaning mentally lacking
See also *Ivy's Last*.

halfback flanker — wanker, as in masturbator
From Australian Rules football position. **See also** *J. Arthur Rank* (2), *merchant banker, sheep shanker, Westpac banker*.

Halley's Comet — vomit
After the comet of the same name that approaches the earth from time to time. **See also** *Wallace and Gromit*.

ham and eggs — legs
Originating in Australia. **See also** *bacon and eggs, clothes pegs, Dutch pegs, fried eggs, Ginger Meggs, Gregory Pegs, Neville Beggs, nine gallon kegs, Scotch pegs*.

ham shank — Yank, meaning American
A nautical usage. **See also** *army tank, iron tank* (2), *Jodrell Bank, mutton shanks, septic tank/s, ship's tank, tin tank* (2).

hammer — police officer
Recorded in children's speech. Possibly from a rhyming slang *hammer and saw* for 'law'. Otherwise unrecorded.

hammer and tack (1) — smack, meaning the drug heroin
From the 1980s, although 'smack' has been in use for 'heroin' since the '40s.

hammer and tack (2) — sack, as in to lose one's job
World War II. **See also** *tin tack* (2).

hammer and tack (3) — tobacco
Thought to have been a rhyme on 'black', as in the colour of tobacco. Gaol slang. Current 1950.

hammer and tack (4) — track, meaning road
Often abbreviated to *hammer*. *c.* 1940s and still current? **See also** *Johnny Mack* (2).

hammer and tack (5) — zac, meaning a sixpenny coin (pre-decimal currency)
See also *Andy Mac, Brodie Mack, I'll be back, Jill and Jack, tin tack* (3).

hammer and tack (6) — back
Often abbreviated to *hammer*. From World War II. **See also** *George Alfred Black, Johnny Mack* (1), *Melbourne, tin tack* (1).

Hampstead Heath — teeth
Usually abbreviated to *Hampsteads*. Of English origin. **See also** *cricket bats, Barrier Reef, Barry Beath, Ted Heath*.

hanky panky — cranky, meaning irritable or silly
World War II.

hansom cab — scab, meaning a non-unionised worker
Probably of considerable age as the hansom cab was horse-drawn. Obsolete. **See also** *Jack McNab, Sandy MacNab* (2).

happy and sad — dad
Recorded in children's speech abbreviated to *happy and*.

happy hour — shower (of rain)
Australianism from the 1950s. **See also** *Eiffel Tower*.

hard hit — shit, as in defecate
See also *big hit, brace and bit, Dinny Hayes-er, Eartha Kitt, Edgar Britt, gravel pit, Jimmy Britt* (1), *king hit, Mickey Fritt, Oscar Britt, Tom tit*.

haricot bean — queen, meaning a male homosexual
See also *baked bean, in-between, pork and bean, submarine*.

Harold — see *Harold Holt* (1)

Harold Holt (1) — bolt, meaning to flee
Often as in to 'do a/the *Harold*' or to do 'a *Harry*'. After the Prime Minister Harold Holt (1908–67), who disappeared while swimming at Cheviot Beach, Vic.

Harold Holt (2) — salt
A usage depending on the usual Australian pronunciation of salt as 'solt'. From the 1970s. **See also** *Tim Holt*.

Harolds — knickers
From Harry Taggs, meaning bags, or trousers. 20th century.

Harry — see Harold Holt (1)

Harry Lime — time
From the main character in the famous espionage film *The Third Man* (1949); reinforced by the novel of the same name by Graham Green (who also wrote the screenplay) first published in 1950. Obsolete? **See also** *bird's lime* (1).

Harry Lauder — order (a meal)
Harry Lauder (1870–1950) was a noted performer of the Scottish music hall and later. From British speech.

Harry Monk — spunk, meaning sperm
English origin, referring apparently to no historical person, though the name sometimes appears in relation to pornography. Current WA 2007. **See also** *New York junk*.

Harry Randle — candle
See also *broom handle, Ron Randle*.

Harry Taggs — bags, meaning trousers
See also *Harolds*.

Harry Tait — plate
See also *five-eight* (1), *Michael Pate, Reg Date*.

Harry Tate — RE8 (World War I reconnaissance plane)
Two-seater used in No. 3 Squadron Australian Flying Corps and possibly more broadly. Obsolete. **See also** *Henry Tate*.

Harry Wragg — fag, meaning cigarette
See also *oily rag, Twelfth Street Rag*.

Harvey Drew — spew, meaning vomit
See also *Chunderloo, Dan McGrew* (1), *Danny La Rue* (2), *Spiro Agnew*.

Hawkesburies — see *Hawkesbury Rivers*

Hawkesbury Rivers — shivers
Usually occurs as *Hawkesburies*. After the major river of the same name. In use since at least 1941. Mainly NSW. See also *Murray Rivers, Swannee Rivers*.

Hawkie — lie
A rhyme on another rhyming slang for a lie, *porky*, short for *pork pie*. See also *Nellie Bligh* (6), *porkie pie, Sargents Pie/s* (2), *2KY* (2).

Heart and soul of the goanna — Varsovienna (a dance)
See also *arsehole of the goanna, arse-over-Anna, arse-over-header, Var Susy Anne*.

hearts of oak — broke, meaning to have lost a bet (horseracing) in this usage
See also *wood, coal and coke* (1).

heavenly plan — man
From the late 19th century. See also *meat and gravy, pot and pan* (1).

Hedy Lamarr — car
After the stage name of Hollywood actress Hedwig Eva Maria Kiesler (1913–2000), who came to prominence in the 1940s. See also *church bazaar, jam jar, Kirk's Bazaar, lah de dah* (1), *Malvern Star, Marie La Var, Mars Bar, near and far* (2).

Henry Berry (1) — jerry, meaning to suddenly understand
As in 'now I *Henry Berry*'. From the name of a business, Henry Berry & Co. World War II. Obsolete.

Henry Berry (2) — sherry

Henry the Third — turd, as in defecate
Heard in gaol 1950. See also *elephant's herd, George the Third, King George the Third, King Henry the Third, King Richard the Third, mocking bird, Richard the Third* (2), *William the Third*.

Henry Tate — **RE8 (World War I reconnaissance plane)**
Two-seater used in No. 3 Squadron Australian Flying Corps and possibly more broadly. Obsolete. **See also** *Harry Tate*.

Herb Alpert — **arse, as in bottom**
From the name of a popular instrumental band of the 1960s and '70s, Herb Alpert's Tijuana Brass. **See also** *Aris, bottle and glass, Bulli Pass, Coke and sars(parilla), Khyber Pass, lemonade and sars(parilla)* (1), *Mark Ella, Reg Gasnier*.

Herby de Groote — **root, meaning sexual intercourse**
See also *Angus and Coote, gumboot, juicy fruit, silly galoot, tin flute, Wellington boot*.

here and now — **chow, meaning Chinese or other Asian person**
From the long-standing general Australian slang derogation of Chinese and other Asian peoples. **See also** *Jersey cow*.

here and there — **hair**
Australian in origin. From *c.* 1930s. **See also** *Barnet Fair, Dublin Fair, Fred Astaire* (2), *over there, preference share, table and chair*.

hers and hims — **hymns**
Australian in origin. In use since at least the early 20th century.

hey diddle diddle (1) — **middle**
World War II. **See also** *hi diddle diddle* (1).

hey diddle diddle (2) — **piddle, as in urinate**
World War II. **See also** *Gerry Riddle, hi diddle diddle* (2), *Jimmy Riddle, Nelson Riddle, Shannon* (2).

hi diddle diddle (1) — **middle, especially in relation to Australian Rules football**
See also *hey diddle diddle* (1).

hi diddle diddle (2) — **piddle**
See also *Gerry Riddle, hey diddle diddle* (2), *Jimmy Riddle, Nelson Riddle, Shannon* (2).

hickery dickery dock — **clock**
See also *dickory dock, Eva Bartok, tick tock*.

hickey hockey — **jockey**
Horseracing term since around 1920.

highland fling **(1) — king (playing cards)**
Since the 1960s.

highland fling **(2) — string**
Australian original since at least World War II. **See also** *Oscar King*.

hit and/or miss **— piss, as in urinate**
From at least the 1940s in Australia and in the form *hit or miss* from 19th-century British usage. **See also** *angel's kiss*, *cat's hiss*, *Gypsy's kiss*, *horse's hiss*, *Johnny Bliss*, *Les Kiss*, *Shirley Bliss*, *snake's hiss*, *swing and a miss*.

hit and swerve **— perve, meaning one who ogles the opposite sex**
May also refer to the act of perving. **See also** *hors d'oeuvre*, *optic nerve*, *sway and swerve*, *Uncle Merve*.

hit the deep **— sleep**
20th century. **See also** *bo-peep*, *rolling deep*.

Hoffman brick **— dick, meaning penis**
See also *Pogo stick* (1).

hollow log **(1) — dog**
Unclear whether this refers to the animal or to the underworld term for an informer. Mid-20th century. Melbourne? **See also** *hollow log* (2).

hollow log **(2) — dog; also (in children's folk speech) one who spoils the game or otherwise breaks the rules**
In this respect similar to the criminalism *chocolate frog*, meaning one who colludes with and/or informs to the police.

hollow log (3) — wog, meaning a person of southern European/ Mediterranean origin
See also *Alsatian dog*, *chocolate frog/s* (2), *Dapto dog*, *Freddo Frog*, *spotty dog*, *woolly dog*.

hollow log **(4) — bog, as in defecate**
See also *Rodney Hogg*.

Holmes à Court **— short, meaning with insufficient money**
After the prominent businessman Robert Holmes à Court (1937–90).

holy friar **— liar**

holy ghost (1) — **post, mail**
Used in this sense in 'Duke' Tritton's rhyming slang letter dated 1905.

holy ghost(2) — **toast**
1950s.

holy ghost (3) — **(fence) post**
Sometimes in the plural form *holy ghosts*. 20th century.

holy ghost(4) — **(starting or finishing) post (horseracing)**
20th century.

holy ghost(5) — **the coast**

home on the range — **change (money)**
Presumably from the title of the popular song composed in the 1870s, although only recorded in 20th-century usage. Australian. **See also** *Kembla Grange, rifle range.*

Home Pride — **see *Home Pride bread***

Home Pride bread — **head**
Usually abbreviated to *Home Pride*, as in 'He must be off his *Home Pride*.' After the name of a well-known bakery brand. Mid-20th century. Melbourne? **See also** *Kelly Ned, loaf of bread, lump of lead* (3), *3KZ.*

honky tonk — **plonk, meaning cheap wine**
Australian, probably World War I or shortly after. **See also** *horse and donk, plink plonk, plinketty-plonk.*

Horace Tottle — **bottle**
World War II. **See also** *Aristotle, charming mottle.*

hors d'oeuvre — **perve, meaning one who ogles the opposite sex**
Barely a rhyming slang? 1960s? **See also** *hit and swerve, optic nerve, sway and swerve, Uncle Merve.*

horse and cart (1) — **fart, as in break wind**
Current WA 2007. **See also** *apple tart, bacon and egg tart, bottle mart, cupcake, Dicky Bart, fairy dart jam tart* (2), *raspberry tart, Stevey Hart.*

horse and cart (2) — **(from the) start**
From at least the early 20th century.

horse and donk — **plonk, meaning cheap wine**
See also *honky tonk, plink plonk, plinketty-plonk.*

horse and dray — trey, meaning a threepenny coin (pre-decimal currency)
Obsolete. See also *Alma Grey, Dolly Gray, Dora Gray.*

horse and foal — dole, meaning unemployment benefit
Australian. See also *Nat King Cole* (2), *rock and roll, strum and stroll, strut and stroll.*

horse's doovers — hors d'oeuvres
Probably not rhyming slang as it depends on the written rather than the verbal form — and it does not rhyme very well.

horse's hiss — piss, as in urinate
Usually abbreviated to *horses.* See also *angel's kiss, cat's hiss, Gypsy's kiss, hit and/or miss, Johnny Bliss, Les Kiss, Shirley Bliss, snake's hiss, swing and a miss.*

horse's hoof — poof, meaning a male homosexual
World War II. See also *cloven hoofter, cow's hoof, willy woofter, woolly boof, woolly woofter.*

hot cross bun — sun
From at least the early 20th century. See also *Atilla the Hun, currant bun* (2), *Peter Gunn.*

hot potater or potato (1) — later
Current during World War II.

hot potato (pronounced 'pertater') (2) — waiter

hot scone — John, meaning police officer
See also *bottle and stopper, bottle stopper, grasshopper, greasy mop, John Cleese, Johnhop/s, Johnhopper.*

Howard Keel — meal
After the stage name of the actor and singer Harry Clifford Keel (1917–2004), most widely known for his role in the musical and film *Annie, Get Your Gun* (1950). See also *Leonard Teale.*

Huckleberry Finn — gin
Often abbreviated to *Huckleberry.* From the famous novel by Mark Twain (Samuel Clemens), published in 1884. In use since at least the early 20th century and current into World War II. See also *Gunga Din, mortal sin, thick and thin* (2), *Vera Lynn* (2).

hugs and kisses — missus, meaning wife
On the worldwide web 2009. **See also** *cows and kisses, cheese and kisses.*

hutch — crutch (of a sheep)
Possibly occupational argot and not rhyming slang or possibly derived
from the British *rabbit hutch* for crutch. **See also** *Mister Mutch.*

hydraulics — bollocks, as in testicles
See also *flowers and frolics, Jackson Pollocks.*

I

I don't care — chair, meaning the electric chair
Said among American criminals to be Australian rhyming slang,
although highly unlikely, as the electric chair has never been used in
Australia for executions.

I suppose — nose
Said to be used in Australia in shearing sheds to refer to a sheep's nose.
One of the earliest rhyming slang terms, recorded in London during the
late 1850s. **See also** *Lionel Rose, Piccadilly rose, rubberan, rubber and
hose, these and those* (1).

**I'll be back — zac, meaning a sixpenny coin (pre-decimal
currency)**
World War II. Obsolete. **See also** *Andy Mac, Brodie Mack, hammer and
tack* (5), *Jill and Jack, tin tack* (3).

I'm afloat — coat, overcoat
Recorded Australia 1902. In the 1850s in London, used to rhyme with
'boat'. **See also** *armour float, Collier and Moat, motorboat.*

in-between — queen, meaning male homosexual
See also *baked bean, haricot bean, pork and bean, submarine.*

Indian brave — wave (ocean)

Innocent Mary — Len Incigneri
Rhyming slang nickname for the Victorian AFL footballer Len Incigneri
(?–1964), prominent in the early 20th century. Obsolete.

Irish folly — brolly (short for umbrella)
See also *Aunt Ella, Aunt Molly, Lake's folly.*

Irish jig — **wig**
See also *Moreton Bay Fig* (3), *syrup and fig*.

iron tank (1) — **bank**
See also *J. Arthur Rank* (1), *septic tank* (2), *tin tank* (1), *Tommy Tank*.

iron tank (2) — **Yank, meaning an American**
World War II. See also *army tank, ham shank, Jodrell Bank, mutton shanks, septic tank/s* (1), *ship's tank, tin tank* (2).

itch and scratch — **match (firelighter)**
See also *Captain scratches, Darryl Patch, fleas and scratches*.

ivory towers — **flowers**
1960s? See also *Cobar shower/s, David Gower/s* (1), *half an hour* (2).

ivy's last — **past**
World War II. See also *half mast*.

J

J. Arthur — **see J. Arthur Rank (1) and (2)**

J. Arthur Rank (1) — **bank**
Sometimes abbreviated to *J. Arthur*. J. Arthur Rank was the trade name of a film distribution company that was displayed prominently in cinemas before the screening of the movie. From at least the 1950s. See also *iron tank* (1), *septic tank* (2), *tin tank* (1), *Tommy Tank*.

J. Arthur Rank (2) — **wank, as in masturbate**
Usually abbreviated to *J. Arthur*. See also *halfback flanker, merchant banker, sheep shanker, Westpac banker*.

J. Carroll Nash — **cash**
Often abbreviated to *J. Carroll*. See also *Arthur Ashe, Charlie Ash, Christopher Ash, Oscar Asche, sausage and mash, smash, splash*.

Jack — **see Jack McNab**

Jack and Jill (1) — **bill, meaning the amount due for a product or service**
Also used in British rhyming slang. See also *Beecham pill*.

Jack and Jill (2) — **dill, meaning a foolish or naive person**
World War II. Australian. See also *Beecham's Pill/s, Burke and Wills*.

Jack and Jill (3) — hill
World War II.

Jack and Jill (4) — pill
See also *Mick Mills*.

Jack and Jill (5) — till (cash register)
Also used in this sense in British rhyming slang. Current in Sydney 1970s.

Jack Benny — penny
After the American comedian Jack Benny, born Benjamin Kubelsky (1894–1974). World War II. Obsolete.

Jack Flash — hash, hashish
Probably after the Rolling Stones 1968 hit song 'Jumpin' Jack Flash'. Australian; from the late 1960s. See also *Johnny Cash*.

Jack Jones — loan(s?)
After the American singer (born 1938). See also *Darby and Joan* (1), *on your own*, *Vic Damone*.

Jack Lang — slang
May also be applied specifically to rhyming slang, as in to *talk the old Jack Lang*. Jack Lang (1876–1975) was a controversial Labor Premier of NSW during the Depression years of the 1930s. See also *Bill Lang*.

Jack McNab — scab, meaning a non-unionised worker
Often abbreviated to *Jack*. Applied since the 1940s to the Permanent and Casual Waterside Workers Union, considered to be strikebreakers by other wharfies. See also *hansom cab*, *Sandy MacNab* (2).

Jack Malone — alone
As in the general slang term 'on your *jack*', meaning by yourself. 20th century. See also *eau de Cologne* (2), *Pat Malone*, *Tod Sloane*.

Jack Palance — dance
After the one-time boxer and Hollywood actor (*c*. 1918–2006).

Jack Rees — fleas
From at least the early 20th century; current in World War II. See also *Joe Rees*, *2UEs*, *Willy Lees*.

Jack-in-the-box — pox, meaning sexually transmissible infection, usually syphilis
As in 'the *jack*', derived from the rhyming slang term. **See also** *Adrian Knox, boots and sox.*

Jack Scratch/es — match/es (firelighter/s)
Australian original from World War II.

Jack Shay (1) — tea (as in the Irish pronunciation 'tay')
Can also be used to refer to a billycan, according to Franklyn. A 'Jack Shay' was a 19th-century tin kit for brewing tea, within which was nested a tin cup for drinking the beverage. **See also** *Dicky Lee* (2), *Gypsy Lee, Jenny Lee, Jimmy Lee, Mother Machree, Rosie Lee, wasp and bee* (1), *you and me* (3).

Jack Shay (2) — stay
20th century.

Jack Shea — slay

Jack Spratt — fat
Presumably after the nursery rhyme, 'Jack Spratt could eat no fat, his wife could eat no lean/ And so between the two of them, they licked the platter clean.'

Jack the dancer — cancer
This rhyme depends on the standard Australian pronunciation of 'dance/r'. **See also** *ballet dancer, Bengal lancer, candy dancer, Charlie Dancer, civil answer, Jimmy Dancer, Johnny Dancer, Mario Lanza, Spanish dancer.*

Jack the Ripper — kipper (fish)
Of English origin; after the notorious serial killer of 1888.

Jack's alive — five (Bingo)
See also *beehive, eat 'em alive, man alive.*

(the) jacks — police
From *Johnhops*, the diminutive of 'John' being 'Jack'. From World War I, when the term was used for military police. **See also** *John Cleese, johnhop/s.*

Jackson Pollocks — bollocks, as in testicles
After the American painter, whose work 'Blue Poles' was famously

purchased for $1.2 million by the Australian National Gallery under the Whitlam Labor government in 1973. While 'bollocks' is widely used in British folk speech, it may be of Australian origin, being first recorded by Downing during World War I. Current 2007. **See also** *flowers and frolics, hydraulics*.

Jacky Lancashire — handkerchief (with the 19th-century Cockney pronunciation 'hankacher')
Recorded in Australia from 1900 but almost certainly older as the term was recorded in the earliest English rhyming slang collection in the late 1850s as *Charley Lancaster*.

Jacob's Creek — leak, as in urinate
After the popular Australian wine label. **See also** *bubble and squeak* (2), *Werris Creek* (2).

Jake La Motta — trotter, meaning a horse for harness racing
After the American middleweight boxer (born 1921).

jam and honey — dunny, meaning toilet
Melbourne 2006. **See also** *don't be funny, Gene Tunney* (2).

jam jar — car
English rhyming slang, but also heard in Perth 2007. **See also** *church bazaar, Hedy Lamarr, Kirk's Bazaar, lah de dah* (1), *Malvern Star, Marie La Var, Mars Bar, near and far* (2).

jam tart (1) — heart
See also *grocer's cart*.

jam tart (2) — fart, as in break wind
See also *apple tart, bacon and egg tart, bottle mart, cupcake, Dicky Bart, fairy dart, horse and cart* (1), *raspberry tart, Stevey Hart*.

Jarrah blocks — socks
Northwest WA, *c.* mid-20th century. **See also** *almond rocks, Bobby rocks, curly locks, Goldilocks, Joe Rocks, keys and locks, ton o' my rocks*.

Jatz crackers — knackers, meaning testicles
After the well-known cracker biscuits manufactured by the iconic Arnott's biscuits company. Current WA 2007. **See also** *Christmas crackers, Kerry Packers*.

Jayden Leskie — Esky, meaning container, most noted for keeping beer cool
Jayden Leskie was a Victorian child who was kidnapped and murdered in 1997. The case remains unresolved. Current early 21st century.

Jekyll and Hydes — strides, meaning trousers
20th century.

Jenny Lee — tea
See also *Dicky Lee* (2), *Gypsy Lee*, *Jack Shay* (1), *Jimmy Lee*, *Mother Machree*, *Rosie Lee*, *wasp and bee* (1), *you and me* (3).

Jersey cow — chow, meaning a Chinese or other Asian person
Mid-20th century. Melbourne? See also *here and now*.

Jersey Flegg — keg (of beer)
Jersey Flegg (1878–1960) was a NSW Rugby League administrator. See also *Auntie Meg*.

Jew chum — new chum, meaning migrant
Playing on 'new chum', the earlier Australianism for a newcomer. From the 1930s. Obsolete.

Jill and Jack — zac, meaning a sixpenny coin (pre-decimal currency)
From at least World War II. Obsolete. See also *Andy Mac*, *Brodie Mack*, *hammer and tack* (5), *I'll be back*, *tin tack* (3).

Jim Gerald — Herald (a newspaper in Sydney and Melbourne)
Jim Gerald (1891–1971), Australian comedian and entertainer noted — among other achievements — for his World War II efforts to entertain AIF troops. World War II. See also *Barry Fitzgerald*.

Jimminy Cricket — wicket
After the Disney cartoon character.

Jimmy Britt (1) — shit, as in defecate
After the American boxer Jimmy Britt (1879–1940), who toured Australia during World War I. Since at least World War II. See also *big hit*, *brace and bit*, *Dinny Hayes-er*, *Eartha Kitt*, *Edgar Britt*, *gravel pit*, *hard hit*, *king hit*, *Mickey Fritt*, *Oscar Britt*, *Tom tit*.

Jimmy Britt (2) — good, as in 'not shit'
Derived by reversal from the usual rhyming of shit, meaning undesirable,

a linguistic routine of children's folk speech. **See also** *plum pud*, *Robin Hood*, *Wee Georgie Wood*.

Jimmy Britts (1) — shits, as in to be irritated as in, 'she is really giving me the Jimmies'
See also *Edgar Britts*, *Tom tits*, *trey bits* (1), *trizzy bits*.

Jimmy Britts (2) — shits, meaning diarrhoea
See also *trey bits* (1).

Jimmy Carruthers — one another
An imperfect rhyme, after the Australian bantamweight boxer Jimmy Carruthers (1929–90).

Jimmy Dancer — cancer
Requires the Australian pronunciation to make the rhyme. Current late 20th century to present. **See also** *ballet dancer*, *Bengal lancer*, *candy dancer*, *Charlie Dancer*, *civil answer*, *Jack the dancer*, *Johnny Dancer*, *Mario Lanza*, *Spanish dancer*.

Jimmy Grant — immigrant
Said to have led to the term for a British migrant, 'pommie'. *Jimmy Grant* became *Pommy Grant* from the alleged similarity between the red colour of the pomegranate and the ruddy complexions of British migrants. By the early 20th century this had inevitably become *pommie* and then abbreviated to *pom*, as it remains today. First noted in Australia in the 1850s (although a decade earlier in New Zealand). Current until at least the 1920s and perhaps beyond. Also used *c*. '50s in form of *Jimmy* — for 'immi'. Obsolete. **See also** *atom bomb*, *to and from*.

Jimmy Hix — fix

Jimmy Lee — tea
From at least the early 20th century. **See also** *Dicky Lee* (2), *Gypsy Lee*, *Jack Shay* (1), *Jenny Lee*, *Mother Machree*, *Rosie Lee*, *wasp and bee* (1), *you and me* (3).

Jimmy Pike — bike
After the Australian jockey James Pike (1892–1969). **See also** *do as you like*.

Jimmy Riddle — piddle, as in urinate
See also *Gerry Riddle*, *hey diddle diddle* (2), *hi diddle diddle* (2), *Nelson Riddle*, *Shannon*.

Joan of Arc/s — shark/s
From the female soldier martyr known as 'the maid of Orleans' (1412–31). From the 1940s. See also *after darks*, *Cutty Sark* (2), *Joe Marks*, *Jonah*, *Luna Park*, *Marcus Clark*(e), *Noah's Ark* (6).

Joanna — piano (pronounced 'pianner')
One of the earliest recorded rhyming slangs, in London 1846. See also *goanna*.

Jodrell Bank — Yank, meaning an American
After the famous British observatory. See also *army tanks*, *ham shank*, *iron tank* (2), *mutton shanks*, *septic tank/s* (1), *ship's tank*, *tin tank* (2).

Joe Baxi — taxi
From the American heavyweight boxer Joe Baxi (1919–77). See also *Joe Maxi*, *slapsie maxie*.

Joe Blake/s (1) — shakes, usually those induced by excess consumption of alcohol and its after-effects
Often abbreviated to the *Joes* which, in this form from the 1910s, could also simply mean being depressed or nervous. Used from the late 19th century in relation to bodily shivers; from around World War II becomes associated specifically with the after-effects of excess alcohol, or delirium tremens, 'the DTs'. See also *ducks and drakes*, *Sexton Blakes* (1).

Joe/y Blake/s (2) — snake/s
Probably from the early 20th century. See also *Sexton Blakes* (2).

Joe Blake (3) — steak
1940s. See also *off break*, *quiver and shake*.

Joe Brown — town
See also *knock me down*, *penny brown*.

Joe Buck (1) — fuck, as in sexual intercourse
From at least the 1930s. See also *Bill Buck* (2), *Donald Duck* (1), *Friar Tuck*, *Mickey Duck* (1).

Joe Buck (2) — truck
See also *Bill Buck* (1), *Donald Duck* (2), *Frank Buck*, *goose and duck*, *Mickey Duck* (2).

Joe Cocker — shocker, a descriptive term for something awful
After the English rock singer Joe Cocker (born 1944). **See also** *Barry Crocker*.

Joe Goss — boss, meaning someone whose signature is valid on a cheque (forgers' jargon); can mean police officer
Probably originating in the USA after the name of a late 19th-century prizefighter. *c.* 1940s. **See also** *pitch and toss*.

Joe Hope — soap
See also *Band of Hope, Bob Hope* (1), *Cape of Good Hope*.

Joe Hunt — cunt, as in female genitalia
See also *All Quiet on the Western Front, Ballina Punt, Berkshire Hunt, Billy Hunt, drop kick and punt, grumble and grunt, mumble and grunt, Stockton Punt.*

Joe Loss — toss
After the English bandleader Joe Loss (1909–90).

Joe Marks — sharks
Possibly after the 19th-century woolbuying firm. World War II. **See also** *after darks, Cutty Sark* (2), *Joan of Arc/s, Jonah, Luna Park, Marcus Clark(e), Noah's Ark* (6).

Joe Maxi — taxi
See also *Joe Baxie, slapsie maxie*.

Joe Morgan — street organ
1890s–1940s. Obsolete.

Joe Palooka — snooker
After the soft-hearted cartoon heavyweight boxer created by American Ham Fisher in 1921. By the late '40s it had become one of the most popular comic strips in the world.

Joe Rees — fleas
World War II. **See also** *Jack Rees, 2UEs, Willy Lees*.

Joe Rocks — socks
Australian. **See also** *almond rocks, Bobby rocks, curly locks, Goldilocks, Jarrah blocks, keys and locks, ton o' my rocks.*

Joe Soap — Pope

(the) Joes — see *Joe Blake/s* (1)

John Bull (1) — **full, meaning drunk**
After the personification of England, John Bull. See also *Roy Bull* (2).

John Bull (2) — **pull, as in male masturbation**
Current in the first decade of the 21st century and probably considerably older. See also *cotton wool*, *Roy Bull* (1).

John Cleese — **police**
After the English comedian John Cleese (born 1939). See also *(the) jacks*.

John Dilling — **shilling (pre-decimal currency)**
Obsolete. See also *John Dillon, rogan, rogue and Dillon, rogue and villain*.

John Dillon — **shilling (pre-decimal currency)**
Obsolete. See also *John Dilling, rogan, rogue and Dillon, rogue and villain*.

John Dory — **story, usually with the connotation of fabrication or exaggeration**
Presumably from the name of the fish. See also *grim and gory*.

John Dunn — **one, as in one pound (pre-decimal currency)**
Perhaps after the notorious NSW bushranger of the 1860? From at least 1908. Obsolete.

Johnhop/s — **cop/s, meaning police officers**
Usually abbreviated to the *johns*. Appears in 'Duke' Tritton's rhyming slang letter dated 1905 and in the writings of C. J. Dennis as John 'Op/Jonop around 1915. Current in World War II. Also used in New Zealand. See also *bottle and stopper, bottle stopper, grasshopper, greasy mop, hot scone, John Cleese, Johnhopper*.

Johnhopper — **copper, meaning police officer**
In relatively recent usage. See also *bottle and stopper, bottle stopper, grasshopper, greasy mop, hot scone, John Cleese, Johnhop/s*.

Johnnie Russell — **hustle, meaning to hurry**
Of Australian origin. In use among American criminals in the 1930s and '40s.

Johnny Bliss — piss, as in urinate
Johnny Bliss, known as 'blistering Johnny Bliss', was a prominent Rugby League player during the 1940s, noted for his speed, and also a surf lifesaver. See also *angel's kiss, cat's hiss, Gypsy's kiss, hit and/or miss, horse's hiss, Les Kiss, Shirley Bliss, snake's hiss, swing and a miss*.

Johnny Cash — hash, hashish
After the late American country singer Johnny Cash (1932–2003), for many years a known drug user. In Britain the term is rhymed with 'slash', as in to urinate. Probably from the 1960s. See also *Jack Flash*.

Johnny Dancer — cancer
See also *ballet dancer, Bengal lancer, candy dancer, Charlie Dancer, civil answer, Jack the dancer, Jimmy Dancer, Mario Lanza, Spanish dancer*.

Johnny Horner — corner; often a euphemism for the pub, as in 'I'm just going round the corner'
Late 19th–early 20th-century origin.

Johnny Mack (1) — back
See also *George Alfred Black, hammer and tack* (6), *Melbourne, tin tack* (1).

Johnny Mack (2) — track
See also *hammer and tack* (4).

Johnny Moyes — noise
Possibly after the noted cricket commentator Alban George Moyes (1893–1963). See also *box of toys*.

Johnny Raper — newspaper
After the famous NSW Rugby League footballer Johnny Raper (born 1939), prominent in the 1960s and '70s. See also *Canadian caper*.

Johnny Ray — lay, as in sexual intercourse
After the American singer Johnny Ray (1927–90). See also *Martha Ray*.

Johnny Rustle/Russell — bustle, meaning to struggle (as in 'on the bustle'); may also mean to be in haste
Thought to be after the British politician Lord John Russell (1792–1878). 1890s. Obsolete.

Johnny Rutter — butter
See also *chuck me in the gutter, Dark Town strutter, kerb and gutter, lisp and stutter, mumble and stutter, mutter and stutter, roll me in the gutter, stammer and stutter.*

Johns — see *Johnhop/s*

Jonah — shark
After Joan of Arc. Perhaps also a biblical reference to the fate of Jonah, who was swallowed by a whale. **See also** *after darks, Cutty Sark* (2), *Joan of Arc/s, Joe Marks, Luna Park, Marcus Clark(e), Noah's Ark* (6).

juice harp — Jew's harp (musical instrument)
The Jew's harp is played on the mouth, often producing excess saliva. Folk musician's rhyming slang.

juicy fruit — root, as in sexual intercourse
Probably after the brand of chewing gum. From at least 1950. **See also** *Angus and Coote, gumboot, Herby de Groote, silly galoot, tin flute, Wellington boot.*

jump and jive — thirty-five (Bingo)

Jungle Jim — swim
After a character from a 1950s and '60s television series. **See also** *dark and dim, Tiger Tim.*

K

kanga/s — see *kangaroo* (1) and (2)

kangaroo (1) — screw, meaning prison warder
Often abbreviated to *kanga*. From at least the 1920s and current in '40s. **See also** *four b' two* (2).

kangaroo/s (2) — shoe(s)
Usually abbreviated to *kanga*(s). **See also** *Basin Street blues, Ben Blues, canoes, ones and twos, Peggy Sue, Pete Kelly's blues, Saint Louis blues, splash throughs, ten to two.*

kangaroo (3) — screw, meaning wages
1950s.

kangaroo Ted — dead

Also occurs as *kangaroo Edward*, in which formation it is sometimes said to be constructed from abbreviations of its constituent elements. Thus kangaroo = 'roo' and Edward = 'Ted', which combined give 'rooted', meaning without hope; in this case, dead. Current 2007. **See also** *brown bread, garden shed, lump of lead* (2), *wombat*.

Kansas City Max — tax

See also *sealing wax.*

Kathleen Mavourneen — morning

Of Australian rather than Irish origin, although derived from the sentimental Irish ballad of the same name, composed in 1837 and in print from at least 1849. A silent film based on the ballad was produced in 1906. The term was also used in general Australian slang to indicate the passing of an indeterminate period of time, a meaning stemming from the ballad's refrain, 'It may be for years, it may be forever.' Also used in crime-speak to mean a lengthy prison sentence. First recorded in 1903 in its non-rhyming slang usage, but almost certainly older. Obsolete?

Kelly Ned — head

A reversal of the famous bushranger's name. This also seems to have been in use among Pacific coast American criminals in the 1930s and '40s. **See also** *Home Pride bread, loaf of bread, lump of lead* (3), *3KZ*.

Kembla Grange — small change (money)

After a NSW south coast town. World War II. Current in prison slang 1950s. **See also** *home on the range, rifle range.*

Kennedy rot — sot, meaning one who is drunk, often habitually

Originating in Australia, where the term refers to a scurvy-like disease. In use among American criminals on the West Coast in the 1930s and '40s. **See also** *dot, plonk dot, wine dot.*

kerb and gutter — butter

World War II. **See also** *chuck me in the gutter, Dark Town strutter, Johnny Rutter, lisp and stutter, mumble and stutter, mutter and stutter, roll me in the gutter, stammer and stutter.*

Kerry Packered — knackered, meaning defeated or exhausted

Sometimes abbreviated to *Kerried*. After the late media magnate

Kerry Packer (1937–2005). The term originally meant that someone or something had been bested or otherwise defeated, but it has been extended to also mean exhausted.

Kerry Packers — knackers, meaning testicles
Australian from *c.* the 1970s. See also *Christmas crackers*, *Jatz crackers*.

Kevin — see *Kevin Sheedy*

Kevin Rudd — dud, meaning ineffectual
After Prime Minister of that name (born 1957). In use since at least 2009. See also *Elmer Fudd*, *potato and spud*.

Kevin Sheedy — greedy
Sometimes abbreviated to *Kevin*. After the legendary coach of the Essendon Football Club, Kevin Sheedy (born 1947). Current early 21st century.

Kewpie Doll (1) — gangster's kept woman and/or prostitute
Usually abbreviated to *Kewpie*. Current in the 1990s.

Kewpie Doll (2) — moll, meaning a girl or woman of ill repute
Usually abbreviated to *Kewpie*. Current in the 1990s, although the Australian pronunciation of moll has usually been 'mole'.

keys and locks — socks
World War II. See also *almond rocks*, *Bobby rocks*, *curly locks*, *Goldilocks*, *Jarrah blocks*, *Joe Rocks*, *ton o' my rocks*.

Khyber Pass — arse, as in bottom
Cockney. See also *Aris*, *bottle and glass*, *Bulli Pass*, *Coke and sars(parilla)*, *Herb Alpert*, *lemonade and sars(parilla)* (1), *Mark Ella*, *Reg Gasnier*.

kid blister — sister
20th century. See also *blood blister*, *skin and blister*.

Kidstake/s! — fake/s, an exclamation of falsity
Perhaps after an early Australian silent film of the same name. Also related to slang term 'fig' for kid. Early 20th century. Also used in New Zealand.

King George the Third — turd, as in faeces
After the King of England (1738–1820). See also *elephant's herd*, *George the Third*, *Henry the Third*, *King Henry the Third*, *King Richard the Third*, *mocking bird*, *Richard the Third*, *William the Third*.

King Henry the Third — turd, as in faeces; usually a dog's
After the King of England (1207–72). **See also** *elephant's herd, George the Third, Henry the Third, King George the Third, King Richard the Third, mocking bird, Richard the Third* (2), *William the Third.*

king hit — shit, as in defecate
See also *big hit, brace and bit, Dinny Hayes-er, Eartha Kitt, Edgar Britt, gravel pit, hard hit, Jimmy Britt* (1), *Mickey Fritt, Oscar Britt, Tom tit.*

King of Spain (1) — 'plane, aeroplane
See also *airy Jane.*

King of Spain (2) — rain
World War II. **See also** *France and Spain, Frankie Laine* (2), *Geoffrey Lane* (2).

King of Spain (3) — train
World War II. **See also** *Frankie Laine* (3), *Geoffrey Lane* (2), *hail and rain, Lois Lane, pouring rain, roaring rain, shower of rain, thunder and rain, wind and rain.*

King Richard the Third — turd, as in faeces
After the King of England (1452–85). **See also** *elephant's herd, George the Third, Henry the Third, King George the Third, King Henry the Third, mocking bird, Richard the Third* (2), *William the Third.*

King Roto — photo

Kirk's Bazaar — car
Kirk's Bazaar was a famous horsetrading venue in Melbourne in the mid-19th century. The name has subsequently been used by other Victorian businesses. Mid-20th century, Melbourne. **See also** *church bazaar, Hedy Lamarr, jam jar, lah de dah* (1), *Malvern Star, Marie La Var, Mars Bar, near and far* (2).

Kirribilli — silly
Probably after the Sydney suburb. **See also** *auntie, dilly, Uncle Willy, Wollondilly.*

Kiss me Kate — date (romantic meeting)
Presumably after the Broadway musical by Cole Porter first staged, to acclaim, in 1948.

kitchen sink — drink
20th century. **See also** *cuff link*, *pen and ink*, *Silver Link* (1), *tiddlywink*.

kitchen stoves — cloves
Abbreviation of '*Tom Thumb* and *kitchen stoves*', meaning the drink rum and cloves. 20th-century Australian origin. Obsolete?

knock at the door — four (Bingo)

knock me — see *knock me silly*

knock me silly — billy (can)
Sometimes abbreviated to *knock me*. From at least the early 20th century. Obsolete?

L

La Perouse — booze
Often abbreviated to *Larpa*. After the Sydney suburb. **See also** *mud and ooze*, *pick and choose*.

lady from Bristol — pistol
Has obvious criminal connotations. Thought to have originated in Australia. Obsolete?

lager beers — ears
See also *Germaine Greer/s* (2), *ginger beer/s* (2), *Melbourne Piers*, *Perc Galeas*, *Port Melbourne Pier/s* (1), *Terry Dears*, *Williamstown Piers*.

lah de dah (1) — car
See also *church bazaar*, *Hedy Lamarr*, *jam jar*, *Kirk's Bazaar*, *Malvern Star*, *Marie La Var*, *Mars Bar*, *near and far* (2).

lah de dah (2) — cigar

Lake's folly — brolly (short for umbrella)
See also *Aunt Ella*, *Aunt Molly*, *Irish folly*.

lamb's fried — died
As in, 'He's *lamb's fried*.' Mid-20th century. Melbourne?

lamb's fries — eyes
See also *meat pies*, *mince pies*, *mud pies*, *Nelly Bligh/s* (4), *Sargents Pie/s* (1), *2KYs*.

lamb's fry — (neck)tie
1890s. See also d*og's eye, Fourth of July, mud in your eye, Nazi spy* (2),
Nellie Bligh (5), *Russian spy, stock and die* (1), *2KY* (1).

Lane Cove — stove
Presumably afer the Sydney suburb. Australian original from World
War II. See also *purple and mauve.*

larrikin's hat — fat, meaning an erection
See also *Ballarat* (3), *State election, Yasser Arafat.*

laugh and joke — smoke (cigarette)
See also *Don Doak; Sentimental Bloke; wood, coal and coke* (2).

laughs and smiles — piles, meaning haemorrhoids
See also *asteroids, Bea Miles, Chalfont St Giles, Farmer Giles, metric
miles.*

lazy hour — shower (as in bathing)
See also *David Gower* (2), *fairy bower, now is the hour, Tyrone Power.*

lean and lurch — church
Recorded in London in the 1850s. See also *left in the lurch, rock and
lurch, roll and lurch.*

left in the lurch — church
See also *lean and lurch, rock and lurch, roll and lurch.*

left jab — cab, meaning taxi
Current WA 2007. See also *Sandy McNab* (1), *smash and grab.*

leg of pork (1) — fork(lift)
Melbourne wharfie term from mid-20th century.

leg of pork (2) — stalk, meaning penis

lemon squash — wash
Australianism from *c.* the early 20th century.

lemonade and sars(parilla) (1) — arse, as in bottom
From at least early to mid-20th century in Melbourne; current WA
2007. See also *Aris, bottle and glass, Bulli Pass, Coke and sars(parilla),
Herb Alpert, Khyber Pass, Mark Ella, Reg Gasnier.*

lemonade and sars(parilla) **(2) — lucky, as in a lucky person**
Recorded in children's speech. Presumably from the general slang term 'arsey' for someone who is considered to have been fortunate in some way.

Leonard Teale **— meal**
Usually abbreviated to a *Leonard*. After the Australian actor Leonard Teale (1922–94). **See also** *Howard Keel*.

Les Kiss **— piss, as in urinate, urine**
Les Kiss was a Rugby League player of the 1980s. Obsolete? **See also** *angel's kiss, cat's hiss, Gypsy's kiss, hit and/or miss, horse's hiss, Johnny Bliss, Shirley Bliss, snake's hiss, swing and a miss.*

Leslie Howard **— coward**
Possibly after English actor Leslie Howard (1893–1943), featured in the film *Gone With the Wind* (1939). **See also** *Charlie Howard.*

let me loose **— goose, meaning a silly person**
See also *letme.*

letme **— goose, meaning a silly person**
Used in this form by children.

let's rejoice **— voice**
Since at least the early 20th century.

Lew Hoad **— load, meaning sexually transmissible infection**
After Australian tennis player Lewis Alan Hoad (1934–94).

Lewis and W(h)itties **— titties, meaning female breasts**
After a Melbourne law firm. From at least 1940s. Obsolete. **See also** *Bristol Cities, cats and kitties, Denver Cities, Elsie Whitty/ies, Manchester City/ies, Salt Lake Cities, Vatican Cities.*

lies and dead horse **— pies and sauce**
Children's form. **See also** *dead horse, flies and dead horse.*

Lillian Gish **(1) — dish**
After the Hollywood actress Lillian Gish (1893–1993), who was especially prominent in the early days of the silent screen. **See also** *Dorothy Gish.*

Lillian Gish (2) — fish
Current WA 2007. See also *dirty dish*.

Lily of Laguna — schooner (NSW measurement of beer)
After the name of a popular song of 1912. In use since at least World
War II. Obsolete? See also *Senator Spooner*.

Lindsay Kline — wine
After Australian Test cricketer Lindsay Kline (born 1934). See also
Andy Devine, Randall Vines, Tilly Devine.

Lionel Rose — nose
After well-known boxer Lionel Rose (born 1948), Australia's first
Aboriginal world champion boxer. From the 1960s. See also *I suppose,
Piccadilly rose, rubberan, rubber and hose, these and those* (1).

lisp and stutter — butter
See also *chuck me in the gutter, Dark Town strutter, Johnny Rutter, kerb
and gutter, mumble and stutter, mutter and stutter, roll me in the gutter,
stammer and stutter*.

LKS Mackinnon Stakes — water
After this horse race, which is run over a mile and a quarter. See also *Cole
Porter, fisherman's daughter, mother and daughter, squatter's daughter*.

little boys (1) — saveloys, meaning penis

little boys (2) — saveloys (sausages)

loaf of bread — head
Note the variation *use your loaf*, meaning 'think clearly'. 19th-century
English origin. See also *Home Pride bread, Kelly Ned, lump of lead* (3),
3KZ.

locket — pocket
See also *Davey Crockett* (2), *Lucy Locket, sky rocket*.

Lois Lane — train
After the name of Superman's girlfriend, first appearing in the Superman
comics from the late 1930s. Current WA 2007. See also *Frankie Laine*
(3), *Geoffrey Lane* (2), *hail and rain, King of Spain* (3), *pouring rain,
roaring rain, shower of rain, thunder and rain, wind and rain*.

lolly — pee, meaning urinate
From 'lolly' for a confection, referencing 'sweetpea' (the flower) as a partial rhyming slang for 'pee'. World War II. Obsolete. **See also** *Dicky Lee, Nancy Lee, one hundred and three, Robert E. Lee, wasp and bee* (2), *you and me* (2).

London fog — log, meaning a stupid person

Long Jetty — sweaty
After the NSW coastal town. *c.* 1980s and '90s?

loop-the-loop (1) — hoop, meaning jockey
World War II.

loop-the-loop (2) — soup
Perhaps an Australian original. Since at least the 1920s.

Lord Gowrie — Maori
After Sir Alexander Gore Arkwright Hore-Ruthven Gowrie, 1st Earl (1872–1955), and Governor-General of Australia (1936–45).

Lord Rex — sex
1950s–60s? **See also** *Vincent's and Bex.*

Loretta Young — tongue
After American film actress Loretta Young (1913–2000), prominent in the 1940s. Melbourne from *c.* '40s? **See also** *Robert Young.*

lost and found (1) — pound (pre-decimal currency)
World War II. Obsolete. **See also** *stereophonic sound.*

lost and found (2) — sound
World War II.

lubra — Yarborough (term used in the card game of Bridge)
World War II. **See also** *gerbera.*

Lucy Locket — pocket
See also *Davey Crockett* (2), *locket, sky rocket.*

lump of lead (1) — bread
From the 1890s and, in this usage, solely Australian. **See also** *Uncle Fred, Uncle Ned* (2).

lump of lead (2) — dead
As in 'He's *lump of lead*.' Mid-20th century. Melbourne? **See also** *brown bread, garden shed, kangaroo Ted, wombat.*

lump of lead (3) — head
Since at least the early 20th century in Australia and probably long before, as the same term appears in the first collection of English rhyming slang published in the late 1850s. **See also** *Home Pride bread, Kelly Ned, loaf of bread, 3KZ.*

Luna Park — shark
After the Sydney amusement park. **See also** *after darks, Cutty Sark* (2), *Joan of Arc/s, Joe Marks, Jonah, Marcus Clark(e), Noah's Ark* (6).

M

macaroni (1) — baloney, meaning a nonsense or an untruth
From *c.* 1920s.

macaroni (2) — pony, a horse
Also abbreviated to *macker*. Mainly horseracing term. World War II.

macaroni (3) — pony (smallest glass of beer served in NSW)
In this 19th-century form sometimes said to mean 'rubbish'.

macker — see *macaroni* (2)

mad Mick (1) — pick (digging tool)
From World War I.

mad Mick (2) — prick, as in penis
World War II. **See also** *dipstick, drop kick* (1), *Pogo stick* (2), *Rickety Dick* (1), *Uncle Dick, zubrick.*

made in heaven — sixty-seven (Bingo)

Mae West/s — breast/s
After the film star, celebrity and author Mae West (1892–1980). From the early 20th century.

Maggies — see *Maggie Moors*

Maggie Moors — drawers (women's underpants)
Usually abbreviated to *Maggies*. 20th century.

magic wand — blonde

Major Stephens — evens, meaning an even money bet

make another — brother
Children's folk speech. **See also** *maken, once another* (1), *one another* (1).

make them wait — fifty-eight (Bingo)

maken — brother
Children's folk speech. **See also** *make another, once another* (1), *one another* (1).

Mal Meninga/s — finger/s
Mal Meninga (born 1960), is a Rugby League player. **See also** *bell ringer, Manly-Warringahs, Onkaparingas.*

Malcolm Bright — light (for a cigarette)
Probably after Australian Rules Footballer Malcolm Bright. Current 2008.

Malcolm Clift (1) — lift (in a car)
Malcolm Clift is a NSW Rugby League player and coach.

Malcolm Clift (2) — lift (elevator)
After the NSW Rugby League player and coach.

mallee root — prostitute
A play on the slang term for sexual intercourse. Also used in the USA. **See also** *Charlie* (2).

Malvern Star — car
From the name of a popular brand of bicycle. **See also** *church bazaar, Hedy Lamarr, jam jar, Kirk's Bazaar, lah de dah* (1), *Marie La Var, Mars Bar, near and far* (2).

man alive — five (Bingo)
See also *beehive, eat 'em alive, Jack's alive.*

Manchester City/ies — titty/ies, meaning female breasts
An Englishism. **See also** *Bristol Cities, cats and kitties, Denver Cities, Elsie Whitty/ies, Lewis and W(h)itties, Salt Lake Cities, Vatican Cities.*

Manly-Warringahs — fingers
NSW homage to a prominent Sydney football club. **See also** *bell ringer, Mal Meninga/s, Onkaparingas.*

Marcus Clark(e) — shark
Usually said to be named after the 19th-century author of *For the Term of His Natural Life* (1874), Marcus Clarke (1846–81), and so spelled, although the average rhymster was, and is, unlikely to have been acquainted with this literary work. Instead, the term is almost certainly derived from the Sydney department store of that name, established in the early 1920s. **See also** *after darks, Cutty Sark* (2), *Joan of Arc/s, Joe Marks, Jonah, Luna Park, Noah's Ark* (6).

Marcus Welby — might as well be
After the main character in the American medical TV series of the same name that began in the 1960s and was revived in the '80s.

Marie La Var — car
World War II. **See also** *church bazaar, Hedy Lamarr, jam jar, Kirk's Bazaar, lah de dah* (1), *Malvern Star, Mars Bar, near and far* (2).

Mario Lanza — cancer
After the stage name of American tenor and film star Alfredo Arnold Cocozza (1921–59). **See also** *ballet dancer, Bengal lancer, candy dancer, Charlie Dancer, civil answer, Jack the dancer, Jimmy Dancer, Johnny Dancer, Spanish dancer.*

Marjorie Moon — spoon
See also *by the light, David Boon, Ruby Moon.*

Mark Boucher — voucher
After the South African cricketer (born 1976), prominent in the early 21st century. Melbourne, 2006.

Mark Ella — arse, as in bottom
From the ability of this Rugby League player (born 1959) to perform a flick pass, hence the implied rhyme. **See also** *Aris, bottle and glass, Bulli Pass, Coke and sars(parilla), Herb Alpert, Khyber Pass, lemonade and sars(parilla)* (1), *Reg Gasnier.*

Mark Foy — boy
After the now-defunct Sydney department store. Possibly implies victim of a predatory homosexual, as in the term 'mark' used by criminals to

denote a victim, or possibly derives from a firm of 19th-century London cartage contractors and is therefore of Cockney rather than Australian origin. From at least 1940s. **See also** *cocky's joy, mother's joy/s, pride and joy*.

Mars Bar — car
After the confection first manufactured in England in 1932. Current 2008. **See also** *church bazaar, Hedy Lamarr, jam jar, Kirk's Bazaar, lah de dah* (1), *Malvern Star, Marie La Var, near and far* (2).

Mars Bars — scars

Martha Ray — lay, as in sexual intercourse
See also *Johnny Ray*.

Martin Place — face
A NSW term after the central Sydney open area and site of a cenotaph. **See also** *boat race, Chevvy Chase, first base, first place, Melrose Place, Princess Grace, smile place*.

Mary-Lou — blue, meaning credit (horseracing)
As in 'bet on the blue', meaning bet on credit. From *c*. 1920s. Obsolete?

Matt Monroes — toes
After the stage name of English singer Terry Parsons (born 1930). **See also** *buttons and bows, GPOs, Old Black Joe/s, these and those (2), Uncle Joes*.

meat and gravy — man
Recorded as children's speech. From rhyming slang *gravy* for *Davey Cloak*, meaning 'bloke'. Cloak was a well-known Australian Rules footballer of the 1980s. **See also** *Davey Cloak, heavenly plan, pot and pan*.

meat pie — try (a score in rugby football)
First decade of the 21st century, although probably in use in the previous century.

meat pies — eyes
Recorded in children's speech as *meaties*. **See also** *lamb's fries, mince pies, mud pies, Nelly Bligh/s* (4), *Sargents Pie/s* (1), *2KYs*.

meat with rubber — cover
Imperfect rhyme. Recorded in children's speech.

Melbourne — back
From *Melbourne Grammar* as a rhyming slang on *hammer*, itself a shortened version of the rhyming slang *hammer and tack* (6) for 'back'. This could be stretched even further by an accomplished rhymster and in the appropriate context, with *Melbourne* meaning sixpence, from the slang term of 'zac' for this amount. **See also** *George Alfred Black*, *hammer and tack* (6), *Johnny Mack* (1), *tin tack* (1).

Melbourne Grammar (1) — hammer
See also *windjammer*.

Melbourne Grammar (2) — hammer, meaning penis
Early to mid-20th century.

Melbourne Piers — ears
Also as *East Melbourne Piers*. From at least the 1940s. **See also** *Germaine Greer/s* (2), *ginger beer/s* (2), *lager beers*, *Perc Galeas*, *Port Melbourne Pier/s* (1), *Terry Dears*, *Williamstown Piers*.

Melrose Place — face
After the popular late 20th-century American television series of that name. Melbourne 2006. **See also** *boat race*, *Chevvy Chase*, *Epsom Races*, *first base*, *first place*, *Martin Place*, *Princess Grace*, *smile place*.

merchant banker — wanker
Probably originating in the UK during the 1980s, when followers of this calling first came to public notice. **See also** *halfback flanker*, *J. Arthur Rank* (2), *sheep shanker*, *Westpac banker*.

Merri Creek — Greek
Melbourne version of *Werris Creek*. **See also** *bubble and squeak* (1), *ox cheek*, *Tennant Creek*, *Werris Creek* (1).

metric miles — piles, meaning hemorrhoids
See also *asteroids*, *Bea Miles*, *Chalfont St Giles*, *Farmer Giles*, *laughs and smiles*.

Michael Pate — plate
After the Australian actor Michael Pate (1920–2008). **See also** *five-eight* (1), *Harry Tait*, *Reg Date*.

Mick Mills — pills
English origin? Current WA 2007. See also *Jack and Jill* (4).

Mickey Duck (1) — fuck, as in sexual intercourse
See also *Bill Buck* (2), *Donald Duck* (1), *Friar Tuck*, *Joe Buck* (1).

Mickey Duck (2) — truck
See also *Bill Buck* (1), *Donald Duck* (2), *Frank Buck*, *goose and duck*, *Joe Buck* (2).

Mickey Finn (1) — spin, meaning five pounds (pre-decimal currency)
World War II.

Mickey Finn (2) — sin
See also *Vickers Gin*.

Mickey Fritt — shit, as in defecate
See also *big hit*, *brace and bit*, *Dinny Hayes-er*, *Eartha Kitt*, *Edgar Britt*, *gravel pit*, *hard hit*, *Jimmy Britt* (1), *king hit*, *Oscar Britt*, *Tom tit*.

Mickey Mouse (1) — grouse, meaning good
After the evergreen Disney character who first came to public notice from the late 1920s. The term 'Mickey Mouse' is also used in non-rhyming slang form as a description of someone or something considered unreliable or faulty. Possibly mainly Victoria, where 'grouse' persists in current folk speech.

Mickey Mouse (2) — house
Recorded in children's speech. See also *fleas and louse*, *Minnie Mouse*.

Mickey Mouse (3) — louse
World War II.

Mickey Spillane — game
After American crime writer Mickey (properly Frank) Spillane (1918–2006). From the 1950s.

mild and meek — cheek
Australian coinage. From World War II.

mile and a quarter (1) — daughter
Mid-20th century. Melbourne? See also *soap and water*, *soapy water*, *ten furlongs*.

mile and a quarter (2) — **gin and water**

milk jug — **mug, meaning a fool or a dupe**
Often abbreviated to *milkie*. Underworld term since at least 1920.

milkie — **see** *milk jug*

mince pies — **eyes**
In the singular form, appears in the first collection of English rhyming slang published in the late 1850s. Since at least the 1890s. **See also** *lamb's fries*, *meat pies*, *mud pies*, *Nelly Bligh/s* (4), *Sargents Pie/s* (1), *2KYs*.

Minnie Mouse — **house**
After the Disney cartoon character. **See also** *fleas and louse*, *Mickey Mouse* (2).

misbehave — **shave**
Australian original. **See also** *Dad and Dave*, *dig a grave*, *digging in a grave*.

Mister Mutch — **crutch (groin)**
Australian invention of the 20th century. **See also** *hutch*.

moan and wail — **gaol**
From the 1930s. Also used in the USA.

mockingbird — **turd, as in faeces**
Often occurs as a *mocka*. Current 2009. **See also** *elephant's herd*, *George the Third*, *Henry the Third*, *King Henry the Third*, *King George the Third*, *King Richard the Third*, *Richard the Third* (2), *William the Third*.

Mollo the monk — **drunk**
Often abbreviated to *Molly*. Australian original from the 1960s; still current in 2007. **See also** *elephant's trunk*, *Molly Monk*.

Molly — **see** *Mollo the Monk*

Molly Maguire — **fire (conflagration)**
Australianism from World War II. **See also** *Andy McGuire*, *Anna Maria*, *Barney McGuire*, *Bob Dyer*.

Molly Monk — **drunk**
Sometimes *Molly the Monk*. **See also** *elephant's trunk*, *Mollo the Monk*.

Moonbeam — clean
WA *c.* 1940s?

more than eleven — thirty-seven (Bingo)

Moreton Bay bugs — drugs
Moreton Bay is in Queensland. Current 2007. See also *Persian rug* (2).

Moreton Bay Fig (1) — gig, fizzgig, meaning an informer (criminal jargon)
Usually abbreviated to *Moreton Bay*. From around 1940, although the term 'fizzgig' is from the late 19th century. See also *Wally Prig*.

Moreton Bay Fig (2) — gig, meaning someone who is irritatingly curious, possibly a detective (?); a stickybeak
Recorded in children's speech as *Moreton*. From at least the 1950s. See also *Wally Prig*.

Moreton Bay Fig (3) — wig
See also *Irish jig, syrup and fig*.

Moriarty — party
World War II. See also *gay and hearty*.

mortal sin — gin
See also *Gunga Din, Huckleberry Finn, thick and thin* (2), *Vera Lynn* (2).

Mort's Dock — cock, meaning penis
Sometimes abbreviated to *Morts*. Historic Sydney shipbuilding site. World War II. See also *eight day clock, Rock Around the Clock, Victoria Dock*.

mother and daughter — water
From at least the early 20th century. See also *Cole Porter, fisherman's daughter, LKS Mackinnon Stakes, squatter's daughter*.

Mother Goose — deuce, meaning a florin (two shilling coin) (pre-decimal currency)
World War II. Obsolete. See also *Paterson, Laing and Bruce* (2); *Roy Sluice* (2).

Mother Machree — tea
Probably from the sentimental and enormously popular ballad of the

same name composed in 1910. Australian original from at least World War II. **See also** *Dicky Lee* (2), *Gypsy Lee*, *Jack Shay* (1), *Jenny Lee*, *Jimmy Lee*, *Rosie Lee*, *wasp and bee* (1), *you and me* (3).

mother of pearl — girl
See also *Barossa Pearl*, *twist/s and twirl/s*.

mother's joy/s — boy/s
Since at least the early 20th century; current in the 1940s and since. **See also** *cocky's joy*, *Mark Foy*, *pride and joy*.

motorboat — overcoat
See also *armour float*, *Collier and Moat*, *I'm afloat*.

mottle — see *charming mottle*

mouse organ — mouth organ (harmonica)
In use among folk musicians.

Mozart and Liszt — pissed, meaning drunk
See also *Adrian Quist*, *Brahms and Liszt*, *Franz Liszt*, *Oliver Twist (1)*, *Schindler's List*, *sisters apart*.

Mrs Murphy's chowder — powder

mud and ooze — booze, meaning alcoholic beverage
Probably since at least the early 20th century. **See also** *La Perouse*, *pick and choose*.

mud in your eye — (neck)tie
See also *dog's eye* (2), *Fourth of July*, *lamb's fry*, *Nazi spy* (2), *Nellie Bligh* (5), *Russian spy*, *stock and die* (1), *2KY* (1).

mud pies — eyes
Australian in origin. **See also** *lamb's fries*, *meat pies*, *mince pies*, *Nellie Bligh/s* (4) *Sargents Pie/s* (1), *2KYs*.

Mulligatawny — horny, meaning sexually aroused
Mulligatawny is a highly spiced soup.

mum and dad — mad
World War II.

mum and daddo — shadow
Obsolete?

mumble and grunt — cunt, as in female genitalia
See also *All Quiet on the Western Front, Ballina Punt, Berkshire Hunt, Billy Hunt, drop kick and punt, grumble and grunt, Joe Hunt, Stockton Punt.*

mumble and stutter — butter
See also *chuck me in the gutter, Dark Town strutter, Johnny Rutter, kerb and gutter, lisp and stutter, mutter and stutter, roll me in the gutter, stammer and stutter.*

Murray cod (1) — on the nod, meaning to bet or to be on credit
As in 'on the *Murray cod*'. After the iconic Murray River fish. From at least the 1960s.

Murray cod (2) — nod (the head)

Murray Rivers — shivers
See also *Hawkesbury Rivers, Swannee Rivers.*

Mutt and Jeff — deaf
After the characters in a long-running American newspaper comic strip by H. C. Fisher (1884–1954), which began in 1907 and became widely popular by World War I. These comic strips also appeared in Australian newspapers. See also *AIF.*

mutter and stutter — butter
See also *chuck me in the gutter, Dark Town strutter, Johnny Rutter, kerb and gutter, lisp and stutter, mumble and stutter, roll me in the gutter, stammer and stutter.*

mutton flaps — Japs, Japanese people
Originating among prisoners-of-war from 1942; used generally into the 1950s and, perhaps, beyond. Obsolete?

mutton shanks — Yanks, meaning Americans
Reported in Australian circus talk in World War II. See also *army tank, ham shank, iron tank* (2), *Jodrell Bank, septic tank/s* (1), *ship's tank, tin tank* (2).

my mother's away — (the) other day
Recorded in 1902, although thought to have been used in the late 19th century.

mystery bags — snags, meaning sausages
Possibly derived from the Cockneyism for sausages, 'bags of mystery'.

N

nails and screws — news
Since at least the early 20th century. **See also** *bottle of booze.*

Nancy Lee — pee, as in urinate
See also *Dicky Lee* (1), *lolly, one hundred and three, Robert E. Lee, wasp and bee* (2), *you and me* (2).

nanny goat (1) — throat
See also *billy goat* (1).

nanny goat (2) — tote, totalisator (horseracing)
World War II. Also in English rhyming slang from at least 1961. **See also** *billy goat* (2), *canal boat, giddy goat.*

Napper Tandy — shandy, a drink of beer and lemonade
After the Irish revolutionary James Napper Tandy (1740–1803). Australian original from at least World War II.

Nat King Cole (1) — bowl (cricket)
After the American singer Nat(haniel) King Cole (1917–65). **See also** *sausage roll* (2).

Nat King Cole (2) — dole, meaning unemployment benefit
See also *horse and foal, rock and roll, strum and stroll, strut and stroll.*

Nazi spy — (1) meat pie
Australian invention from World War II. **See also** *dog's eye* (1), *Nellie Bligh* (3), *pig's eye* (1), *stock and die* (2), *2KY* (3).

Nazi spy (2) — (neck)tie
See also *dog's eye* (2), *Fourth of July, lamb's fry, mud in your eye, Nellie Bligh* (5), *Russian spy, stock and die* (1), *2KY* (1).

near and far (1) — bar, meaning a surface for serving alcoholic beverages; in recent usage can refer to the establishment
Since at least the early 20th century.

near and far (2) — car
See also *church bazaar, Hedy Lamarr, jam jar, Kirk's Bazaar, lah de dah* (1), *Malvern Star, Marie La Var, Mars Bar.*

Ned Kelly (1) — belly, meaning stomach
After the bushranger turned national hero Edward Kelly (1857–80). From the 1920s; used in World War II. **See also** *Aunt Nelly, Darby Kelly, Nelly Kelly.*

Ned Kelly (2) — telly, short for television
Since the 1970s in Britain. **See also** *custard and jelly*.

needle and thread — bed
Mid-20th century. Melbourne? **See also** *Bill and Ted*, *God strike me dead*, *Rocky Ned*, *roses red*, *Uncle Ned* (1), *white and red*.

Nellie and dead — red, meaning wine

Nellie Bligh (1) — fly (in trousers)
Probably after a famous song of this name (variously spelt) written by American composer Stephen Foster in 1850.

Nellie Bligh (2) — fly, meaning in state of alertness, possibly sharp
World War II?

Nellie Bligh (3) — (meat) pie
1950s. **See also** *dog's eye* (1), *Nazi spy* (1), *pig's eye* (1), *stock and die* (2), *2KY* (3).

Nellie Bligh/s (4) — eye/s
See also *lamb's fries*, *meat pie/s*, *mince pies*, *mud pies*, *Sargents Pie/s* (1), *2KYs*.

Nellie Bligh (5) — (neck)tie
From 1940s. **See also** *dog's eye* (2), *Fourth of July*, *lamb's fry*, *mud in your eye*, *Nazi spy* (2), *Russian spy*, *stock and die* (1), *2KY* (1).

Nellie Bligh or Bly (6) — lie
Recorded in the 1980s. **See also** *Hawkie*, *pork/ie pie*, *Sargents Pie/s* (2), *2KY* (2).

Nelly Kelly — belly, meaning (usually a woman's) stomach
20th century. **See also** *Aunt Nelly*, *Darby Kelly*, *Ned Kelly* (1).

Nelson — see Nelson Riddle

Nelson Mandela — quinella, type of bet in horseracing
After the famous South African political leader Nelson Mandela (born 1918).

Nelson Riddle — piddle, as in urinate
Usually abbreviated to 'a *Nelson*'. After the American composer and musician Nelson Riddle (1921–85). Australian origin. World War II. **See also** *Gerry Riddle*, *hey diddle diddle* (2), *hi diddle diddle* (2), *Jimmy Riddle*, *Shannon*.

nervous wreck — cheque
Often abbreviated to 'a *nervous*'. **See also** *duck's neck, goose's neck, Gregory Peck* (1), *total wreck*.

never better/s — letter/s
Since at least World War II. **See also** *carburettor, don't forget her* (2).

Neville Beggs — legs
After the racehorse trainer of that name. **See also** *bacon and eggs, clothes pegs, Dutch pegs, fried eggs, Ginger Meggs, Gregory Pegs, ham and eggs, nine gallon kegs, Scotch pegs.*

Neville Wran — can (tin)
After one-time NSW Labor Premier Neville Wran (born 1926).

New South — mouth
Probably derived from Cockney rhyming slang form *north and south* for 'mouth' rather than the folk abbreviation for the state of NSW? Also used in the USA. 20th century. **See also** *north and south.*

New York junk — spunk, meaning semen
Mid-to-late 20th century? **See also** *Billy Dunk, Harry Monk.*

Niagara Falls — balls, as in testicles
Usually abbreviated to *Niagaras*. Current 2007. **See also** *cobblers' awls, orchestra stalls, Queenie Pauls, town halls, Wentworth Falls.*

Niagaras — see Niagara Falls

Nine and ten — pen, for sheep

nine gallon kegs — legs
See also *bacon and eggs, clothes pegs, Dutch pegs, fried eggs, Ginger Meggs, Gregory Pegs, ham and eggs,, Neville Beggs, Scotch pegs.*

Noah/s — see Noah's Ark (6)

Noah's Ark (1) — dark

Noah's Ark (2) — park

Noah's Ark (3) — lark, meaning having fun, as in having a 'lark'

Noah's Ark (4) — nark, meaning a spoilsport, or possibly one who is in a bad mood, as in 'narky'
World War II.

Noah's Ark (5) — narc/k, meaning informer
Since the late 19th century, criminals have used the term with this meaning. **See also** *Cutty Sark* (1), *dog and bark*.

Noah's Ark (6) — shark (fish)
Often abbreviated to *Noah* or *Noah's*, after the biblical figure. In this sense, usage dates from at least 1940s. **See also** *after darks*, *Cutty Sark* (2), *Joan of Arc/s*, *Joe Marks*, *Jonah*, *Luna Park*, *Marcus Clark(e)*.

Noah's Ark (7) — shark, meaning an individual believed to be an untrustworthy dealer, especially in business matters, such as a moneylender
Often abbreviated to *Noah* or *Noah's*, after the biblical figure. In this sense, usage dates from at least 1940s.

Noel McGrowdie — cloudy
Noel 'Digger' McGrowdie (1920–61) was a jockey, prominent in the 1940s and '50s. Perhaps restricted to Victoria? Mid-20th century.

north and south — mouth
In use since at least the early 20th century in Australia. Also Cockney. **See also** *New South*.

North Sydney — kidney
NSW only? 20th century. **See also** *east o' Sydneys*, *South Sydney*.

now is the hour — shower (as in bathing)
See also *David Gower* (2), *fairy bower*, *lazy hour*, *Tyrone Power*.

number two — poo, as in defecate
Mainly recorded in children's speech and that of adults to children. From at least the mid-20th century.

nuts and bolts — colts, meaning junior cricketers and rugby players
Probably NSW only.

O

ocean liner (1) — cliner (girl, woman)
'Cliner' was a 19th-century slang term for a larrikin's girlfriend or wife, probably derived from the German term for a woman. In use since at least the early 20th century.

ocean liner (2) — mate, meaning friend; likely to be male
A play on rhyming slang *China plate* for 'mate'. Probably World War II origins. **See also** *China plate, five-eight* (2), *old China plate, Royal Doulton.*

off break — steak
A croquet term. **See also** *Joe Blake/s* (3), *quiver and shake.*

off-shore — four (Bingo)

oh my dear — beer
Recorded 1902. **See also** *Britney Spears, cherry cheer, Crimea, Germaine Greer/s* (1), *Perc Galea, pig's ear, Port Melbourne Pier* (2), *pot of good cheer, Ray Stehr, Terry Dear.*

oily rag — fag, meaning a cigarette
See also *Harry Wragg, Twelfth Street Rag.*

okey doke — coke, cocaine
A whimsical reworking of 'okay' adapted to rhyming slang. Current among cocaine users in the 1990s.

Old Black Joe/s — toe/s
After the Stephen Foster song of the same name composed in 1860. Originated in Australia during the 20th century. **See also** *buttons and bows, GPOs, Matt Monroes, these and those* (2), *Uncle Joes.*

old China plate — old mate
Often abbreviated to *old China*. A classical Cockneyism widely used in Australia, probably from the 19th century. **See also** *China plate, five-eight* (2), *ocean liner* (2), *Royal Doulton.*

old nags — fags
See also *bones and rags.*

old pot — see *pot and pan* **(1) and (2)**

Oliver — see *Oliver Twist* **(2)**

Oliver Twist (1) — pissed, meaning drunk
After the hero of Charles Dickens' famous novel, first published in 1828. **See also** *Adrian Quist, Brahms and Liszt, Franz Liszt, Mozart and Liszt, Schindler's List, sisters apart.*

Oliver Twist **(2) — wrist**
Often abbreviated to *Oliver*. From late 19th-century Australian speech. Current to World War II at least. Obsolete?

Oliver Twist **(3) — fist**

on the beak — reek, meaning stink.
Beak is slang for 'nose'. Current 2008.

on the floor — poor
See also *Archie Moore*.

on your own — loan
See also *Darby and Joan* (1), *Jack Jones*, *Vic Damone*.

once another (1) — brother
World War II. **See also** *make another*, *maken*, *one another*.

once another (2) — mother
See also *one another* (2), *strangle and smother*, *tell us another*.

one alone — moan

one another (1) — brother
See also *make another*, *maken*, *once another* (1).

one another (2) — mother
See also *once another* (2), *strangle and smother*, *tell us another*.

one hundred and three — pee, as in urinate
See also *Dicky Lee* (1), *lolly*, *Nancy Lee*, *Robert E. Lee*, *wasp and bee* (2), *you and me* (2).

one more time — seventy-nine (Bingo)

ones and twos — shoes
See also *Basin Street blues*, *Ben Blues*, *canoes*, *kangaroo/s* (2), *Peggy Sue*, *Pete Kelly's blues*, *Saint Louis blues*, *splash throughs*, *ten to twos*.

Onkaparingas **— fingers**
Often abbreviated to *onkas*; also in the singular form *Onkaparinga*. From the SA town of Onkaparinga; a placename and brand of woollen blanket made by a company established there in 1869. **See also** *bell ringer*, *Mal Meninga/s*, *Manly-Warringahs*.

Onkas **— see *Onkaparingas***

(an) optic — see *optic nerve*

optic nerve — **perve, meaning one who ogles the opposite sex**
As in 'Cop *an optic* at that', usually an enthusiastic comment on the attractiveness of a woman. In use since at least the early 1970s. **See also** *hit and swerve, hors d'oeuvre, sway and swerve, Uncle Merv.*

orchestra stalls — **balls, as in testicles**
Mid-20th century and current 2007. **See also** *cobblers' awls, Niagara Falls, Queenie Pauls, town halls, Wentworth Falls.*

Oscar — see *Oscar Asche*

Oscar Asche — **cash**
Usually abbreviated to *Oscar*. After Australian actor Oscar Asche (1871–1936). In use since at least the early 20th century. Current into World War II. **See also** *Arthur Ashe, Charlie Ash, Christopher Ash, J. Carroll Nash, sausage and mash, smash, splash.*

Oscar Britt — **shit, as in defecate**
See also *big hit, brace and bit, Dinny Hayes-er, Eartha Kitt, Edgar Britt, gravel pit, hard hit, Jimmy Britt* (1), *king hit, Mickey Fritt, Tom tit.*

Oscar King — **string**
Recorded in children's folk speech. **See also** *highland fling* (2).

over there — **hair**
World War II. **See also** *Barnet Fair, Dublin Fair, Fred Astaire* (2), *here and there, preference share, table and chair.*

overweight — **twenty-eight (Bingo)**

ox cheek — **Greek**
Mid-20th century. Melbourne? **See also** *bubble and squeak* (1), *Merri Creek, Tennant Creek, Werris Creek* (1).

Oxford scholar — **dollar**
From the British slang term for five shillings, once the equivalent of an American dollar. Used in Australia before the introduction of decimal currency in 1966 and continued since as a rhyme on the Australian dollar. **See also** *Rhodes scholar.*

ozone — **phone, telephone**
World War II. **See also** *Al Capone, Darby and Joan* (2), *dog and bone, eau de Cologne* (1).

P

paddy melt — **belt**
See also *dark felt*, *South African Veldt*.

paper doll **(1) — moll, meaning a gangster's kept woman and/or prostitute**
'Moll' as underworld slang for a woman, usually a criminal's consort, was in use since at least the mid-19th century.

paper doll **(2) — moll, meaning a girl or woman whose sexual favours are widely distributed**
From *c.* 1950s–60s.

paraffin lamp — **tramp, a vagrant**

pass — **see *Bulli Pass***

passing by **(1) — swy, meaning two shillings (a florin) (pre-decimal currency)**
World War II? Obsolete.

passing by **(2) — swy, meaning the gambling game two-up**

Pat and Mick **(1) — lick, as in defeat or best someone**
Also occurs as *Pat and Micked* (licked). See also *Tom and Dick* (1).

Pat and Mick **(2) — sick**
See also *Tom and Dick* (2).

Pat Malone — **on one's own, alone**
In this form in 'Duke' Tritton's rhyming slang letter dated 1905; also in *We of the Never Never* (1908) by Mrs Aeneas Gunn. As 'on my *pat*', it appears in 1908 and later in the writing of C. J. Dennis as larrikin slang. *c.* 1915. See also *eau de Cologne* (2), *Jack Malone*, *Tod Sloane*.

Paterson, Laing and Bruce **(1) — deuce, meaning two items**
Usually abbreviated to *Paterson Laing*, or even just *Paterson*. After a Sydney company. Restricted to that city. Obsolete.

Paterson, Laing and Bruce **(2) — deuce, meaning two shillings (a florin) (pre-decimal currency)**
Usually abbreviated to *Paterson Laing*, or even just *Paterson*. After a Sydney company. Restricted to that city. Obsolete. **See also** *Mother Goose*, *Roy Sluice* (2).

pay me (the) rent — tent
World War II.

pear and quince — prince
Australian World War II invention. **See also** *curried mince.*

peas in a pot — hot

Peggy Lee — three
After the American jazz singer Peggy Lee (Norma Egstrom, 1920–2002). **See also** *Sammy Lee.*

Peggy Lou — two
See also *button my shoe.*

Peggy Sue — shoe
Probably from the title of a famous popular song by Buddy Holly and the Crickets, released in 1957. **See also** *Basin Street blues, Ben Blues, canoes, kangaroo/s* (2)*, ones and twos, Pete Kelly's blues, splash throughs, ten to twos.*

pen and ink — drink (alcoholic?)
A contrast to the London version, which is a rhyme for 'stink'. **See also** *cuff link, kitchen sink, Silver Link* (1)*, tiddlywink.*

penny brown — town
World War II. **See also** *Joe Brown, knock me down.*

penny dips — lips
1950s–60s? **See also** *slippery dip* (1)*.*

Perc Galea — beer
After the well-known and well-liked Sydney racing identity Percival John Galea (died 1977). **See also** *Britney Spears, cherry cheer, Crimea, Germaine Greer/s* (1)*, oh my dear, pig's ear, Port Melbourne Pier* (2)*, pot of good cheer, Ray Stehr, Terry Dear.*

Perc Galeas — ears
See also *Germaine Greer/s* (2)*, ginger beer/s* (2)*, lager beers, Melbourne Piers, Terry Dears, Williamstown Piers.*

Persian rug (1) **— tug, as in male masturbation**
Current 2007.

Persian rug (2) — drug
See also *Moreton Bay bugs*.

Pete Kelly's blues — shoes
After a 1955 film based on a 1951 radio series. **See also** *Basin Street blues, Ben Blues, canoes, kangaroo/s* (2), *ones and twos, Peggy Sue, Saint Louis blues, splash throughs, ten to twos*.

Pete Tong — wrong
After a prominent British club DJ. The term was used in the title of a feature film *It's All Gone Pete Tong* (2005), further popularising the rhyming slang term among followers of Tong's music, and beyond. Current from the early 2000s.

Peter Gunn — sun
After an early American TV detective series of the late 1950s and early '60s. **See also** *Attila the Hun, currant bun* (2), *hot cross bun*.

Peter Mertens — curtains, as in to have lost or failed
Probably after the Victorian jockey of the same name. Current 2008.

petrol bowsers — trousers
Usually abbreviated to *bowsers* or *petrols*. The term 'bowser' is from the name of the company that manufactured commercial petrol pumps, so the rhyming slang is possibly pre-World War II. Current NSW 2007. **See also** *council houses, dead wowsers, rammy rousers, round the houses, terrace houses*.

petrols — see ***petrol bowsers***

philharmonic — tonic

Piccadilly — chilly
See also *Dennis Lillee*.

Piccadilly rose — nose
See also *I suppose, Lionel Rose, rubberan, rubber and hose, these and those* (1).

pick and choose — booze, meaning alcoholic beverage
See also *La Perouse, mud and ooze*.

pick and mix — twenty-six (Bingo)

pickle and pork — walk
Sometimes occurs as *pickled pork*. From World War II. **See also** *Duke of York* (2), *stick of chalk*.

pig's arse — glass
Australian original. World War II or before. **See also** *forward pass/es*.

pig's ear — beer
Since the late 19th century in British folk speech. **See also** *Britney Spears, cherry cheer, Crimea, Germaine Greer/s* (1), *oh my dear, Perc Galea, Port Melbourne Pier* (2), *pot of good cheer, Ray Stehr, Terry Dear*.

pig's eye (1) — pie
See also *dog's eye* (1), *Nazi spy* (1), *Nelly Bligh* (3), *stock and die* (2), *2KY* (3).

pig's eye (2) — try, meaning a score in rugby football

pitch and toss — boss
World War II. **See also** *Joe Goss*.

plate of meat — sweet, meaning all clear, all is well
Recorded in children's speech.

plates of meat — feet
A Cockneyism; in use in Australia from at least the 1890s. Still current after World War II.

plink plonk — vin blanc (white wine)
Used during World War I, after which the shortened form 'plonk' — meaning wine in general — moved into the broader Australian vernacular, where it is still heard. **See also** *honky tonk, horse and donk, plinketty-plonk*.

plinketty-plonk — vin blanc (white wine)
World War I soldiers had many terms for the French *vin blanc*, including 'vin blank', 'von blink' and 'point blank'. Eventually 'plonk' emerged as the general slang term for wine. Obsolete. **See also** *honky tonk, horse and donk, plink plonk*.

plonkdot — sot, meaning one who is drunk, often habitually
See also *dot, Kennedy rot, wine dot*.

plum jam — ram (sheep)

plum pud — good
Australian original from at least World War II. **See also** *Jimmy Britt* (2), *Robin Hood*, *Wee Georgie Wood*.

poddy calf — half (a crown), the equivalent of two shillings and sixpence (pre-decimal currency)
From *poddy calf* as a rhyme on 'half-a-caser', a caser being five shillings. A motherless calf or lamb is a 'poddy'. 20th century. In this form obsolete, but persisted until the introduction of decimal currency in 1966 as shorthand for 'two and six' (two shillings and sixpence).

Pogo — see Pogo stick (1) and (2)

Pogo stick (1) — dick, meaning penis
Usually abbreviated to *Pogo*; recorded as *Pogo* in children's speech. From the spring-loaded jumping toy invented in 1919 by American George Hansburg. **See also** *Hoffman brick*.

Pogo stick (2) — prick, meaning penis
Usually abbreviated to *Pogo*. **See also** *dipstick, drop kick* (1), *mad Mick* (2), *Rickety Dick* (1), *Uncle Dick, zubrick*.

Pollywaffle — brothel
After the name of a popular Australian confection. Not a perfect rhyme, but a memorable one. Current in the first decade of the 21st century. **See also** *Timothy*.

poofter's bum — rum
See also *dad and mum* (1), *deaf and dumb* (2), *finger and thumb*, T*om Thumb* (1).

pork and bean — queen, a male homosexual
Often in the plural *pork and beans*. From at least the 1940s; current in the '60s. **See also** *baked bean, haricot bean, in-between, submarine*.

pork and beans — Portuguese (troops)
World War I. Obsolete. **See also** *pork and cheese*.

pork and cheese — Portuguese (troops)
World War I. Obsolete. **See also** *pork and beans*.

pork/ie pie — lie
From Cockney and broader British usage. **See also** *Hawkie, Nellie Bligh* (6), *Sargents Pie/s* (2), *2KY* (2).

Port Melbourne Pier/s (1) — ear
In children's speech, shortened to *porties*. Melbourne; since at least World War II. See also *Germaine Greer/s* (2), *ginger beer/s* (2), *lager beers, Melbourne Piers*.

Port Melbourne Pier (2) — beer
See also *Britney Spears, cherry cheer, Crimea, Germaine Greer/s* (1), oh *my dear, pig's ear, pot of good cheer, Ray Stehr, Terry Dear*.

post and rail — fairytale, meaning a lie
From *c.* 1910.

pot and pan (1) — man
Often abbreviated to *pot*. From at least the early 20th century with this meaning. See also *heavenly plan, meat and gravy*.

pot and pan (2) — old man, meaning husband or father
Usually occurs as *pot* or *old pot*. Cockney. In use in Australia in the 1890s. Appears in the form *old pot* in the writings of C. J. Dennis as larrikin slang *c.* 1915 and in prison usage from the '40s. Obsolete? See also *heavenly plan, meat and gravy*.

pot of good cheer — beer
Current 2007. See also *Britney Spears, cherry cheer, Crimea, Germaine Greer/s* (1), *oh my dear, Perc Galea, pig's ear, Port Melbourne Pier (2), Ray Stehr, Terry Dear*.

potato and spud — dud, meaning ineffectual
Recorded in children's speech. See also *Elmer, Elmer Fudd, Kevin Rudd*.

potato peeler — sheila, a girl or woman
Recorded from the late 1950s, but almost certainly older. See also *Charlie Wheeler, rock-wheeler, two wheeler*.

pouring rain — train
See also *Frankie Laine* (3), *Geoffrey Lane* (2), *hail and rain, King of Spain* (3), *Lois Lane, roaring rain, shower of rain, thunder and rain, wind and rain*.

preference share — hair
See also *Barnet Fair, Dublin Fair, Fred Astaire* (2), *here and there, over there, table and chair*.

pride and joy — boy
1940s. See also *cocky's joy*, *Mark Foy*, *mother's joy/s*.

Princess Grace — face
After Princess Grace of Monaco (1930–82). See also *boat race*, *Chevvy Chase*, *Epsom Races*, *first base*, *first place*, *Martin Place*, *Melrose Place*, *smile place*.

purple and mauve — stove
Australian 20th-century original. See also *Lane Cove*.

Q

queen bee — seventy-three (Bingo)

Queenie Paul — wall
Queenie Paul OAM (1893–1982) was an all-round Australian entertainer. See also *bat and ball* (2), *Duncan Hall*.

Queenie Pauls — balls, as in testicles
See also *cobblers' awls*, *Niagara Falls*, *orchestra stalls*, *town halls*, *Wentworth Falls*.

quiver and shake — steak
20th century. See also *Joe Blake* (3), *off break*.

R

rabbit in the thicket — cricket
See also *Wilson Pickett*.

rabbit's paw — jaw

racehorse — (tomato) sauce
See also *clerk of the course*, *dead horse*, *rocking horse*, *Tommy Farter*.

rammy rousers — trousers
According to the *Bulletin* of 20 December 1906, this is the Australianised version of the Cockney rhyming slang for trousers — 'rahand me 'ouses'. Also occurs in 'Duke' Tritton's rhyming slang letter dated 1905. See also *council houses*, *dead wowsers*, *petrol bowsers*, *round the houses*, *terrace houses*.

ram's horn — pawn(?)
Appears in print in 1918 in relation to anger. Obsolete. **See also** *bullock('s) horn*.

Randall Vines — wine(s?)
See also *Andy Devine, Lindsay Kline, Tilly Devine*.

Randwick Races — braces
After the Sydney racecourse. **See also** *airs and graces, Flemington Races*.

raspberry ripple — cripple

raspberry tart — fart, as in break wind
Most widely used in the shortened form *raspberry*. One of the oldest rhyming slangs in English, going back to at least the late 19th century. **See also** *apple tart, bacon and egg tart, bottle mart, cupcake, Dicky Bart, fairy dart, horse and cart* (1), *jam tart* (2), *Stevey Hart*.

rats and mice — rice

Ray Bright — light, meaning low-alcohol beer
See also *scare and fright*.

Ray Millands — hands
After the Welsh-born Hollywood actor Ray Milland (1907–86). **See also** *brass bands, Brighton le Sands, Dave Sands, German band/s*.

Ray Stehr — beer
After the Australian Rugby League footballer of the 1930s. **See also** *Britney Spears, cherry cheers, Crimea, Germaine Greer/s* (1), *oh my dear, Perc Galea, pig's ear, Port Melbourne Pier* (2), *pot of good cheer, Terry Dear*.

red hot — pot, meaning ten-ounce (pre-metric) glass of beer
Australian original. **See also** *Sir Walter Scott*.

red hots (1) **— trots, meaning dysentery**
See also *dry rots*.

red hots (2) **— trots, meaning harness racing**
Probably from the 1950s.

red Ned — red (wine)
Not a true rhyming slang? Perhaps derived from the World War I usage 'Ned Kelly's blood' for *vin rouge*.

red raw — sixty-four (Bingo)

Reg Date — plate
After an early Australian soccer player. See also *five-eight* (1), *Harry Tait*, *Michael Pate*.

Reg Gasnier — arse, as in bottom
From this NSW Rugby League footballer's ability with the 'flick pass', hence the implied rhyme. Reg Gasnier (born 1939), was a prominent player in the 1950s and '60s. See also *Aris*, *Bulli Pass*, *bottle and glass*, *Coke and sars(parilla)*, *Herb Alpert*, *Khyber Pass*, *lemonade and sars(parilla)*(1), *Mark Ella*.

Reg Grundies — undies (short for underpants)
Usually abbreviated to *Reginalds* or *Reggies*. After Reg Grundy (born 1924), a prominent television producer.

Reginalds — see *Reg Grundies*

Rhodes scholar — one dollar
Also in the plural form. See also *Oxford scholar*.

rice and sago — dago, meaning a Greek, Italian or other person of Mediterranean background

Richard Dix — six (cricket)
See also *Dorothy Dix*, *Tom Mix*.

Richard the Third (1) — bird, as in to 'get the bird', meaning to lose one's job
See also *had the Richard*.

Richard the Third (2) — turd, as in faeces
Usually abbreviated to 'a *Richard*'. Current WA, 2007. See also *elephant's herd*, *George the Third*, *Henry the Third*, *King George the Third*, *King Henry the Third*, *King George the Third*, *King Richard the Third*, *mocking bird*, *William the Third*.

Rickety Dick (1) — prick, meaning penis
World War II. See also *dipstick*, *drop kick* (1), *mad Mick* (2), *Pogo stick* (2), *Uncle Dick*, *zubrick*.

Rickety Dick (2) — stick
World War II. See also *clicketty-click* (1).

Rickety Kate — **gate**
Australian original. Probably since at least the 1960s.

Ricky May — **way, as in 'the way home'**
After New Zealand jazz/pop singer Ricky May (1944–88), who sang in
Australia from the early 1960s.

ridgy didge — **fridge, refrigerator**
In general slang, *ridgy didge*, or *ridge* is an expression of approval, usually
signifying that something is genuine. **See also** *Brooklyn Bridge*.

ridgy-dite — **'all right'**
Used to indicate that someone or something is genuine, to be trusted.
Recorded in the 1950s but likely to be older. **See also** *ridgy didge*.

rifle range — **change (money)**
See also *home on the range, Kembla Grange*.

rinkydinks — **stinks, as in something is bad**
Current WA 2007.

rise and shine — **twenty-nine (Bingo)**

River Murray — **curry**
See also *Angus Murray, Arthur Murray*.

River Murrays — **worries**
As in 'No *River Murrays*', indicating that all is well. Since the 1970s?

Riverina — **deaner (one shilling)**
Obsolete. **See also** *dog's dinner* (1).

roaring horsetails — **Aurora Australis (astronomy)**
Perhaps not really rhyming slang and probably highly restricted? World
War II. Obsolete.

roaring rain — **train**
World War II. **See also** *Frankie Laine* (3), *Geoffrey Lane* (2), *hail and
rain, King of Spain* (3), *Lois Lane, pouring rain, shower of rain, thunder
and rain, wind and rain*.

roast pork — **talk**
Also used in English rhyming slang, although the term *rabbit and pork*,
hence to 'rabbit on', is probably more common there. To 'rabbit on', of

course, is used in general Australian slang, although few people, if any, would be aware of its rhyming slang derivation.

Robert E. Lee — pee, as in urinate
After General Robert E. Lee (1807–70), a Confederate leader of the American Civil War. See also *Dicky Lee* (1), *lolly*, *Nancy Lee*, *one hundred and three*, *wasp and bee* (2), *you and me* (2).

Robert Young — tongue
After American film and television actor Robert Young (1907–98), probably best known in Australia from the 1950s–60s television series *Father Knows Best* and, in the late '60s and '70s as Marcus Welby, MD. See also *Loretta Young*.

Roberta Flack — sack, meaning bed
After American singer Roberta Flack (born 1937). Australian original from the 1970s.

Robertson and Moffat — profit
Usually abbreviated to *Robertson*. After a Melbourne department store. Since the 1940s.

Robin Hood — good
A rhyme on the legendary English outlaw. See also *Jimmy Britt* (2), *plum pud*, *Wee Georgie Wood*.

rock and lurch — church
In the form *lean and lurch*, among the first recorded rhyming slang terms in London during the late 1850s. See also *lean and lurch*, *left in the lurch*, *roll and lurch*.

rock and roll — dole, meaning unemployment benefit
Probably since the 1950s only. See also *horse and foal*, *Nat King Cole* (2), *strum and stroll*, *strut and stroll*.

rock and rollers — bowlers (lawn bowls)

Rock Around the Clock — cock, meaning penis
From the name of a famous rock and roll song popularised by Bill Haley and the Comets from 1954. See also *eight-day clock*, *Mort's Dock*, *Victoria Dock*.

rock boulder/s — shoulder/s

Australian version of the late 19th-century English *rock and boulder*.
Still in currency mid–late 20th century. Melbourne.

rock of ages — wages
See also *greengages*.

rocking horse — tomato sauce
Recorded in children's speech. **See also** *clerk of the course, racehorse, Tommy Farter*.

rocks — see *almond rocks*

rock-wheeler — sheila, meaning girl or woman
Recorded in children's speech. Probably also a play on rottweiler (dog breed). **See also** *Charlie Wheeler, potato peeler, two wheeler*.

Rocky Ned — bed
After a famously unrideable bucking horse of the 1930s, celebrated in a song of this title by New Zealand-born country singer 'Tex' Morton, born Robert Lane (1916–83). **See also** *Bill and Ted, God strike me dead, needle and thread, roses red, Uncle Ned* (1), *white and red*.

Rodney Hogg — bog, meaning toilet; also the act of going to the toilet
See also *hollow log* (4).

Rodney Rude — food
Sometimes abbreviated to *Rodney*. After the Australian comedian of that name.

rogan — shilling (pre-decimal currency)
From English rhyming slang *rogue and villain*, meaning shilling. World War II. Obsolete. **See also** *John Dilling, John Dillon, rogue and Dillon, rogue and villain*.

Roger Moore — floor
After the English actor Sir Roger Moore (born 1927). **See also** *Rory O'Moore*.

rogue and Dillon — shilling (pronounced shillin') (pre-decimal currency)
Obsolete. **See also** *John Dilling, John Dillon, rogan, rogue and villain*.

rogue and villain — shilling (pronounced shillin') (pre-decimal currency)
Usually abbreviated to *rogan*. Derived from English rhyming slang. Current at least in the 1850s. Obsolete. **See also** *John Dilling, John Dillon, rogan, rogue and Dillon*.

roll and lurch — church
In the form *lean and lurch* appears in the first collection of English rhyming slang, published in the late 1850s. Since at least the early 20th century. **See also** *lean and lurch, left in the lurch, rock and lurch*.

roll me in the gutter — butter
Since at least the early 20th century. **See also** *chuck me in the gutter, Dark Town strutter, Johnny Rutter, kerb and gutter, lisp and stutter, mumble and stutter, mutter and stutter, stammer and stutter*.

rolling deep — sleep
Australian since *c*.World War II. **See also** *Bo-peep, hit the deep*.

Ron Randle — candle
Said to be after Australian actor Ron Randell (1918–2005), although his name is usually pronounced to rhyme with 'bell'. **See also** *broom handle, Harry Randle*.

Rory O'Moore — floor
Often abbreviated to 'the *Rory*'. Rory O'Moore was a mythical Irish revolutionary celebrated in the early 19th century. Current in London during the 1850s and probably since then, or shortly after, in Australia. Obsolete. **See also** *Roger Moore*.

roses red — bed
Also used in America. 20th century. **See also** *Bill and Ted, God strike me dead, needle and thread, Rocky Ned, Uncle Ned* (1), *white and red*.

Rosewall and Hoad — road
After Australian tennis stars Ken Rosewall (born 1934) and Lew Hoad (1934–94). **See also** *frog and toad*.

Rosie Lee — tea
See also *Dicky Lee* (2), *Gypsy Lee, Jack Shay* (1), *Jenny Lee, Jimmy Lee, Mother Machree, wasp and bee* (1), *you and me* (3).

rotary hoe — righty-o (a term of agreement)
Since the 1960s.

round the houses — trousers
See also *council houses, dead wowsers, petrol bowsers, rammy rousers, terrace houses*.

Roy Bull (1) — pull, as in male masturbation
After NSW Rugby League player Roy Bull, prominent in the 1950s.
See also *cotton wool, John Bull* (2).

Roy Bull (2) — full, meaning drunk
See also *John Bull* (1).

Roy Bull (3) — full, as in 'out on the full' (Rugby League)

Roy Rogers and Trigger — nigger, from the folk name 'blackfish' for the *Girella tricuspidata*
After the stage name of American cowboy actor Roy Rogers (Leonard Slye, 1911–98) and his horse, Trigger.

Roy Sluice (1) — deuce (in cards)
From combination of the stage name of *Roy* Rene, the comedian known as 'Mo', and his proper name, Harry van der *Sluice* (1891–1954). Obsolete.

Roy Sluice (2) — deuce, meaning a florin (two shilling coin) (pre-decimal currency)
May also be spelled 'Sluys'. World War II. See also *Mother Goose; Paterson, Laing and Bruce* (2).

Royal Doulton — mate, meaning friend; likely to be male
From Royal Doulton plate, the famous English pottery brand. See also *China plate, five-eigh*t (2), *ocean liner* (2), *old China plate*.

rubber and hose — nose
Possibly a take on the British *fireman's hose*. Recorded in children's speech as *rubberan*. See also *I suppose, Lionel Rose, Piccadilly rose, rubberan, these and those* (1).

rubberan — nose
From children's folk speech. See also *I suppose, Lionel Rose, Piccadilly rose, rubber and hose, these and those* (1).

(the) rubbidy — see rubbidy dub

rubbidy dub — **a pub (short for public house)**
Often shortened to *rubbidy*. A usage recorded in the late 1890s, although certainly older on the common tongue. Still in wide use today, even if most users are probably unaware that it is rhyming slang. Its many variations include *rubadub, rubadubdub, rubberty* and *rubbie*. **See also** *Bib and Bub* (1).

Ruby Moon — **spoon**
World War II. **See also** *by the light, David Boon, Marjorie Moon.*

Russian spy — **(neck)tie**
See also *dog's eye* (2), *Fourth of July, lamb's fry, mud in your eye, Nazi spy* (2), *Nellie Bligh* (5), *stock and die* (1), *2KY* (1).

S

Saint Louis blues — **shoes**
After the song of that name made popular from 1917 when American musician W. C. Handy composed then re-composed it. Current in Sydney's Long Bay Gaol during the 1960s. **See also** *Basin Street blues, Ben Blues, canoes, kangaroo/s* (2), *ones and twos,, Peggy Sue, Pete Kelly's blues, splash throughs, ten to twos.*

Saint Vitus' Dance — **pants**
Probably an Australian original. 20th century. **See also** *bull ants, fleas and ants.*

salmon and trout — **snout, meaning nose**
See also *Wally Grout* (2).

Salt Lake Cities — **titties, meaning female breasts**
After the capital of the American state of Utah. **See also** *Bristol Cities, cats and kitties, Denver Cities, Elsie Whitty/ies, Lewis and W(h)itties, Manchester City/ies, Vatican Cities.*

salty bananas — **sultanas**
c. mid-20th century.

Sammy Hall — **ball, meaning a single testicle**
Applied to horses with this anatomical feature.

Sammy Lee — three
After the Canadian Samuel Lee (1912?–75), a colourful Sydney nightclub owner from the 1930s to the '60s. **See also** *Peggy Lee.*

Sandy McNab (1) — cab, meaning taxi
See also *left jab, smash and grab.*

Sandy MacNab (2) — scab, meaning a non-unionised worker
See also *hansom cab, Jack McNab.*

Sandy McNabs — crabs, meaning body lice (sexually transmissible infection)
See also *dibs and dabs, dribs and drabs, smash and grabs.*

Sarah Vaughan — horn, meaning an erection
After the American singer Sarah Vaughan (1924–90). **See also** *early morn, Somerset Maugham.*

Sargents Pie/s (1) — eye/s
From the brand name of a Sydney meat pie. From at least the 1940s. See also *lamb's fries, meat pies, mince pies, mud pies, Nellie Bligh/s (4), 2KYs.*

Sargents Pie/s (2) — lie
See also *Hawkie, Nellie Bligh* (6), *pork/ie pie, 2KY* (2).

saucepan lids — kids, meaning children
See also *billy lid/s, Captain, God-forbids, tin lid/s* (1).

sausage — see *sausage roll* (1) and (2)

sausage and mash — cash
See also *Arthur Ashe, Charlie Ash, Christopher Ash, J. Carroll Nash, Oscar Asche, smash, splash.*

sausage roll (1) — goal (football)
As in 'He kicked a *sausage*.' Mostly used in Australian Rules football. From the 1960s.

sausage roll (2) — bowl (cricket)
See also *Nat King Cole* (1).

saving Grace — sixty-eight (Bingo)
An imperfect rhyme.

scare and fright — light, meaning low-alcohol beer
Late 20th century. Melbourne? **See also** *Ray Bright*.

Schindler's List — pissed, meaning drunk
After the feature film of the same name (1993), created from the book
by Australian author Thomas Kenneally titled *Schindler's Ark* (1982).
See also *Adrian Quist, Brahms and Liszt, Franz Liszt, Mozart and Liszt,
Oliver Twist* (1), *sisters apart*.

Scotch — see *Scotch tape*

Scotch pegs — legs
See also *bacon and eggs, clothes pegs, Dutch pegs, fried eggs, Ginger Meggs,
Gregory Pegs, ham and eggs, Neville Beggs, nine gallon kegs*.

Scotch tape — rape
Often abbreviated to *scotch*. Probably of Australian origin. Perhaps from
the 1960s. **See also** *sour grape*.

scrum half — scarf
See also *cry and laugh*.

sealing wax — tax
Australian. Since World War II. **See also** *Kansas City Max*.

second look — crook, meaning a criminal
See also *babbling brook* (3).

Senator Spooner — schooner, a NSW beer glass
Also abbreviated to 'a *Senator*'. **See also** *Lily of Laguna* (1).

sentimental — see *Sentimental Bloke*

Sentimental Bloke — smoke, meaning a cigarette, cigar or pipe
Sometimes abbreviated to 'a *sentimental*'. Presumably after the collection
of ballads *Songs of a Sentimental Bloke* by C. J. Dennis (1914), reinforced
by subsequent film and stage versions. *c.* World War I–1970s. **See also**
Don Doak; *laugh and joke*; *wood, coal and coke* (2).

seppo — see *septic tank/s* (1)

septic — see *septic tank/s* (1)

septic tank/s (1) — Yank, meaning an American
Usually abbreviated to *septic* or *seppo*. Recorded as Australian naval

usage for American sailors. From the 1960s, possibly earlier. **See also** *army tanks, ham shank, iron tank* (2), *Jodrell Bank, mutton shanks, ship's tank, tin tank* (2).

septic tank (2) — bank
From at least the 1960s. **See also** *iron tank* (1), *J. Arthur Rank* (1), *tin tank* (1), *Tommy Tank*.

Sexton Blakes (1) — shakes
After the fictional detective hero featured in many books by various authors from 1893 and also in film and television until the late 1970s. World War II. **See also** *ducks and drakes, Joe Blake/s* (1).

Sexton Blakes (2) — snakes
See also *Joe/y Blakes* (2).

shake and shiver — river
World War II. **See also** *bacon and liver, bullock's liver*.

Shannon — piddle, as in urinate
After Peter Riddle, trainer of champion racehorse Shannon. **See also** *Gerry Riddle, hey diddle diddle* (2), *hi diddle diddle* (2), *Jimmy Riddle, Nelson Riddle*.

sheep shanker — wanker, as in a male who masturbates
Recorded in children's speech. **See also** *halfback flanker, J. Arthur Rank* (2), *merchant banker, Westpac banker*.

ship's tank — Yank, meaning an American
World War II. **See also** *army tanks, ham shank, iron tank* (2), *Jodrell Bank, mutton shanks, septic tank/s* (1), *tin tank* (2).

Shirley Bliss — piss, as in urinate
Sometimes abbreviated to 'a *Shirley*'. After Shirley Bliss, Miss Australia in 1955. **See also** *angel's kiss, cat's hiss, Gypsy's kiss, hit and/or miss, horse's hiss, Johnny Bliss, Les Kiss, snake's hiss, swing and a miss*.

short ease — Schottische (a dance)
Folk musicians' usage. **See also** *short squeeze*.

short squeeze — Schottische (a dance)
Folk musicians' usage. **See also** *short ease*.

shovel — see *shovel and broom*

shovel and broom — room
Often abbreviated to *shovel*. Since the 1920s in the UK. Also in use in the USA.

shower of rain — train
See also *Frankie Laine* (3), *Geoffrey Lane* (2), *hail and rain*, *King of Spain* (3), *Lois Lane*, *pouring rain*, *roaring rain*, *thunder and rain*, *wind and rain*.

silly galoot — root, as in sexual intercourse
World War II. See also *Angus and Coote*, *gumboot*, *Herby de Groote*, *juicy fruit*, *tin flute*, *Wellington boot*.

silly galoots — boots
World War II. See also *daisy roots*, *fiddles and flutes*.

Silver Link (1) — drink
After a champion racehorse. See also *cuff link*, *kitchen sink*, *pen and ink*, *tiddlywink*.

Silver Link (2) — stink, meaning trouble
See also *WA Inc*.

silver spoon (1) — hoon, meaning a prostitute's pimp in this usage
The term 'hoon' has since broadened to mean antisocial behaviour, particularly driving fast, noisy cars in a dangerous manner. See also *blue moon*, *silvery moon*.

silver spoon (2) — moon
From at least the early 20th century.

silvery moon — hoon, meaning a prostitute's pimp in this usage
Said to be current *c*. early 21st century. See also *blue moon*, *silver spoon* (1).

Simon and Garfunkel — uncle
After the American singing duo popular since the 1960s.

Simple Simon — diamond
Possibly from the children's game.

Sinbad the Sailor — tailor
See also *Bunkey Naylor*.

Sir Walter Scott — **pot, meaning ten-ounce (pre-metric) glass of beer**
After the Scots author and poet Sir Walter Scott (1771–1832). Appears in the earliest English collection of rhyming slang, published in the late 1850s, with the same meaning, although perhaps only a general pot, rather than a pot of beer? Vic. and possibly SA? (Not NSW or WA.) Mid-20th century. **See also** *red hot*.

sisters apart — **pissed as a fart, meaning extremely drunk**
See also *Adrian Quist, Brahms and Liszt, Franz Liszt, Mozart and Liszt, Oliver Twist* (1), *Schindler's List*.

sixteen ton — **son**
See also *bath bun, buttered bun*.

skin and blister — **sister**
See also *blood blister, kid blister*.

sky — **Eyetie, meaning an Italian**
Barely a rhyming slang. Said to have been coined in the 1920s and apparently not heard since.

sky rocket — **pocket**
British underworld slang from 1870s. In general use in Australia from at least 1902. **See also** *Davey Crockett* (2), *locket, Lucy Locket*.

slapsie maxie — **taxi**
After 'Slapsie' Maxie Rosenbloom (1904–76), American boxer. Current in the 1930s. **See also** *Joe Baxi, Joe Maxi*.

slippery dip (1) — **lip, meaning cheekiness**
20th century. **See also** *penny dips*.

slippery dip (2) — **hip**
World War II.

smash — **cash**
See also *Arthur Ash, Charlie Ash, Christopher Ash, J. Carroll Nash, Oscar Asche, sausage and mash, splash*.

smash and grab — **cab, meaning taxi**
See also *left jab, Sandy McNab* (1).

smash and grabs — **crabs, meaning body lice (sexually transmissible infection)**
See also *dibs and dabs*, *dribs and drabs*, *Sandy McNabs*.

Smellbourne — **Melbourne**
Not genuine rhyming slang? From the 1890s and also in World War II.

smile place — **face**
See also *boat race*, *Chevvy Chase*, *Epsom Races*, *first base*, *first place*, *Martin Place*, *Melrose Place*, *Princess Grace*.

smoked haddock — **paddock**

snake's — **see *snake's hiss***

snake's hiss — **piss, as in urinate**
Usually abbreviated to 'a *snake's*'. In general slang, a male toilet may be referred to as a 'snake's house'. Sometimes said to be an Australian original. From at least the early 20th century. See also *angel's kiss*, *cat's hiss*, *Gypsy's kiss*, *hit and/or miss*, *horse's hiss*, *Johnny Bliss*, *Les Kiss*, *Shirley Bliss*, *swing and a miss*.

snakes alive — **fifty-five (Bingo)**

soap and water — **daughter**
See also *mile and a quarter* (2), *soapy water*, *ten furlongs*.

soapy water — **daughter**
From *c.* early 20th century. Melbourne? Obsolete? See also *mile and a quarter* (2), *soap and water*, *ten furlongs*.

soft as silk — **milk**
Australian original. World War II. See also *Acker Bilk*.

soldiers — **see *soldiers bold***

soldiers bold — **cold**
Usually abbreviated to *soldiers*. Possibly from the long obsolete 19th-century English rhyming slang *soldier bold* for 'a cold'. See also *brave and bold*, *Cheltenham bold*, *young and old*.

Somerset Maugham — **horn, meaning erection**
An imperfect rhyme, after the famous author Somerset Maugham (1874–1965). See also *early morn*, *Sarah Vaughan*.

sons of guns — gums (in the mouth)
World War II. Obsolete?

soup and gravy — navy

sour grape — rape
See also *Scotch tape*.

South African veldt — belt
See also *dark felt*, *paddy melt*.

South Sydney — kidney
20th century. See also *east o' Sydneys*, *North Sydney*.

Spanish dancer — cancer
See also *ballet dancer*, *Bengal lancer*, *candy dancer*, *Charlie Dancer*, *civil answer*, *Jack the dancer*, *Jimmy Dancer*, *Johnny Dancer*, *Mario Lanza*.

spire and steeple — people
Since at least the early 20th century.

Spiro Agnew — spew, meaning to vomit
After the American Vice-President convicted of bribery in 1981. See also *Chunderloo*, *Dan McGrew* (1), *Danny La Rue* (2), *Harvey Drew*.

splash — cash
Not a genuine rhyming slang? Current. See also *Arthur Ashe*, *Charlie Ash*, *Christopher Ash*, *J. Carroll Nash*, *Oscar Asche*, *sausage and mash*, *smash*.

splash throughs — shoes
See also *Basin Street blues*, *Ben Blues*, *canoes*, *kangaroo/s* (2), *ones and twos*, *Peggy Sue*, *Pete Kelly's blues*, *Saint Louis blues*, *ten to twos*.

spotty dog — wog, meaning a person of southern European/ Mediterranean origin
London rhyming slang, said to be used of Africans, Aborigines and Indians. (It is also used to mean 'bog', or toilet, in London rhyming slang.) See also *Alsatian dog*, *chocolate frog/s* (2), *Dapto dog*, *Freddo Frog*, *hollow log* (3), *woolly dog*.

sprouse — spouse
Probably not rhyming slang?

squatter's daughter — water
See also *Cole Porter, fisherman's daughter, LKS Mackinnon Stakes, mother and daughter.*

squiz — look
Said to be derived from the name of the Melbourne criminal 'Squizzy' Taylor (1888–1927) insofar as he was a 'crook', which rhymed with 'look', producing 'Have a *squiz* at that', and similar formations. **See also** *butcher's hook* (3), *Captain Cook, cook.*

stammer and stutter — butter
Since the late 1930s at least. **See also** *chuck me in the gutter, Dark Town strutter, Johnny Rutter, kerb and gutter, lisp and stutter, mumble and stutter, mutter and stutter, roll me in the gutter.*

stand at ease — cheese
See also *Annie (Anna) Louise, cough and sneeze, piper's knees.*

State election — erection
See also *Ballarat* (3), *larrikin's hat, Yasser Arafat.*

staying alive — eighty-five (Bingo)

steak and kidney — Sydney (city)
Appears in 'Duke' Tritton's rhyming slang letter dated 1905. **See also** *bullock's kidney.*

steam tug (1) — pug, meaning a pugilist or boxer
steam tugs (2) — bugs (insects)

Steele Rudds — spuds, meaning potatoes
Presumably after the pen name of the creator of 'Dad and Dave', Arthur Hoey Davis (1868–1935). 20th century. **See also** *Captain Bloods.*

stereophonic sound — pound (pre-decimal currency)
See also *lost and found* (1).

Stevey Hart — fart, as in break wind
Steve Hart was a member of the Kelly gang, 1878–80, although this may or may not refer to him. **See also** *apple tart, bacon and egg tart, bottle mart, cupcake, Dicky Bart, fairy dart, horse and cart* (1), *jam tart* (2), *raspberry tart.*

stick of chalk — **walk**
See also *Duke of York* (2), *pickle and pork*.

sticky beak — **peek**

stiff shitty — **city**

stock and die (1) — **(neck)tie**
See also *dog's eye* (2), *Fourth of July*, *lamb's fry*, *mud in your eye*, *Nazi spy* (2), *Nellie Bligh* (5), *Russian spy*, *2KY* (1).

stock and die (2) — **pie**
See also *dog's eye* (1), *Nazi spy* (1), *Nelly Bligh* (3), *pig's eye* (1), *2KY* (3).

Stockton Punt — **cunt, as in female genitalia**
See also *All Quiet on the Western Front*, *Ballina Punt*, *Berkshire Hunt*, *Billy Hunt*, *drop kick and punt*, *grumble and grunt*, *Joe Hunt*, *mumble and grunt*.

stop thief — **beef**

straight on through — **eighty-two (Bingo)**

(the) strangle — **see** *strangle and smother*

strangle and smother — **mother**
Also abbreviated to 'the *strangle*'. See also *once another* (2), *one another* (2), *tell us another*.

strum and stroll — **dole, meaning unemployment benefit**
Australian. Probably since the 1930s. See also *horse and foal*, *Nat King Cole* (2), *rock and roll*, *strut and stroll*.

strut and stroll — **dole, meaning unemployment benefit**
See also *horse and foal*, *Nat King Cole* (2), *rock and roll*, *strum and stroll*.

Stuart Diver — **survivor**
From the linguistically fortuitous name of a man who survived the Thredbo avalanche of 1997.

stuck in the tree — **fifty-three (Bingo)**

stuck pig — **gig, meaning a public performance by musicians**
Used by jazz musicians, mid–late 20th century?

submarine — queen, or male homosexual
World War II. **See also** *baked bean, haricot bean, in-between, pork and bean.*

sudden death — breath
Usually bad breath.

sugar and honey — money
See also *bees and honey, Bugs Bunny, Gene Tunney* (1).

sugar and spice — nice
See also *apples and rice, apples and spice.*

Swannee Rivers — shivers
Often abbreviated to *Swannees.* World War II. **See also** *Hawkesbury Rivers, Murray Rivers.*

Swannees — see Swannee Rivers

sway and swerve — perve, meaning one who ogles the opposite sex
Current first decade of the 21st century. **See also** *hit and swerve, hors d'oeuvre, optic nerve, Uncle Merv.*

swear and cuss — bus
See also *Uncle Gus.*

swiftly flowing — going
Also occurs as *swiftly flow* (go). From late 19th century. Obsolete.

swing and a miss — piss, as in urinate
Said to derive from an American baseball term. Current first decade of the 21st century. **See also** *angel's kiss, cat's hiss, Gypsy's kiss, hit and/or miss, horse's hiss, Johnny Bliss, Les Kiss, Shirley Bliss, snake's hiss.*

Sydney Harbour — barber
From at least 1940s; in the USA from '20s. **See also** *Coffs Harbour.*

Syngman Ree(s) — knees
Syngman Ree was President of South Korea during the Korean War (1950–53) in which Australian troops fought. **See also** *biscuits and cheese, bugs and fleas, bumblebees, gum tree/s, Gypsy Rose Lee/s.*

syrup and fig — wig
See also *Irish jig, Moreton Bay Fig* (3).

T

table and chair — hair
See also *Barnet Fair, Dublin Fair, Fred Astaire* (2), *here and there, over there, preference share.*

tadpole — hole
Mid-20th century. Melbourne.

tea leaf — thief
See also *chunk of beef* (2), *tea leafing.*

tea leafing — thieving
See also *chunk of beef* (2), *tea leaf.*

Ted Heath — teeth
After the British bandleader Ted Heath (1902–69), prominent in the 1940s to the early '60s. See also *Barrier Reef, Barry Beath, cricket bats, Hampstead Heaths.*

teddy bear — lair, as in a man given to flashy dress and behaviour
From around 1930 and current in Sydney's Long Bay Gaol during the '60s. Also used more widely since at least World War II. See also *Fred Astaire* (3).

tell us another — mother
See also *once another* (2), *one another* (2), *strangle and smother.*

teller of tales — nails
World War II. Obsolete.

ten furlongs — daughter
Ten furlongs equals a mile and a quarter (pre-metric measurement), hence the deferred rhyme. See also *Gordon and ten, mile and a quarter* (2), *soap and water, soapy water.*

ten to twos — shoes
See also *Basin Street Blues, Ben Blues, canoes, kangaroo/s* (2), *ones and twos, Peggy Sue, Pete Kelly's blues, Saint Louis blues, splash throughs.*

Tennant Creek — a Greek
The Northern Territory version of the rhyming slang term for a Greek person. See also *bubble and squeak* (1), *Merri Creek, ox cheek, Werris Creek* (1).

terrace houses — trousers
Often shortened to *terraces*; also occurs as *terrace of houses*. World War II. **See also** *council houses, dead wowsers, petrol bowsers, rammy rousers, round the houses.*

terraces — see terrace houses

terrible Turk — work
From a 19th-century term for a dominating person. **See also** *dodge and shirk.*

Terry Dear — beer
After Terry Dear (1913–95), New Zealand-born personality in Australian radio and TV. **See also** *Britney Spears, cherry cheer, Crimea, Germaine Greer/s* (1), *oh my dear, Perc Galea, pig's ear, Port Melbourne Pier* (2), *pot of good cheer, Ray Stehr.*

Terry Dears — ears
See also *Germaine Greer/s* (2), *ginger beer/s* (2), *lager beers, Melbourne Piers, Perc Galeas, Port Melbourne Pier/s* (1), *Williamstown Piers.*

Terry Toon (1) **— hoon, meaning a noisy lout**
Probably after Terry Toons cartoons for television. 1970s. **See also** *dish ran away with the spoon, egg and spoon* (1).

Terry Toon (2) **— coon, meaning a coloured person**
See also *egg and spoon* (3).

Theatre Royal — boil, meaning a skin abscess
After a Sydney theatre. Current *c.* 1950s–70s? **See also** *Conan Doyle.*

thee and me — twenty-three (Bingo)

these and those (1) **— nose**
World War II. **See also** *I suppose, Lionel Rose, Piccadilly rose, rubberan, rubber and hose.*

these and those (2) **— toes**
World War II. **See also** *buttons and bows, GPOs, Matt Monroes, Old Black Joe/s, Uncle Joes.*

thick and thin (1) **— chin**
Also used in the USA. 20th century. **See also** *Errol Flynn, Vera Lynn* (1).

thick and thin (2) — gin
See also *Gunga Din*, *Huckleberry Finn*, *mortal sin*, *Vera Lynn* (2).

thick and thin (3) — skin
Apparently an Australian original.

thief and robber — cobber, meaning friend
From at least the early 20th century. Used in 'Duke' Tritton's rhyming slang letter dated 1905.

thirty-first of May — gay, meaning a fool or a dupe
Underworld slang. Since the mid-1920s.

this and that (1) — bat (cricket)

this and that (2) — hat
1940s? See also *ball and bat*, *Ballarat* (1), *barrel of fat*, *bowl of fat*, *thises and thats*, *tit for tat* (1).

thises and thats — hats
See also *ball and bat*, *Ballarat* (1), *barrel of fat*, *bowl of fat*, *this and that* (2), *tit for tat* (1).

three bags full — bull, meaning nonsense or lies
20th century.

3KZ — head
From the call sign for a Melbourne AM radio station, since renamed. Early 21st century; Melbourne only. Obsolete? See also *Home Pride bread*, *Kelly Ned*, *loaf of bread*, *lump of lead* (3).

thunder and rain — railway train
Since at least the early 20th century. See also *Frankie Laine* (3), *Geoffrey Lane* (2), *hail and rain*, *King of Spain* (3), *Lois Lane*, *pouring rain*, *roaring rain*, *shower of rain*, *wind and rain*.

tick tock — clock
In Australia from at least 1950; dates back to the 19th century in British usage. See also *dickory dock*, *Eva Bartok*, *hickery dickery dock*.

tiddlywink — drink (alcoholic)
In use 1890s. See also *cuff link*, *kitchen sink*, *pen and ink*, *Silver Link* (1).

Tiger Tim — swim
Thought to be after the cartoon character created in 1904 by Julius Stafford Baker. See also *dark and dim*, *Jungle Jim*.

Tilly Devine — wine
Tilly Devine (1900–70) was a colourful member of the Sydney underworld. See also *Andy Devine*, *Lindsay Kline*, *Randall Vines*.

Tim Holt — salt
See also *Harold Holt* (2).

time for fun — forty-one (Bingo)

time for tea — eighty-three (Bingo)

Timothy — brothel
Possibly descended from a rhyming slang such as *Timothy Grass* for 'arse' or *Timothy titmouse* for 'house (of ill fame)'. Early 1950s. Obsolete? See also *Pollywaffle*.

tin flute — root, as in sexual intercourse
See also *Angus and Coote*, *gumboot*, *Herby de Groote*, *juicy fruit*, *silly galoot*, *Wellington boot*.

tin lid/s (1) — kid/s, meaning child/ren
Australian original. From at least the early 20th century. See also *billy lid/s*, *Captain*, *God-forbids*, *saucepan lids*.

tin lid (2) — yid, meaning a Jewish person

tin lid (3) — quid, meaning a pound (pre-decimal currency)
See also *fiddly-did*, *yid*.

tin tack (1) — back (anatomy)
See also *George Alfred Black*, *hammer and tack* (6), *Johnny Mack* (1), *Melbourne*.

tin tack (2) — sack, as in losing one's job
See also *hammer and tack* (2).

tin tack (3) — zac, meaning a sixpenny coin (pre-decimal currency)
World War II. See also *Andy Mac*, *Brodie Mack*, *hammer and tack* (5), *I'll be back*, *Jill and Jack*.

tin tank (1) — bank
See also *iron tank* (1), *J. Arthur Rank* (1), *septic tank* (2), *Tommy Tank*.

tin tank (2) — Yank, meaning an American
Still current 2007. See also *army tanks*, *ham shank*, *iron tank* (2), *Jodrell Bank*, *mutton shanks*, *septic tank/s* (1), *ship's tank*.

tingaling — ring (jewellery)
See also *Frank Thring*, *gin sling*.

tipsy Jap — Gypsy tap (a dance)
Folk musicians' rhyming slang, possibly from the 1950s. An example of rhyming slang as spoonerism?

tit for tat (1) — hat
Usually occurs as *titfer*. Cockney. In use during World War I and since. Now rare in Australia. See also *ball and bat*, *Ballarat* (1), *barrel of fat*, *bowl of fat*, *this and that* (2), *thises and thats*.

tit for tat (2) — rat, meaning a non-unionised worker
From the late 19th century. See also *cabbage tree hat*.

to and fro (1) — go

to and fro (2) — mo' (short for moustache)

to and from — pom, pommie, meaning a person from Britain
Used by Australian POWs to refer to English servicemen. Since the 1940s. See also *atomic bomb*, *Jimmy Grant*.

Tod Sloane — alone
As in 'on my *tod*'. Tod Sloane (1874–1923) was an American jockey. This form is now rarely heard. See also *eau de Cologne* (2), *Jack Malone*, *Pat Malone*.

Tom and Dick (1) — lick
See also *Pat and Mick* (1).

Tom and Dick (2) — sick
See also *Pat and Mick* (2).

Tom and Sam — jam
20th century.

Tom Cruise — snooze
After the Hollywood actor (born 1962).

Tom Mix — six (cricket)
Note that a cricket player earns six runs for batting a ball over the

boundary line. After Tom Mix (1880–1940), the star of many early Hollywood Western movies, prominent in the 1920s. **See also** *Dorothy Dix, Richard Dix.*

Tom tart — sweetheart
More likely to be a woman, and perhaps the origin of 'tart'? Since the late 19th century. Obsolete. **See also** *jam tart* (1).

Tom Thumb (1) — rum
Possibly from the stage name of a famous 19th-century dwarf. Since at least the early 20th century. **See also** *dad and mum* (1), *deaf and dumb* (2), *finger and thumb, poofter's bum.*

Tom Thumb (2) — drum, meaning the truth or useful information of some kind, as in 'give us the drum'
From at least the 1940s. **See also** *deaf and dumb* (1).

Tom tit — shit, as in defecate
See also *big hit, brace and bit, Dinny Hayes-er, Eartha Kitt, Edgar Britt, gravel pit, hard hit, Jimmy Britt* (1), *king hit, Mickey Fritt, Oscar Britt.*

Tom tits — shits, as in to be irritated
As in 'The boss is really giving me the *Tom tits*.' **See also** *Edgar Britts, Jimmy Britts* (1), *trey bits* (1), *trizzy bits.*

tomato sauce/s (1) — course/s (horseracing)
From at least the early 20th century. **See also** *apple sauce, condiments and sauces, Ella May Morse.*

tomato sauce/s (2) — horse/s (horseracing)
From at least the early 20th century. **See also** *apple sauce, condiments and sauces, Ella May Morse.*

tomfoolery — jewellery

Tommy — see Tommy Rook

Tommy Farter — tomato (pronounced 'tomarter') (sauce)
Recorded in children's speech. **See also** *dead horse, lies and dead horse, racehorse, rocking horse.*

Tommy Rook — book, meaning a bookmaker's list of odds; also bookmaker
Usually abbreviated to *Tommy*. Also in New Zealand. From the 1920s. **See also** *docker's hook.*

Tommy Tank — (savings) bank
See also *iron tank* (1), *J. Arthur Rank* (1), *septic tank* (2), *tin tank* (1).

Tommy Tucker — supper
Probably after the nursery rhyme character of the same name who sang for his supper. Obsolete? **See also** *chock-a-block up 'er*.

ton o' my rocks — socks
See also *almond rocks*, *Bobby rocks*, *curly locks*, *Goldilocks*, *Jarrah blocks*, *Joe Rocks*, *keys and locks*

Tony's den — ten (Bingo)
See also *Big Ben*, *cock and hen*, *clucky hen*.

tosh and waddle — twaddle, meaning nonsense
An unusual term in which a blended word 'twaddle', derived from combining *tosh* and *waddle*, is rhymed with its constituent elements. Late 19th century. Obsolete.

total wreck — cheque
Also used in the American West Coast underworld in the 1930s and '40s, although thought to be of Australian origin. **See also** *duck's neck*, *goose's neck*, *Gregory Peck* (1), *nervous wreck*.

town halls — balls, as in testicles
See also *cobblers' awls*, *Niagara Falls*, *orchestra stalls*, *Queenie Pauls*, *Wentworth Falls*.

tracy-bit/s — tit/s, meaning female breast(s)
In underworld speech since the 1920s. See also *braces and bits*, *Eartha Kitts*, *trey bits* (2), *Vita Brits*.

trams and trains (1) — brains
Current in WA 2007. See also *Frankie Laine* (1).

trams and trains (2) — drains

tree and sap — tap (bathroom or kitchen)
Australian. 20th century.

trey bits (1) — shits, as in to be irritated
Trey means threepenny coin (pre-decimal currency); also used in card-playing to mean a three of any suite. Obsolete. **See also** *Edgar Britts*, *Jimmy Britts* (1), *Tom tits*, *trizzy bits*.

trey bits (2) — tits, meaning female breasts
From at least 1950. **See also** *brace and bits*, *Eartha Kitts*, *tracy-bit/s*, *Vita Brits*.

trick cyclist/s — psychiatrist/s
An imperfect but evocative rhyme originating among British military
personnel in the 1930s. Still heard on Australian lips in Perth 2007 and
on the worldwide web 2008.

trizzy bits — shits, as in to be annoyed
Abbreviation *trizzy* is a rendering of *trey*, slang for a threepenny coin
(pre-decimal currency). See also *Edgar Britts, Jimmy Britts* (1), T*om
tits, trey bits* (1).

trot and paces — races (horseracing)
Current from *c.* early 20th century. Melbourne? See also *airs and graces,
braces, fireman's braces.*

trouble and strife — wife
Cockney and at least early 20th century in Australia. Still current during
World War II and, like a number of other classic rhyming slangs, widely
known, if not used. See also *drum and fife.*

Tuggerah Lake — cake
After a coastal town in NSW.

turn on the screw — sixty-two (Bingo)

turtledove — love

turtledoves — gloves

Twelfth Street rag — fag, meaning cigarette
After a popular ragtime tune composed by Euday L. Bowman in 1914.
See also *Harry Wragg, oily rag.*

twist/s — see twist/s and twirl/s

twist/s and twirl/s — girl/s
Often abbreviated to *twist/s*. Since at least the 1920s in Australia.
Apparently taken up in British usage and also in American speech,
particularly that of the carnival. See also *Barossa Pearl, mother of pearl.*

2KY (1) — tie
After the Sydney radio station. See also *dog's eye* (2) *Fourth of July,
lamb's fry, mud in your eye, Nazi spy* (2), *Nellie Bligh* (5), *Russian spy,
stock and die* (1).

2KY (2) — lie
See also *Hawkie, Nellie Bligh* (6), *pork/ie pie, Sargents Pie/s* (2).

2KY (3) — pie
See also *dog's eye* (1), *Nazi spy* (1), *Nelly Bligh* (3), *pig's eye* (1), *stock and die* (2).

2KYs — eyes
See also *lamb's fries*, *meat pies*, *mince pies*, *mud pies*, *Nellie Bligh/s* (4), *Sargents Pie/s* (1).

2UEs — fleas
2UE is a Sydney radio station and this rhyme was probably restricted to NSW. Perhaps from the late 1920s to the mid-20th century. See also *Jack Rees*, *Joe Rees*, *Willy Lees*.

two wheeler — sheila, meaning a girl or woman
See also *Charlie Wheeler*, *potato peeler*, *rock-wheeler*.

Tyrone Power — shower (as in bathing)
After the Hollywood star Tyrone Power (1914–58). See also *David Gower* (2), *fairy bower*, *lazy hour*, *now is the hour*.

U

(an) uncle — see Uncle Merve

uncle — see Uncle Willy

Uncle Bert — shirt
See also *decky dirt*, *Dicky dirt*, *dinky dirt*, *dirty Bert*, *Ernie and Bert*, *Val Quirk*.

Uncle Dick — prick, as in penis
See also *dipstick*, *drop kick* (1), *mad Mick* (2), *Pogo stick* (2), *Rickety Dick* (1), *zubrick*.

Uncle Fred — bread
See also *lump of lead* (1), *Uncle Ned* (2).

Uncle Gus — bus
Current WA 2007. See also *swear and cuss*.

Uncle Joes — toes
Mid-20th century. Melbourne? See also *buttons and bows*, *GPOs*, *Matt Monroes*, *Old Black Joe/s*, *these and those* (2).

Uncle Merv — perve, meaning to ogle the opposite sex
Sometimes abbreviated to *uncle*, as in 'Have an *uncle*.' See also *hit and swerve, hors d'oeuvre, optic nerve, sway and swerve*.

Uncle Ned (1) — bed
See also *Bill and Ted, God strike me dead, needle and thread, Rocky Ned, roses red, white and red*.

Uncle Ned (2) — bread
Since at least the early 20th century. See also *lump of lead* (1), *Uncle Fred*.

Uncle Willy — silly
Usually abbreviated to *uncle*. In Australia may be inverted as 'auntie', meaning 'uncle' and so short for the full form of 'Uncle Willy'. From at least the early 20th century. Obsolete? See also *auntie, dilly, Kirribilli, Wollondilly*.

up and under — chunder, meaning vomit
Rhyming slang on rhyming slang. Thought to have originated in the 1950s as a term for a rugby kick. See also *Chunderloo*.

up to tricks — forty-six (Bingo)

V

Val Quirk — shirt
Thought to be from the name of a Melbourne boxing referee. An imperfect rhyme. Obsolete. See also *decky dirt, Dicky dirt, dinky dirt, dirty Bert, Ernie and Bert, Uncle Bert*.

Var Susy Anne — Varsovienna (a dance)
Folk musicians' rhyming slang. See also *arsehole of the goanna, arse-over-Anna, arse-over-header, heart and soul of the goanna*.

varicose vein — sain, meaning a ten shilling note (pre-decimal currency)
Melbourne only? From *c.* early 20th century and possibly earlier. Obsolete.

Vatican City/ies — titties, meaning female breasts
Mid-20th century. See also *Bristol Cities, cats and kitties, Denver Cities,*

Elsie Whitty/ies, Lewis and W(h)itties, Manchester City/ies, Salt Lake Cities.

Vera Lynn (1) — chin
After Vera Lynn (born 1917), English singer who rose to fame during World War II. Australian original. **See also** *Errol Flynn, thick and thin* (1).

Vera Lynn (2) — gin
After Vera Lynn (born 1917), English singer who rose to fame during World War II. **See also** *Gunga Din, Huckleberry Finn, mortal sin, thick and thin* (2).

Vic Damone — loan
After the stage name of American singer Vito Rocco Farinola (born 1928). **See also** *Darby and Joan* (1), *Jack Jones, on your own.*

Vickers Gin — sin
After the well-known gin label. **See also** *Mickey Finn* (2).

Victor Trumper — bumper, meaning cigarette butt
Victor Trumper (1877–1915) was a famous Australian Test batsman. The term is said to be based on a colloquialism for a cigarette butt, a 'dumper' or a 'bumper'. **See also** *African nigger, forgive and forget.*

Victoria Dock — cock, meaning penis
See also *eight-day clock, Mort's Dock, Rock Around the Clock.*

Vincent's and Bex — sex
After the once well-known Australian headache remedies. **See also** *Lord Rex.*

Violet Crumble — tumble, meaning to suddenly understand something
As in 'Oh, now I *Violet Crumble*!' After the Violet Crumble bar, an Australian confectionery of chocolate-coated honeycomb, introduced in 1923. To 'tumble' (or 'rumble') to something has been in use among Cockneys and costers since at least the 19th century.

virgin bride — ride, as in a lift in a car
Recorded 1902. Obsolete?

Vita Brits — tits, meaning female breasts
Often abbreviated to *vitas*. Recorded in children's speech. From the
brand name of a breakfast cereal manufactured in Australia from 1935.
See also *brace and bits, Eartha Kitts, tracy bits, trey bits* (2).

W

WA Inc — stink, meaning trouble
After the name given to a notoriously corrupt WA State government.
See also *Silver Link* (2).

Wallace and Gromit — vomit
From the popular cartoon characters created by Nick Parks in the 1990s.
Current early 2000s as children's playground speech and probably
earlier. See also *Halley's Comet*.

Wally — see *Wally Grout* (1)

Wally Grout (1) — shout, meaning buy a round of drinks
Usually abbreviated to *Wally*, as in 'It's my *Wally*.' Wally Grout (1927–
68) was an Australian Test wicketkeeper in the 1950s and '60s renowned
for shouting out catches and lbws.

Wally Grout (2) — snout, meaning nose
2007. See also *salmon and trout*.

Wally Grout (3) — stout, the alcoholic beverage
2007.

Wally Prig — gig, meaning an informer
See also *Moreton Bay Fig* (1) and (2).

Warwick Farm/s — arm/s
After the well-known NSW racecourse. World War II and since. See
also *chalk farms*.

wasp and bee (1) — tea
World War II. See also *Dicky Lee* (2), *Gypsy Lee, Jack Shay* (1), *Jenny
Lee, Jimmy Lee, Mother Machree, Rosie Lee, you and me* (3).

wasp and bee (2) — pee, as in urinate
See also *Dicky Lee* (1), *lolly, Nancy Lee, one hundred and three, Robert
E. Lee, you and me* (2).

wattle/s — see *wattle and daub*

wattle and daub — warb: prison slang for a dirty or untidy person
Usually abbreviated to *wattle* or *wattles*. Australian. From at least 1950.

Wee Georgie Wood — good
English entertainer — and midget — George Wood (1894/5–1979) worked until the 1950s. There is a 'Wee Georgie Wood' narrow gauge railway in Tasmania, its small locomotive being named after the entertainer. 20th century. Obsolete. **See also** *Jimmy Britt* (2), *plum pud*, *Robin Hood*.

weeping willow — pillow

weight for age — page
World War II. Obsolete.

Wellington boot — root, as in sexual intercourse
Sometimes in the cheerful form of *wello*. **See also** *Angus and Coote*, *gumboot*, *Herby de Groote*, *juicy fruit*, *silly galoot*, *tin flute*.

Wentworth Falls — balls, as in testicles
After the Blue Mountains town and so probably restricted to NSW. From the 1920s. **See also** *cobblers' awls*, *Niagara Falls*, *orchestra stalls*, *Queenie Pauls*, *town halls*.

Werris — see **Werris Creek** (1) and (2)

Werris Creek (1) — Greek
Usually abbreviated to *Werris*. After the railway town of the same name in NSW, although also used in Victoria. Late 20th century. **See also** *bubble and squeak* (1), *Merri Creek*, *ox cheek*, *Tennant Creek*.

Werris Creek (2) — leak, as in urinate
Usually abbreviated to *Werris*, as in 'I'm going for a *Werris*.' **See also** *bubble and squeak* (2), *Jacob's Creek*.

Westpac banker — wanker, as in masturbator
After the name of a prominent bank and perhaps reflecting the widespread Australian dislike of banking institutions, though 'wanker' is also rhymed with various bank(er)s in British rhyming slang. Current first decade of the 21st century. **See also** *halfback flanker*, *J. Arthur Rank* (2), *merchant banker*, *sheep shanker*.

whirling spray — Wirraway (a training plane)
World War II, Royal Australian Air Force. Obsolete.

whistle — see whistle and flute

whistle and flute — suit (of clothes)
Usually abbreviated to *whistle*. Cockney origin. **See also** *bag of fruit, bowl of fruit, whistle and toot*.

whistle and toot — flute

white and red — bed
See also *Bill and Ted, God strike me dead, needle and thread, Rocky Ned, roses red, Uncle Ned* (1).

white mice — lice
Found in K. S. Prichard's *Kiss on the Lips* (1932). Australian original.

William the Third — turd, as in faeces
After William III (1650–1702), also known as William of Orange, King of England. An Australianism. **See also** *elephant's herd, George the Third, Henry the Third, King George the Third, King Henry the Third, King Richard the Third, mocking bird, Richard the Third* (2).

Williamstown Piers — ears
See also *Germaine Greer/s* (2), *ginger beer/s* (2), *lager beers, Melbourne Piers, Perc Galeas, Port Melbourne Pier/s* (1), *Terry Dears*.

Willow the weep — sheep
Shearing jargon.

Willy Lees — fleas
Australian coinage. From the 1920s. Obsolete? **See also** *Jack Rees, Joe Rees, 2UEs*.

Willy wag — swag, meaning rolled up bedding
From at least the early 20th century. Current in World War II.

willy woofter — poofter, meaning a male homosexual
See also *cloven hoofter, cow's hoof, horse's hoof, woolly boof, woolly woofter*.

Wilson Pickett — cricket
After the American soul singer Wilson Pickett (1941–2006). **See also** *rabbit in the thicket*.

Winchcombe Carson — **parson**
Possibly after the name of a wool company formed in 1910. In use since at least the early 20th century.

wind and rain — **train**
See also *Frankie Laine* (3), *Geoffrey Lane* (2), *hail and rain*, *King of Spain* (3), *Lois Lane*, *pouring rain*, *roaring rain*, *shower of rain*, *thunder and rain*.

windjammer — **hammer**
See also *Melbourne Grammar* (1).

wine dot — **sot, meaning one who is drunk, often habitually**
See also *dot*, *Kennedy rot*, *plonk dot*.

wiss wot — **pisspot, meaning one who frequently drinks too much**

witchetty grub — **cub, meaning junior boy scout**
After the famous indigenous bush tucker. Australian. **See also** *Brussels sprout*, *giddy gout*.

Wollondilly — **silly**
After the rural NSW township. Recorded in 1950. Its use is thought to be restricted. **See also** *auntie*, *dilly*, *Kirribilli*, *Uncle Willy*.

wombat — **'hors de combat' (French, but with Australian pronunciation), meaning dead**
See also *brown bread*, *garden shed*, *kangaroo Ted*, *lump of lead* (2).

wood, coal and coke (1) — **broke, meaning without funds**
See also *hearts of oak*.

wood, coal and coke (2) — **smoke, meaning cigarette**
See also *Don Doak*, *laugh and joke*, *Sentimental Bloke*.

woolly boof — **poof, male homosexual**
See also *cloven hoofter*, *cow's hoof*, *horse's hoof*, *willy woofter*, *woolly woofter*.

woolly dog — **wog, meaning a person of southern European/ Mediterranean origin**
Since World War I at least. **See also** *Alsatian dog*, *chocolate frog/s* (2), *Dapto dog*, *Freddo Frog*, *hollow log* (3), *spotty dog*.

woolly woofter — poofter, meaning male homosexual
Possibly from the 1990s only. **See also** *cloven hoofter, cow's hoof, horse's hoof, willy woofter, woolly boof.*

X

Xerox copy — poppy, as worn on Remembrance Day
An Australian invention from the 1950s, when photomechanical reproduction under the trade name 'Xerox' first became available in offices.

Y

Yasser Arafat — fat, meaning an erection
See also *Ballarat* (3), *larrikin's hat, State election.*

yid — quid, meaning one pound (pre-decimal currency)
Yit is a variation. From the early 20th century, when it was used to mean a sovereign. Later it became a general slang term for one pound, for example as used in Dal Stiven's novel *Jimmy Brockett* (1951). **See also** *fiddly-did, tin lid* (3).

yit — see **yid**

Yogi Bear — boob lair, meaning a prisoner ('boob' means gaol)
After the Hanna-Barbera cartoon character who debuted on *The Huckleberry Hound Show* on American television in 1958 and became especially popular from the 1960s.

you and me (1) — pea (vegetable)
Thought to be an Australian original. **See also** *yous and mes.*

you and me (2) — pee, as in urinate
20th century. **See also** *Dicky Lee* (1), *lolly, Nancy Lee, one hundred and three, Robert E. Lee, wasp and bee* (2).

you and me (3) — tea
See also *Dicky Lee* (2), *Gypsy Lee, Jack Shay* (1), *Jenny Lee, Jimmy Lee, Mother Machree, Rosie Lee, wasp and bee* (1).

you beaut — ute (short for utility wagon)
Said to have been in use *c.* mid-20th century. **See also** *Blundstone boot.*

you're the one — nun
See also *currant bun* (3).

young and frisky — whisky
Australian. Probably since the early 20th century. **See also** *gay and frisky*.

young and old — cold
See also *brave and bold, Cheltenham bold, soldiers bold*.

yous and mes — peas
See also *you and me* (1).

Z

Zane Grey — pay (wages for work performed)
After Zane Grey (1872–1939), American writer of popular adventure stories.

zubrick — prick, as in penis
Derived from Arabic and so almost certainly originating *c*. 1915. **See also** *dipstick, drop kick* (1), *mad Mick* (2), *Pogo stick* (2) *Rickety Dick* (1), *Uncle Dick*.

PART 2

Thematic Categories

This part of the book presents rhyming slang terms in a number of thematic groupings. A few terms appear more than once as they can be classified in two or more different ways.

From the Kelly Ned to the Buttons and Bows — the Body

Expressions for various parts of the body — plus its functions, its adornments and its afflictions — constitute the largest single category of the rhyming slang repertoire. Those items that deal with parts of the body often rhyme on the general slang term, such as twat, tits and arse.

Parts

All Quiet on the Western Front — cunt, as female genitalia; usually abbreviated to *All Quiet*

April fool/s — tool/s, as in penis

Aris — arse, as in bottom

Aunt Nelly — belly, meaning somach

bacon and eggs — legs

Ballina Punt — cunt, as in female genitalia

Barnet Fair — hair

Barrier Reef — teeth

Barry Beath — teeth

bell ringer — finger

billy goat (1) — throat

Billy Hunt — cunt, as in female genitalia

biscuits and cheese — knees

boat race — face; usually abbreviated to *boat*

Boris Becker — pecker, meaning penis

bottle and glass — arse, as in bottom

brace and bits — tits, meaning female breasts

brass bands — hands

Brighton le Sands — hands

Bristol Cities — titties, meaning female breasts; usually abbreviated to *Bristols*

Bugs and fleas — knees

Bulli Pass — arse, as in bottom; sometimes abbreviated to *Bulli* or *Pass*

bumblebees — knees

bundle of socks (2) — think-box, meaning the head
bushel and peck — neck
buttons and bows — toes
cats and kitties — titties, meaning female breasts
chalk farms — arms
Chevvy Chase — face
Christmas crackers — knackers, meaning testicles
clothes pegs — legs
cobbler's awls — balls, as in testicles
Coke and sars(parilla) — arse, as in bottom
comic cuts — guts, meaning intestines
cricket bats — tatts, meaning teeth
Darby Kelly — belly
date and plum — bum
Dave Sands — hands
deaf and dumb (3) — bum
Denver Cities — titties, meaning female breasts; usually abbreviated
    to *Denvers*
Digger's nest — chest (human)
Digger's vest — the chest
dollypot — twat, meaning vagina; also used as an insult, meaning an
    unpleasant person
drop kick and punt — cunt, as in female genitalia
Dublin Fair — hair
Dutch pegs — legs
Eartha Kitts — tits, meaning female breasts
east and west (1) — chest
east o'Sydneys — kidneys
eight-day clock — cock, meaning penis
Elsie Whitty/ies — titty/ies, meaning female breasts
Epsom Races — faces
Errol Flynn — chin
first base — face
first place — face
flick pass — arse, as in bottom
flowers and frolics — bollocks, meaning testicles
Frankie Laine (1) — brain
Fred Astaire (2) — hair

Fred Strutt — gut, meaning intestines, stomach
fried eggs — legs
George Alfred Black — back; usually abbreviated to *George Alfred*
Germaine Greer/s (2) — ear/s
German band/s — hand/s
ginger ale (2) — tail, meaning bottom
ginger beer/s (2) — ear/s
Ginger Meggs — legs
GPOs — toes
Gregory Peck (3) — neck
Gregory Pegs — legs
grocer's cart — heart
grumble and grunt — cunt, as in female genitals; in this usage,
    means sexual intercourse
gum tree/s — knee/s
Gypsy Rose Lee/s — knee/s
hairy chest — vest
ham and eggs — legs
hammer and tack (6) — back
Hampstead Heath — teeth; usually abbreviated to *Hampsteads*
Herb Alpert — arse, as in bottom
here and there — hair
Hoffman brick — dick, meaning penis
Home Pride bread — head
hydraulics — bollocks, meaning testicles
I suppose — nose
Jackson Pollocks — bollocks, meaning testicles
jam tart (1) — heart
Jatz crackers — knackers, meaning testicles
Joe Hunt — cunt, as in female genitalia
Johnny Mack (1) — back
Kelly Ned — head
Kerry Packers — knackers, meaning testicles
Khyber Pass — arse, as in bottom; usually abbreviated to *Khyber*
lager beers — ears
lamb's fries — eyes
leg of pork (2) — stalk, meaning penis
lemonade and sars(parilla) (1) — arse, as in bottom

let's rejoice — voice
Lewis and W(h)itties — titties, meaning female breasts
Lionel Rose — nose
little boys (1)— saveloys, meaning penis
loaf of bread — head
Loretta Young — tongue
lump of lead (3) — head
mad Mick — prick, meaning penis; also used as an insult, meaning
    an unpleasant person
Mae West/s — breast/s
Mal Meninga — finger
Manchester City/ies — titties, meaning female breasts
Manly-Warringahs — fingers
Mark Ella — arse, as in bottom
Martin Place — face
Matt Monroes — toes
meat pies — eyes
Melbourne — back
Melbourne Grammar — hammer, meaning penis
Melbourne Piers — ears
Melrose Place — face
mild and meek — cheek
mince pies — eyes
Mister Mutch — crutch (the groin)
Mort's Dock — cock, meaning penis
mud pies — eyes
mumble and grunt — cunt, as in female genitalia
nanny goat (1) — throat
Ned Kelly (1) — belly, meaning stomach
Nellie Blighs (4)— eyes
Nelly Kelly — belly
Neville Beggs — legs
New South — mouth
Niagara Falls — balls, as in testicles; usually abbreviated to *Niagaras*
nine gallon kegs — legs
north and south — mouth
North Sydney/s — kidney/s
Old Black Joe/s — toe/s

Oliver Twist (2) — wrist
Oliver Twist (3) — fist
Onkaparingas — fingers; often abbreviated to *onkas*
orchestra stalls — balls, as in testicles
over there — hair
penny dips — lips
Perc Galeas — ears
Piccadilly rose — nose
plates of meat — feet
Pogo stick (1) — dick, meaning penis; may be abbreviated to *Pogo*
Pogo stick (2) — prick, meaning penis; may be abbreviated to *Pogo*
Port Melbourne Pier/s (1) — ear/s
preference share — hair
Princess Grace — face
Queenie Pauls — balls, as in testicles
rabbit's paw — jaw
Ray Millands — hands
Reg Gasnier — arse, as in bottom
Rickety Dick (1) — prick, meaning penis; also used as an insult,
    meaning an unpleasant person
Robert Young — tongue
rock around the clock — cock, meaning penis
rock boulder/s — shoulder/s
rubber and hose — nose
rubberan — nose
salmon and trout — snout, meaning nose
Salt Lake Cities — titties, meaning female breasts
Sargents Pie/s (1) — eye/s
Scotch pegs — legs
slippery dip (2) — hip
smile place — face
sons of guns — gums (in the mouth)
Stockton Punt — cunt, as in female genitalia
South Sydney — kidney
Syngman Ree(s) — knees
table and chair — hair
Ted Heath — teeth
Terry Dears — ears

these and those (1) — nose
these and those (2) — toes
thick and thin (1) — chin
thick and thin (3) — skin
3KZ — head
tin tack (1) — back
to and fro (2) — mo (short for moustache)
town halls — balls, as in testicles
Tracy-bit/s — tit/s
trams and trains (1) — brains
trey bits (2) — tits, meaning female breasts
2KYs — eyes
Uncle Dick — prick, meaning penis; also used as an insult, meaning
an unpleasant person
Uncle Joes — toes
Vatican Cities — titties
Vera Lynn (1) — chin
Victoria Dock — cock, meaning penis
Vita Brits — tits
Wally Grout (2) — snout, meaning nose
Warwick Farm/s — arm/s
Wentworth Falls — balls, as in testicles
Williamstown Piers — ears
zubrick — prick, meaning penis

Functions
Andy Capp — crap, as in defecate
angel's kiss — piss, as in urinate
apple tart — fart, as in break wind
bacon and egg tart — fart, as in break wind
big hit — shit, as in defecate
bottle mart — fart, as in break wind
brace and bit — shit, as in defecate
bubble and squeak (2) — leak, as in urinate
butcher's hook (3) — look
Captain Cook — look
cat's hiss — piss, as in urinate
Cook — look
cupcake — fart, as in break wind

Dicky Bart — fart, as in break wind
Dicky Lee (1) — pee, as in urinate
Dinny Hayes-er — shit, as in defecate
Eartha Kitt — shit, as in defecate
Edgar Britt — shit, as in defecate
elephant's herd — turd, as in faeces
fairy dart — fart, as in break wind
George the Third — turd, as in faeces
Gerry Riddle — piddle, as in urinate
gravel pit — shit, as in defecate
Gypsy's kiss — piss, as in urinate
hard hit — shit, as in defecate
Henry the Third — turd, as in faeces
hey diddle diddle (2) — piddle, as in urinate
hi diddle diddle (2) — piddle, as in urinate
hit and/or miss — piss, as in urinate
hollow log (4) — bog, as in defecate
horse and cart (1) — fart, as in break wind
horse's hiss — piss, as in urinate; usually abbreviated to *horses*
Jacob's Creek — leak, as in urinate
jam tart (2) — fart, as in break wind
Jimmy Britt (1) — shit, as in defecate
Jimmy Riddle — piddle, as in urinate
Johnny Bliss — piss, as in urinate
King George the Third — turd, as in faeces
King Henry the Third — turd, as in faeces
king hit — shit, as in defecate
King Richard the Third — turd, as in faeces
Les Kiss — piss, as in urinate
lolly — pee, as in urinate
Mickey Fritt — shit, as in defecate
mockingbird — turd, as in faeces
Nancy Lee — pee, as in urinate
Nelson Riddle — piddle as in urinate; usually abbreviated to *Nelson*
number two — poo, as in defecate
one hundred and three — pee, as in urinate
Oscar Britt — shit, as in defecate
raspberry tart — fart, as in break wind

Robert E. Lee — pee, as in urinate
Rodney Hogg — bog, meaning a toilet; also the act of going to the
    toilet
Shannon — piddle, as in urinate
Shirley Bliss — piss, as in urinate
snake's hiss — piss, as in urinate; usually abbreviated to a *snake's*
squiz — look
Stevey Hart — fart, as in break wind
swing and a miss — piss, as in urinate
Tom tit — shit, as in defecate
wasp and bee (2) — pee, as in urinate
Werris Creek (2) — leak, as in urinate
William the Third — turd, as in faeces
you and me (2) — pee, as in urinate

Ailments, Maladies and Afflictions

AIF — deaf
asteroids — haemorrhoids
babbling brook (2) — crook, meaning unwell, sick
ballet dancer — cancer
Bea Miles — piles, meaning haemorrhoids
Bengal lancer — cancer
butcher's hook (1) — crook, meaning unwell, sick
candy dancer — cancer
Chalfont St Giles — piles, meaning haemorrhoids; usually
    abbreviated to *Chalfonts*
Charlie Britt — fit, as in to 'take a fit' (of anger or frustration)
Charlie Dancer — cancer
chocolate frog (3) — wog, meaning a virus, such as influenza
Chunderloo — spew, meaning vomit
civil answer — cancer
Conan Doyle — boil (skin abscess)
Dan McGrew (1) — spew, meaning vomit
Dan McGrew (2) — 'flu, influenza
Danny La Rue (2) — spew, meaning vomit
dibs and dabs — crabs, meaning body lice (sexually transmissible
    infection)
dry rots — trots, meaning diarrhoea

ducks and drakes — shakes, meaning delirium tremens, or the DTs
elephant's herd — turd, as in faeces
Farmer Giles — piles, meaning haemorrhoids
Gough — cough
Halley's Comet — vomit
Harvey Drew — spew, meaning vomit
Hawkesbury Rivers — shivers
Jack the dancer — cancer
Jimmy Britts (2) — shits, meaning diarrhoea
Jimmy Dancer — cancer
Joe Blake/s (1) — shakes
Johnny Dancer — cancer
King George the Third — turd, as in faeces
King Henry the Third — turd, as in faeces
King Richard the Third — turd, as in faeces
laughs and smiles — piles, meaning haemorrhoids
Mario Lanza — cancer
Mars Bars — scars
metric miles — piles, meaning haemorrhoids
mocking bird — turd, as in faeces
Murray Rivers — shivers
Mutt and Jeff — deaf
Pat and Mick (2) — sick
raspberry ripple — cripple
red hots (1) — trots, meaning dysentery
Richard the Third (2) — turd, as in faeces
Sexton Blakes (1) — shakes
smash and grabs — crabs, meaning body lice (sexually transmissible
    infection)
Spanish dancer — cancer
Spiro Agnew — spew, meaning vomit
sudden death — breath; usually bad breath
Swanee Rivers — shivers
Theatre Royal — boil (skin abscess)
Tom and Dick — sick
up and under — chunder, meaning vomit
Wallace and Gromit — vomit
William the Third — turd, as in faeces

Adornments and Appearances

Annalise — crack, back and sac (hair removal)
basin crop — haircut
Dad and Dave — shave
dig a grave (1) — shave
dig in the grave — shave
digging in a grave — shave
Frank Thring — ring (jewellery)
gin sling — ring (jewellery)
Gregory Pecks — specs (short for spectacles)
Irish jig — wig
Jack Spratt — fat
misbehave — shave
Moreton Bay Fig (3) — wig
syrup and fig — wig
tingaling — ring (jewellery)

Vincent's and Bex — Sex and Gender

Closely following the body in terms of number are rhyming slangs for aspects of human sexual behaviour, sexual orientation, and sexually transmissible infections. Gender identifications also form part of this group.

Sexual Acts, States and Apparatus

Angus and Coote — root, as in sexual intercourse
Ballarat (3) — fat, meaning an erection
cotton wool — pull, as in male masturbation
Donald Duck (1) — fuck, as in sexual intercourse, as in 'Have a
    Donald Duck'
don't forget her (1) — (French) letter, meaning a condom
early morn — horn, meaning an erection
Friar Tuck — fuck, as in sexual intercourse
gumboot — fuck, as in sexual intercourse
Harry Monk — spunk, meaning semen
Herby de Groote — root, as in sexual intercourse
J. Arthur Rank (2) — wank, as in masturbate; usually abbreviated
    to a *J. Arthur*
Joe Buck (1) — fuck, as in sexual intercourse
John Bull (2) — pull, as in male masturbation

Johnny Ray — lay, as in sexual intercourse
juicy fruit — root, as in sexual intercourse
kiss me Kate — date
larrikin's hat — fat, meaning an erection
Lord Rex — sex
Martha Ray — lay, as in sexual intercourse
Mickey Duck (1) — fuck, as in sexual intercourse
Mulligatawny — horny, meaning sexually aroused
New York junk — spunk, meaning semen
Persian rug — tug, as in male masturbation
Sarah Vaughan — horn, meaning an erection
Scotch tape — rape
silly galoot — root, as in sexual intercourse
Somerset Maugham — horn, meaning an erection
sour grape — rape
State election — erection
tin flute — root, as in sexual intercourse
Vincent's and Bex — sex
Wellington boot — root, as in sexual intercourse
Yasser Arafat — fat, meaning an erection

Homosexuality
baked bean — queen, meaning a male homosexual
Charlie or Charley (1) — lesbian
cloven hoofter — poofter, meaning a male homosexual
cow's hoof — poof, meaning a male homosexual
Dave Prince — quince, probably meaning a male homosexual
Doris Day — gay, meaning homosexual
ginger beer (3) — queer, meaning homosexual
haricot bean — queen, meaning a male homosexual
horse's hoof — poof, meaning a male homosexual
in-between — queen, meaning a male homosexual
pork and bean — queen, meaning a male homosexual
submarine — queen, meaning a male homosexual
willy woofter — poofter, meaning a male homosexual
woolly boof — poof, meaning a male homosexual
woolly woofter — poofter, meaning a male homosexual

Prostitution

apple Charlotte — harlot
blue moon — hoon, meaning a prostitute's pimp in this usage
Charlie (2) — prostitute
dish ran away with the spoon — hoon, meaning a prostitute's pimp
  in this usage
mallee root — prostitute
paper doll (1) — moll, meaning a gangster's kept woman and/or
  prostitute
Pollywaffle — brothel
silver spoon (1) — hoon, meaning a prostitute's pimp in this usage
silvery moon — hoon, meaning a prostitute's pimp in this usage
Timothy — brothel

Sexually Transmissible Infections

Adrian Knox — pox, meaning sexually transmissible infection,
  usually syphilis
boots and sox — pox, meaning sexually transmissible infection,
  usually syphilis
dibs and dabs — crabs, meaning body lice (sexually transmissible
  infection)
dribs and drabs — crabs, meaning body lice (sexually transmissible
  infection)
gone or here — gonorrhoea
Jack-in-the-box — pox, meaning sexually transmissible infection,
  usually syphilis
Lew Hoad — load, meaning sexually transmissible infection, usually
  syphilis
Sandy McNabs — crabs, meaning body lice (sexually transmissible
  infection)
smash and grabs — crabs, meaning body lice (sexually transmissible
  infection)

Gender

artichoke — bloke
bag of coke — bloke
Barossa Pearl — girl
bart — tart, meaning a girl
Billy Dunk — spunk, meaning a fit, attractive male

Charlie Wheeler — sheila, meaning a girl or woman; usually
   abbreviated to *Charlie*
cocky's joy — boy
Davey Cloak — bloke, meaning man, person
heavenly plan — man
magic wand — blonde
Mark Foy — boy
meat and gravy — man
mother of pearl — girl
mother's joy/s — boy/s
ocean liner (1) — cliner, meaning a girl or woman
paper doll (1) — moll, meaning a gangster's kept woman and/or
   prostitute
paper doll (2) — moll, meaning a girl or woman whose sexual
   favours are widely distributed
pot and pan (1) — man; often abbreviated to *pot*
potato peeler — sheila, meaning a girl or woman
pride and joy — boy
rock-wheeler — sheila
twist/s and twirl/s — girl/s; sometimes abbreviated to *twist*
two wheeler — sheila, meaning a girl or woman

Moreton Bay Bugs — Drugs
There are many rhyming slang terms for drugs — mainly for alcohol,
followed by nicotine and miscellaneous other illicit substances.

Alcohol
Acker Bilk (2) — rum and milk
Andy Devine — wine
apple fritter — bitter, meaning beer
Aristotle — bottle (usually of beer)
Auntie Meg — keg (usually of beer)
Britney Spears — beers
charming mottle — bottle of beer
cherry cheer — beer
corroboree — spree, or drunken spree
country cousin — dozen (usually bottles or cans of beer)
Crimea — beer
cuff link — drink

dad and mum — rum

deaf and dumb (2) — rum

didn't ought — port (fortified wine)

dimple and blotch — scotch (whisky)

dot — wine drinker

fine and dandy — brandy

finger and thumb — rum

gay and frisky — whisky

Germaine Greer/s (1) — beer/s

Goldsborough Mort — port (fortified wine)

Gordon and Gotch (2) — scotch (whisky)

Gordon and ten — scotch (whisky) and water

Graham Eady — seedy, meaning not in a good condition

Gunga Din — gin

Henry Berry (2) — sherry

honky tonk — plonk, meaning cheap wine

horse and donk — plonk, meaning cheap wine

Huckleberry Finn — gin

Jayden Leskie — Esky, meaning large chilled food container

Jersey Flegg — keg (of beer)

Kennedy rot — sot, meaning one who is drunk, often habitually

kitchen sink — drink

La Perouse — booze, meaning alcoholic beverage; often abbreviated
    to *Larpa*

Lily of Laguna — schooner (a NSW measurement of beer)

Lindsay Kline — wine

macaroni (3) — pony (smallest glass of beer served in NSW)

mile and a quarter (2) — gin and water

mortal sin — gin

mottle (abbreviation of *charming mottle*) — bottle of beer

mud and ooze — booze, meaning alcoholic beverage

Napper Tandy — shandy, meaning beer mixed with lemonade

near and far (1) — bar (for serving alcoholic beverages)

Nellie and dead — red (wine)

oh my dear — beer

pen and ink — drink, meaning alcoholic beverage

Perc Galea — beer

pick and choose — booze

pig's ear — beer
plink plonk — vin blanc
plinketty-plonk — plonk, meaning cheap wine
plonkdot — sot, meaning one who is drunk, often habitually
poofter's bum — rum
Port Melbourne Pier (2) — beer
pot of good cheer — beer
Randall Vines — wine(s)
Ray Bright — light, meaning low-alcohol beer
Ray Stehr — beer
red hot — pot, meaning ten-ounce (pre-metric) glass of beer
red Ned — (cheap) red (wine)
scare and fright — light, meaning low-alcohol beer
Senator Spooner — schooner (a NSW measurement of beer);
    sometimes abbreviated to a *Senator*
Silver Link (1) — drink
Terry Dear — beer
thick and thin (2) — gin
tiddly wink — (alcoholic) drink
Tilly Devine — wine
Tom Thumb (1) — rum
Vera Lynn (2) — gin
Wally Grout (1) — shout, meaning buy a round of drinks
Wally Grout (3) — stout (ale)
wine dot — sot, meaning one who is drunk, often habitually
wiss wot — pisspot, meaning one who often drinks too much
young and frisky — whisky

Tobacco
African nigger (1) — cigger, meaning cigarette
cherry ripe — pipe (smoking)
choof — puff, meaning inhale, inhalation
Don Doak — smoke, meaning cigarette
forgive and forget — cigarette
Great Australian Bight — light (for a cigarette)
hammer and tack (3) — tobacco
Harry Wragg — fag, meaning a cigarette
lah de dah (2) — cigar
laugh and joke — smoke, meaning a cigarette

oily rag — fag, meaning a cigarette
Sentimental Bloke — smoke, meaning a cigarette
Twelfth Street Rag — fag, meaning a cigarette
Victor Trumper — bumper, meaning a cigarette butt
wood, coal and coke (2) — smoke, meaning a cigarette

Other Drugs
billy (bong) — bong, meaning apparatus for smoking marijuana
Bob Hope (2) — dope, meaning drugs
Dan Milecki's — eckies, meaning Ecstasy tablets
Gary Ablett — tablet
hammer and tack (1) — smack, meaning heroin
Jack and Jill (4) — pill
Jack Flash — hash, meaning hashish
Johnny Cash — hash, meaning hashish
Mick Mills — pills
Moreton Bay bugs — drugs
okey doke — coke, meaning cocaine
Persian rug (2) — drug

Bottle Stoppers and Tea Leaves — Crime
Rhyming slang is used among criminals, particularly in prisons, although with a small number of usually specialised meanings.

Amsterdam (1) — ram, meaning a criminal's accomplice; often
    abbreviated to *Amster*
babbling brook (3) — crook, meaning criminal
bottle and stopper — copper, meaning a police officer
cabbage tree hat — rat, meaning an informer
chocolate frog (1) — dog, meaning an informer
chunk of beef (2) — thief
cocky's clip (1) — dip, meaning a pickpocket
Cutty Sark (1) — nark, meaning an informer
dog and bark — nark, meaning an informer
eighteen pence (2) — fence, meaning a receiver of stolen goods
flowery dell — cell (in prison)
four b' two (2) — screw, meaning a prison warder
ginger ale (1) — bail, meaning a bond
half inch — pinch, meaning to steal

hammer — police officer
I don't care — chair, meaning the electric chair
Johnhopper — copper, meaning a police officer
kangaroo — screw, meaning a prison warder; often abbreviated to
  kanga
lady from Bristol — pistol
milk jug — mug, meaning a fool or a dupe; often abbreviated to
  milkie
Moreton — tittle-tattle (in children's speech)
Moreton Bay Fig (1) — fizzgig, or simply gig, meaning an informer
Moreton Bay Fig (2) — gig, possibly meaning a detective and/or a
  stickybeak
Noah's Ark (5) — narc/k, meaning an informer
second look — crook, meaning a criminal
thirty-first of May — gay, meaning a fool or a dupe
Wally Prig — gig, meaning an informer
wattle and daub — warb, meaning a dirty or untidy person (prison
  slang); usually abbreviated to *wattle*

Bull Ants and Jarrah Blocks — Clothing

This is a major category of rhyming slang, closely associated with terms for the body and its parts, and includes accessories.

airs and graces — braces
almond rocks — socks; sometimes abbreviated to *rocks*
armour float — coat, overcoat
Arty Rolla — collar
Aunt Ella — umbrella
Aunt Molly — brolly (short for umbrella)
bag of fruit — suit
ball and bat — hat
Ballarat (1) — hat
barrel of fat — hat
Basin Street blues — shoes
Ben Blues — shoes
Bobby rocks — socks
bowl of fat — hat
bowl of fruit — suit
Brett Parker — afterdarker, meaning a dinner suit

bull ants — pants
canoes — shoes
Charlie Prescott — waistcoat (pronounced 'westcot')
clicketty-click (1) — stick (for walking)
Collier and Moat — coat
council houses — trousers
cry and laugh — scarf
curly locks — socks
daisy roots — boots
dark felt — belt (item of clothing)
Davey Crockett (2) — pocket
dead wowsers — trousers
decky dirt — shirt
Dicky dirt — shirt
dinky dirt — shirt
dirty Bert — shirt
dog's eye (2) — (neck)tie
east and west (2) — vest
Ernie and Bert — shirt
fiddles and flutes — boots
fleas and ants — pants
Flemington Races — braces
Fourth of July — (neck)tie
Freddo Frogs — togs, meaning trousers
Goldilocks — socks
Harolds — knickers, meaning underpants
Harry Taggs — bags, meaning trousers
I'm afloat — coat, overcoat
Irish folly — brolly, meaning umbrella
Jacky Lancashire — handkerchief
Jarrah blocks — socks
Joe Rocks — socks
Kangaroo/s (2) — shoe/s; usually abbreviated to *kanga(s)*
keys and locks — socks
Lake's folly — brolly, meaning umbrella
lamb's fry — (neck)tie
locket — pocket
Lucy Locket — pocket

Maggie Moors — drawers, meaning women's underpants; usually abbreviated to *Maggies*

motorboat — overcoat

Nazi spy (2) — (neck)tie

Nellie Bligh (1) — fly (of trousers)

Nellie Bligh (5) — (neck)tie

ones and twos — shoes

Paddy melt — belt

Peggy Sue — shoe

Pete Kelly's blues — shoes

petrol bowsers — trousers; usually abbreviated to *bowsers*

Randwick Races — braces

rammy rousers — trousers

Reg Grundies — undies, meaning underpants; usually abbreviated to *Reginalds*

Rickety Dick (2) — stick

round the houses — trousers

Russian spy — tie

Saint Louis blues — shoes

Saint Vitus' Dance — pants

scrum half — scarf

silly galoots — boots

sky rocket — pocket

South African veldt — belt

splash throughs — shoes

stock and die (1) — (neck)tie

ten to twos — shoes

terrace houses — trousers; often abbreviated to *terraces*

this and that (2) — hat

thises and thats — hats

tit for tat (1) — hat; usually abbreviated to titfer

ton o' my rocks — socks

turtle doves — gloves

2KY (1) — tie

Uncle Bert — shirt

Val Quirk — shirt

whistle and flute — suit (of clothes); usually abbreviated to *whistle*

whistle and toot — suit

Blood Blister to Thief and Robber— Relationships

These terms for relationships of various kinds are another indication of the everyday nature of most rhyming slang.

baker's dozen — cousin
bath bun — son
blood blister — sister; sometimes abbreviated to *blister*
buttered bun — son
cash and carry — marry
cheese and kisses — missus
cherry plum — mum
China plate — mate, meaning friend; likely to be male; usually abbreviated to *China*
chunk of beef (1) — chief, meaning the leader, or boss; sometimes abbreviated to *chunka*
cows and kisses — missus
dead spotted ling — dead ring, meaning identical, as in 'dead ringer'
drum and fife — wife
eau de Cologne (2) — alone
five-eight (2) — mate, meaning friend; likely to be male
happy and sad — dad
hugs and kisses — missus
Jack Malone — alone
Jimmy Carruthers — one another
Kewpie Doll (2) — moll, meaning a girl or woman of ill repute
kid blister — sister
make another — brother
maken — brother
mile and a quarter — daughter
ocean liner (2) — mate, meaning friend; likely to be male
old China plate — old mate, meaning longtime friend; usually male
once another (1) — brother
once another (2) — mother
one another (1) — brother
one another (2) — mother
Pat Malone — on my own, alone
Royal Doulton — mate, meaning friend; likely to be male
Simon and Garfunkel — uncle

sixteen ton — son
skin and blister — sister
soap and water — daughter
soapy water — daughter
sprouse — spouse
strangle and smother — mother; sometimes abbreviated to
    'the *strangle*'
tell us another — mother
ten furlongs — daughter
thief and robber — cobber, meaning friend; usually male
Tod Sloane — alone; *on my tod* is a common variation
Tom tart — sweetheart
trouble and strife — wife

Just Wollondilly or Totally Mum and Dad? — States of Mind

Silliness is the mental state most frequently treated in rhyming slang,
along with irritation, madness and trouble.

auntie — silly
butcher's hook (2) — to go crook, meaning to express anger
Dalai Lamas — dramas, meaning emotionally complex situations,
    as in 'No dramas'
dilly — silly
Edgar Britts — (the) shits, meaning to be irritated, as in 'He is
    giving me the *Edgars*'
half mast — past, meaning mentally retarded
hanky panky — cranky, meaning irritable or silly
Jimmy Britts (1) — shits, meaning to be irritated, as in
    'He's got the *Jimmy Britts*'
Kirribilli — silly
mum and dad — mad
Nellie Bligh (2) — fly, meaning on the alert
No River Murrays — no worries
Noah's Ark (4) — nark, meaning a spoilsport
Tom tits — shits, meaning to be irritated
trey bits (1) — shits, meaning to be irritated
trizzy bits — shits, meaning to be irritated

turtledove — love
Uncle Willy — silly; usually abbreviated to *uncle*
Wollondilly — silly

Elephants, Moonbeam and Wombat — States of Being

Inebriation and cleanliness are frequently noted in Australian rhyming slang, reflecting two national obsessions. Other bodily states and sensations include sleep, temperature, tiredness and death.

Inebriation
Adrian Quist — pissed, meaning drunk
Brahms and Liszt — pissed, meaning drunk
elephant's trunk — drunk; often abbreviated to *elephants*
Franz Liszt — pissed, meaning drunk
Graham Eady — seedy
John Bull (1) — full, meaning drunk
Mollo the monk — drunk; *Molly* is a common variation
Molly Monk — drunk
Mozart and Liszt — pissed, meaning drunk
Oliver Twist (1) — pissed, meaning drunk
Roy Bull (2) — full, meaning drunk
Schindler's List — pissed, meaning drunk
sisters apart — pissed as a fart, meaning very drunk

Cleanliness
Baden Powell — towel
Band of Hope — soap; often abbreviated to *bander*
Bob Hope (1) — soap
Bob Powell — towel
Cape of Good Hope — soap
David Gower (2) — shower
Dick Powell — towel
dog's growl — towel
fairy bower — shower
Joe Hope — soap
lazy hour — shower
lemon squash — wash
Long Jetty — sweaty

moonbeam — clean
now is the hour — shower
on the beak — reek
Tyrone Power — shower

Fright
bona fide — terrified
Charlie Howard — *coward*
Leslie Howard — coward

Hopelessness
Buckley and Nunn — none
Charlie Chase — race, meaning in the hurly burly, as in
    'Not in the race'
had the Richard — exhausted
Kerry Packered — knackered, meaning exhausted
Peter Mertens — curtains, meaning finished

Survival
Stuart Diver — survivor

Sleep
Bo-peep — sleep
currant cake — awake
hit the deep — sleep
Roberta Flack — sack, meaning bed
rolling deep — sleep
Tom Cruise — snooze, meaning sleep
weeping willow — pillow

Bodily temperature
brave and bold — cold
Cheltenham bold — cold
Dennis Lilley — chilly
Hawkesbury Rivers — shivers
Murray Rivers — shivers
Piccadilly — chilly
soldiers bold — cold; usually abbreviated to *soldiers*
Swannee Rivers — shivers
young and old — cold

Death
brown bread — dead
garden shed — dead
kangaroo Ted /Edward — dead
lamb's fried — died
lump of lead (2) — dead
wombat — 'hors de combat', meaning dead

Trouble
Barney Rubble — trouble
froth and bubble (2) — trouble

Enjoyment
Noah's Ark (3) — lark, meaning fun

Luck
lemonade and sars(parilla) (2) — lucky; one who is 'arsey'

Truth
baby blue — true

Confidence
George Moore (2) — sure

Acquiescence
Marcus Welby — might as well be

Squatter's Daughter in the Bullock's Liver — The Natural World

Animals, insects and a variety of natural features and phenomena, such as flowers and the weather, are commonly encountered in rhyming slang.

General
bacon and liver — river
bullock's liver — river
bundle of socks (1) — rocks
Cobar shower — flower
Cole Porter — water
David Gower/s (1) — flower/s

fisherman's daughter — water
half an hour (2) — flower
Indian brave — wave (the ocean)
ivory towers — flowers
kitchen stoves — cloves (culinary)
LKS Mackinnon Stakes — water
mother and daughter — water
mum and daddo — shadow
Noah's Ark (1) — dark
shake and shiver — river
squatter's daughter — water
Xerox copy — poppy (as worn on Remembrance Day)

Weather
Attila the Hun — sun
currant bun (2) — sun
Eiffel Tower — shower (of rain)
France and Spain — rain
Frankie Laine (2) — rain
Geoffrey Lane (1) — rain
happy hour — shower (of rain)
hot cross bun — sun
King of Spain (2) — rain
Noel McGrowdie — cloudy
peas in a pot — hot
Peter Gunn — sun
roaring horsetails — Aurora Australis (astronomy)
silver spoon (2) — moon

Creatures
after darks — sharks
all stations — Alsatian dog
apple sauce — horse
Ballarat (2) — cat
Bill Picken — chicken
bow and arrow — sparrow
Charles Dickens — chickens
choc and log — dog
condiments and sauces — horses

cries and screeches — leeches
Cutty Sark (2) — shark
dirty dish — fish
Ella May Morse — horse
George the Third — turd, as in faeces
hollow log (1) — dog
Jack the Ripper — kipper (a fish)
Joan of Arc/s — shark/s
Joe/y Blake/s (2) — snake/s
Joe Marks — sharks
Jonah — shark
King Henry the Third — turd, as in faeces
Lillian Gish (2) — fish
Luna Park — shark
macaroni (2) — pony (horse); sometimes abbreviated to *macker*
Marcus Clark(e) — shark
Noah's Ark (6) — shark; often abbreviated to *Noah* or *Noah's*
plum jam — ram (sheep)
Sammy Hall — ball, meaning one single testicle; usually used to
    refer to horses with this anatomical feature
Sexton Blakes (2) — snakes
steam tugs (2) — bugs, meaning insects
tomato sauce/s (2) — horse/s
willow the weep — sheep

Insects
Jack Rees — fleas
Joe Rees — fleas
Mickey Mouse (3) — louse
2UEs — fleas
white mice — lice
Willy Lees — fleas

Jimmy Grants, Chocolate Frogs and Septics — Ethnicity, Race and Nation

Derogatory terms for 'others' of all kinds form a solid category of Australian rhyming slang, reflecting one of our uglier national characteristics.

Alsatian dog — wog, meaning a person of southern European/ Mediterranean origin

army tanks — Yanks, meaning Americans

atomic bomb — pom, short for 'pommie', meaning a person from Britain

Billy the Kid — yid, meaning a Jewish person

bubble and squeak (1) — Greek

chocolate frog/s (2) — wog/s, meaning person/s of southern European/Mediterranean origin

currant bun (1) — Hun, meaning a German

Dapto dog — wog, meaning a person of southern European/ Mediterranean origin; usually abbreviated to a *Dapto*

dink — Chink, meaning a Chinese or other Asian person

egg and spoon (3) — coon, meaning a black-skinned person

Ethel Merman — German

five b' two — Jew

five to two — Jew

five-ter — Jew

four b' two (1) — Jew

Freddo Frog — wog, meaning a person of southern European/ Mediterranean origin; usually abbreviated to *Freddo*

ham shank — Yank, meaning an American

here and now — chow, meaning a Chinese or other Asian person

hollow log (3) — wog, meaning a person of southern European/ Mediterranean origin

iron tank (2) — Yank

Jersey cow — chow, meaning a Chinese or other Asian person

Jew chum — new chum, meaning an immigrant

Jimmy Grant — immigrant

Jodrell Bank — Yank, meaning an American

Lord Gowrie — Maori

Merri Creek — Greek

mutton flaps — Japs, meaning Japanese people
mutton shanks — Yanks, meaning Americans
ox cheek — Greek
pork and beans — Portuguese
pork and cheese — Portuguese
rice and sago — dago, meaning a Greek, Italian or other person of
    Mediterranean background
seppo — Yank, meaning an American
septic — Yank, meaning an American
septic tank/s (1) — Yank/s, meaning (an) American/s
ship's tank — Yank, meaning an American
sky — Eyetie, meaning an Italian
spotty dog — wog, meaning a person of southern European/
    Mediterranean origin
Tennant Creek — Greek
Terry Toon (2) — coon, meaning a black-skinned person
tin tank (2) — Yank, meaning an American
to and from — pom, short for 'pommie', meaning a person from
    Britain
Werris Creek (1) — Greek; usually abbreviated to *Werris*
woolly dog — wog, meaning a person of southern European/
    Mediterranean origin

Beecham's Pills and Terry Toons — Insults
When insults are combined with the many rhyming slangs for 'others',
the result is a large amount of invective.

Stupidity
Beechams Pill — dill, meaning a foolish or naive person
Burke and Wills — dills, meaning foolish or naive persons
dropkick (2) — thick, meaning stupid
egg and spoon (2) — goon, meaning a stupid person
Elmer Fudd — dud, meaning ineffectual; often abbreviated to *Elmer*
Jack and Jill (2) — dill, meaning a foolish or naive person
Kevin Rudd — dud, meaning ineffectual
let me loose — goose, meaning a silly person
letme — goose, meaning a silly person
London fog — log, meaning a stupid person
potato and spud — dud, meaning ineffectual

Honesty
cabbage tree hat — rat, meaning an informer
holy friar — liar

Religion and Politics
cattle tic — catholic
hansom cab — scab, meaning a non-unionised worker
Jack McNab — scab, meaning a non-unionised worker; often
    abbreviated to *Jack*
Sandy MacNab (2) — scab, meaning a non-unionised worker
tit for tat (2) — rat, meaning a non-unionised worker

Vulgarities
Berkshire Hunt — cunt, as in a despicable person
blue moon — hoon, meaning a prostitute's pimp
chow — cow, meaning a vulgar or ill-tempered woman
dillypot — twat, meaning vagina; also used as an insult, meaning
    an unpleasant person
drop kick (1) — prick, meaning penis; also used as an insult,
    meaning an unpleasant person
drop kick and punt — cunt, as in female genitalia; usually
    abbreviated to 'drop kick'
egg and spoon (1) — hoon, meaning a noisy lout
Fred Astaire (3) — lair, as in a man given to flashy dress and
    behaviour
halfback flanker — wanker, as in a male who masturbates
merchant banker — wanker, as in a male who masturbates
sheep shanker — wanker, as in a male who masturbates
silver spoon (1) — hoon, meaning a prostitute's pimp in this usage
silvery moon — hoon, meaning a prostitute's pimp in this usage
teddy bear — lair, as in a man given to flashy dress and behaviour
Terry Toon (1) — hoon, meaning a noisy lout
Westpac banker — wanker, as in a male who masturbates
Yogi Bear — lair, as in a man given to flashy dress and behaviour

Steele Rudds for Deacon Skinner — Food and Drink (Non-alcoholic)

The number and variety of terms related to food and drink strongly reflects the Anglo-Celtic nature of traditional Australian cuisine.

Acker Bilk — milk
Angus Murray — curry
Annie (Anna) Louise — cheese
Army and Navy — gravy
Arthur Murray — curry
Billy Guyatt — diet
Bruce Reed — feed, meaning to eat a meal; also the meal itself
Captain Bloods — spuds, meaning potatoes
cheap and nasty — pasty, as in a pastry with a savoury filling
chock-a-block up 'er — supper
chuck me in the gutter — butter
clerk of the course — sauce
cough and sneeze — cheese
Dark Town strutter — butter
Deacon Skinner — dinner
dead horse — sauce
Derby winner — dinner
Dicky Lee (2) — tea
dirt grime and dust — crust (pie)
dog's eye (1) — pie
flies and dead horse — pies and sauce
Gertie Gitana — banana
Gypsy Lee — tea
half an hour (1) — flour
Harold Holt (2) — salt
holy ghost (2) — toast
horse's doovers — hors d'oeuvres
Howard Keel — meal
Jack Shay (1) — tea (as in the Irish pronunciation 'tay')
Jenny Lee — tea
Jimmy Lee — tea
Joe Blake (3) — steak
Johnny Rutter — butter

kerb and gutter — butter
Kevin Sheedy — greedy; sometimes abbreviated to *Kevin*
kitchen sink — drink
Leonard Teale — meal; usually abbreviated to a *Leonard*
lies and dead horse — pies and sauce
lisp and stutter — butter
little boys — saveloys (sausages)
loop-the-loop (2) — soup
lump of lead (1) — bread
Mother Machree — tea
mumble and stutter — butter
mutter and stutter — butter
*mystery bag*s — snags, meaning sausages
Nazi spy (1) — meat pie
Nelly Bligh (3) — (meat) pie
off break — steak
pig's eye (1) — pie
piper's knees — cheese
quiver and shake — steak
racehorse — (tomato) sauce
rats and mice — rice
River Murray — curry
rocking horse — (tomato) sauce
Rodney Rude — food
roll me in the gutter — butter
Rosie Lee — tea
salty bananas — sultanas
soft as silk — milk
stammer and stutter — butter
stand at ease — cheese
Steele Rudds — spuds, meaning potatoes
stock and die (2) — pie
stop thief — beef
Tim Holt — salt
Tom and Sam — jam
Tommy Farter — tomato (pronounced 'tomarter') (sauce)
Tommy Tucker — supper
Tuggerah Lake — cake
2KY (3) — pie

Uncle Fred — bread
Uncle Ned (2) — bread
wasp and bee (1) — tea
you and me (1) — pea
you and me (3) — tea
yous and mes — peas

Arse-over-Anna at the Gay and Hearty — Leisurely Pastimes and Diversions

The Australian love of leisure — and activities pursued while enjoying it — has generated a solid body of rhymes.

Gambling

barmaid's blush — flush (a hand in the card game of poker)
billy goat (2) — tote, totalisator (horseracing)
Bunsen burner — turner, meaning a cricket wicket that takes the spin from a ball
canal boat — tote, totalisator (horseracing)
cast a net — make a bet
cats and mice — dice
docker's hook — book, meaning a bookmaker's list of odds
dog's dinner (2) — skinner, meaning when the house wins in the gambling game of two-up
dog's dinner (3) — spinner, meaning the tosser of coins in the gambling game of two-up
egg flip — tip, meaning some advice about a possible winner (horseracing)
egg flipper — tipper, meaning one who tips on horse races
fried rice (2) — dice
giddy goat — tote, totalisator (horseracing)
highland fling (1) — king (playing cards)
Major Stephens — evens, meaning a bet in which the winnings is equal to the money staked
Mary-Lou — blue, meaning credit
nanny goat (2) — tote, totalisator (horseracing)
passing by (2) — swy, meaning the gambling game two-up
Tommy Rook — book, meaning a bookmaker's list of odds; often abbreviated to *Tommy*

Sports

airs and graces — races, meaning horseracing
baked dinner — winner (horseracing)
braces — races (horse or dog)
cat cuff — bluff, meaning a feint (boxing)
citronella — quinella, meaning a type of bet (horseracing)
Coca Cola — bowler (cricket)
condiments and sauces — horses
Dorothy Dix — six (cricket)
eagle — bar, meaning two under par (golf)
fireman's braces — races (horse or dog)
froth and bubble (1) — double, a kind of bet (horseracing)
George Moore (1) — four (cricket)
giddy goat — tote, totalisator (horseracing)
gin and water — mile and a quarter
holy ghost (4) — (start and/or finish) post (horseracing)
innocent Mary — Len Incigneri (Melbourne footballer)
Jake La Motta — trotter, meaning a horse for harness racing
Jimminy Cricket — wicket (cricket)
macaroni (2) — pony, meaning a horse
meat pie — try, meaning a score in rugby football
Nat King Cole (1) — bowl (cricket)
pig's eye (2) — try, meaning a score in rugby football
rabbit in the thicket — cricket
red hots (2) — trots, meaning harness racing
Richard Dix — six (cricket)
rock and rollers — bowlers, meaning lawn bowls
Roy Bull (3) — full, as in 'out on the full' (rugby league)
sausage roll (1) — goal (football)
sausage roll (2) — bowl (cricket)
this and that (1) — bat (cricket)
Tom Mix — six (cricket)
tomato sauce/s (2) — horse/s (horseracing)
trot and paces — races
Wilson Picket — cricket

Games
African nigger (2) — jigger, meaning a wooden rest for a billiard cue
bladder and lard — card
Carole Lombard — card
gerbera — Yarborough (term used in the card game of Bridge)
hollow log (2) — dog: in children's folk speech this means one who spoils the game or otherwise breaks the rules
Joe Palooka — snooker
lubra — Yarborough (term used in the card game of Bridge)
Mickey Spillane — game

Dances
arsehole of the goanna — Varsovienna
arse-over-Anna — Varsovienna
arse-over-header — Varsovienna
heart and soul of the goanna — Varsovienna
Jack Palance — dance
short ease — Schottische
short squeeze — Schottische
tipsy Jap — Gypsy tap
Var Susy Anne — Varsovienna

Diversions
Bondi Junction — function (social event)
Brussels sprout — boy scout
constant screamer — concertina
fleas and itches — pictures (pronounced 'pichers'), meaning the cinema
gay and hearty — party
giddy gout — boy scout; usually abbreviated to *giddy*
goanna — piano (pronounced 'pianner')
hers and hims — hymns
Joanna — piano (pronounced 'pianner')
Joe Morgan — street organ
juice harp — Jew's harp (musical instrument)
Moriarty — party
mouse organ — mouth organ, meaning harmonica
whistle and toot — flute
witchetty grub — cub, meaning junior boy scout

Dodge and Shirk — Work

There are roughly as many rhyming slangs related to working life as there are dealing with its opposite.

General

dodge and shirk — work
flick pass — arse (as in to 'get the arse'), meaning to lose one's job
greengages — wages
hammer and tack (2) — sack, meaning to lose one's job
Joe Goss — boss
pitch and toss — boss
rock of ages — wages
soup and gravy — navy
terrible Turk — work
Zane Grey — pay

Occupations

babbling brook (1) — cook; often abbreviated to *babbler*
bag of yeast — priest
bottle (and) stopper — copper, meaning a police officer
breadcrumb — hum, meaning someone who is down and out
Bunkey Naylor — tailor
Christmas card (1) — guard (on a train)
Coffs Harbour — barber
currant bun (3) — nun
curried mince — prince
dingaling — king
ducks and geese — police
four b' two — screw, meaning a prison warder
ginger beer (1) — engineer
girl abductor — conductor (of a tram)
grasshopper — copper, meaning a police officer
greasy mop — cop, meaning a police officer; often abbreviated to *greasy*
hickey hockey — jockey
hot potato (pronounced 'pertater') (2) — waiter
hot scone — John, meaning a police officer
jacks — police
Joe Soap — pope

John Cleese — police
johnhop/s — cop/s, meaning police officer/s; usually abbreviated
   to 'the *johns*'
johnhopper — copper, meaning police officer
loop-the-loop (1) — hoop, meaning jockey (horseracing)
paraffin lamp — tramp, meaning a vagrant
pear and quince — prince
Sinbad the Sailor — tailor
steam tug (1) — pug, meaning a pugilist, or boxer
Sydney Harbour — barber
tea leaf — thief
tea leafing — thieving
trick cyclist — psychiatrist
Winchcombe Carson — parson
you're the one — nun

Tools and Materials
Clark Gable — cable
leg of pork — fork(lift)
mad Mick (1) — pick (digging tool)
Melbourne Grammar (1) — hammer
teller of tales — nails
windjammer — hammer

Specialised
Ashley Mallett — pallet
cattle bruisers — battle cruisers
Charlie's coat — Carley float (nautical item)
deaf adder — ladder
found a nail — round the tail (sheep shearing jargon)
Harry Tate — RE8 (a World War I reconnaissance plane)
Henry Tate — RE8 (a World War I reconnaissance plane)
hutch — crutch (of a sheep)
kangaroo (1) — screw, meaning a prison warder; often abbreviated
   to *kanga*
nine and ten — sheep (pen)
stuck pig — gig, meaning a public performance of musicians
whirling spray — Wirraway, a World War II training plane

Boracic Lint for the Duke of Kent — Money and its Absence

The 'root of all evil' is always an important part of any slang repertoire; it's no different in relation to rhyming slang.

Alma Grey — trey, meaning a threepenny coin (pre-decimal currency)

Andy Mac — zac, meaning a sixpenny coin (pre-decimal currency)

Archie Moore — poor; often abbreviated to *Archie*

Arthur Ashe — cash

Beecham pill — bill (for goods and services, as at a restaurant)

bees and honey — money

boracic lint — skint, meaning without funds

Brodie Mack — zac, meaning a sixpenny coin (pre-decimal currency)

Bugs Bunny — money

bullock('s) horn — pawn, as in being 'in pawn' or having 'to pawn'; meaning to use possessions as security for cash loan

Charlie Ash — cash

Christopher Ash — cash; usually abbreviated to *C. Ash*

curry and rice — price

Darby and Joan (1) — loan

disaster — piastre (Egyptian currency)

dog's dinner (1) — deaner, meaning one shilling (pre-decimal currency)

Dolly Gray — trey, meaning a threepenny coin (pre-decimal currency); or a three in cards

Dora Gray — trey, meaning a threepenny coin (pre-decimal currency); often abbreviated to *Dora*

duck's neck — cheque

Duke of Kent — rent

fiddly-did — quid, meaning one pound (pre-decimal currency); usually abbreviated to a *fiddly*

football pools — jewels

fried rice (1) — price

frog skin — sovereign (pronounced 'sov-rin'), meaning a pound coin (pre-decimal currency)

Gene Tunney (1) — money

goose's neck — cheque

Gregory Peck (1) — cheque

grey nurse — purse

half a neddy — ten shillings, meaning half a pound (pre-decimal currency)

hammer and tack (5) — zac, meaning a sixpenny coin (pre-decimal currency)

hearts of oak — broke, meaning without funds

Holmes à Court — short, meaning with insufficient money

home on the range — change

horse and dray — trey, meaning a threepenny coin (pre-decimal currency)

horse and foal — dole, meaning unemployment benefit

I'll be back — zac, meaning a sixpenny coin (pre-decimal currency)

J. Carroll Nash — cash; often abbreviated to *J. Carroll*

Jack and Jill (1) — bill (for goods and services, as at a restaurant)

Jack and Jill (5) — till, meaning cash register

Jack Benny — penny

Jack Jones — loan(s)

Jill and Jack — zac, meaning a sixpenny coin (pre-decimal currency)

Joe Loss — toss

John Dilling — shilling, meaning twelve pence (pre-decimal currency)

John Dillon — shilling, meaning twelve pence (pre-decimal currency)

John Dunn — one, meaning one pound (pre-decimal currency)

kangaroo (3) — screw, meaning wages; often abbreviated to *kanga*

Kansas City Max — tax

Kembla Grange — small change

lost and found (1) — pound (pre-decimal currency), meaning money

Mark Boucher — voucher

Mickey Finn — five pounds (pre-decimal currency), meaning money

Mother Goose — deuce, meaning a florin (two shilling coin) (pre-decimal currency)

Murray cod — on the nod, meaning to bet; also means to be on credit

Nat King Cole (2) — dole, meaning unemployment benefit

nervous wreck — cheque

on the floor — poor

on your own — loan

Oscar Asche — cash; usually abbreviated to *Oscar*

Oxford scholar — dollar

passing by (1) — florin, meaning a two shilling coin (pre-decimal currency)

poddy calf — half (a crown), meaning a coin worth two shillings and
    sixpence (pre-decimal currency)
ram's horn — pawn? (see *bullock's horn*)
Rhodes scholar — dollar
rifle range — change
Riverina — deaner, meaning one shilling (pre-decimal currency)
Robertson and Moffat — profit; usually abbreviated to *Robertson*
rock and roll — dole, meaning unemployment benefit
rogan — shilling (pre-decimal currency)
rogue and Dillon — shilling (pronounced 'shillin') (pre-decimal
    currency)
rogue and villain — shilling (pronounced 'shillin') (pre-decimal
    currency); usually abbreviated to *rogan*
Roy Sluice (2) — deuce, meaning a florin (two shilling coin)
    (pre-decimal currency)
sausage and mash — cash
sealing wax — tax
Simple Simon — diamond
smash — cash
splash — cash
stereophonic sound — pound (pre-decimal currency)
strum and stroll — dole, meaning unemployment benefit
strut and stroll — dole, meaning unemployment benefit
sugar and honey — money
tin lid (3) — quid, meaning a pound (pre-decimal currency)
tin tack (3) — zac, meaning a sixpenny coin (pre-decimal currency)
tomfoolery — jewellery
total wreck — cheque
varicose vein — sain, meaning a ten shilling note (pre-decimal
    currency)
Vic Damone — loan
wood, coal and coke (1) — broke, meaning without funds
yid — quid, meaning one pound (pre-decimal currency)

From Smellbourne to Steak and Kidney — Place and Location

Rhymes on placenames are, perhaps surprisingly, relatively limited in number and are bolstered by more general rhymes for non-specific locations, such as 'park', 'town' and 'road'.

Bib and Bub (1) — pub
bullock's kidney — Sydney
cock sparra — Yarra (Melbourne's River Yarra)
darling it hurts — Darlinghurst (Sydney)
field of wheat — street
frog and toad — road
fuck shop — tuck shop, meaning school canteen
Gregory Peck (2) — deck (of a ship)
hammer and tack (4) — track, meaning road; often abbreviated
    to *hammer*
hey diddle diddle (1) — middle
hi diddle diddle (1) — middle, especially in relation to Australian
    Rules football
holy ghost (5) — coast
horse and cart (2) — (from the) start
iron tank (1) — bank
J. Arthur Rank (1) — bank
Jack and Jill (3) — hill
Joe Brown — town
Johnny Mack (2) — track, meaning road
lean and lurch — church
left in the lurch — church
moan and wail — gaol
Noah's Ark (2) — park
North Sydney — kidney
penny brown — town
Ricky May — (the) way, meaning 'the way home'
rock and lurch — church
roll and lurch — church
Rosewall and Hoad — road
rubbidy dub — pub; often abbreviated to *rubbidy*
septic tank (2) — bank

Smellbourne — Melbourne
smoked haddock — paddock
steak and kidney — Sydney (city)
stiff shitty — city
tadpole — hole
tin tank (1) — bank
Tommy Tank — (savings) bank
Yogi Bear — boob lair, meaning prisoner ('boob' means gaol)

Clicketty-Click! — Number and Collectivities

There are relatively few rhyming slang terms for numbers and associated concepts. Many of them relate to the gambling game usually known as 'Bingo' and, in Australia, often as 'Housey'. These terms often vary from place to place and caller to caller, so the terms included here are representative rather than exhaustive.

ask for more — thirty-four (Bingo)
baker's bun — sixty-one (Bingo)
bang on the drum — seventy-one (Bingo)
beehive — five
between the sticks — eighty-six (Bingo)
Big Ben — ten
Brighton line — fifty-nine (Bingo)
buckle my shoe — thirty-two (Bingo)
button my shoe — two
candy store — seventy-four (Bingo)
Christmas cake — thirty-eight (Bingo)
clicketty-click (2) — sixty-six (Bingo)
clucky hen — ten
cock and hen — ten
cucumber — number
dancing queen — seventeen (Bingo)
Danny La Rue (1) — fifty-two (Bingo)
Diana Dors — forty-four (Bingo)
dirty Gertie — thirty
Doctor Bevan — seven
dog's date — eight
down on your knees — forty-three(s) (Bingo)
droopy drawers — forty-four(s) (Bingo)

duck and dive — twenty-five (Bingo)
eat 'em alive — five
garden gate — eight (Bingo)
get up and run — thirty-one (Bingo)
goodbye teens — nineteen (Bingo)
Jack's alive — five (Bingo)
jump and jive — thirty-five (Bingo)
knock at the door — four (Bingo)
made in heaven — sixty-seven (Bingo)
make them wait — fifty-eight (Bingo)
man alive — five (Bingo)
more than eleven — thirty-seven (Bingo)
one more time — seventy-nine (Bingo)
overweight — twenty-eight (Bingo)
Paterson, Laing and Bruce (1) — deuce, meaning two items
Peggy Lee — three
Peggy Lou — two
pick and mix — twenty-six (Bingo)
queen bee — seventy-three (Bingo)
red raw — sixty-four (Bingo)
rise and shine — twenty-nine (Bingo)
Roy Sluice (1) — deuce, in cards
Sammy Lee — three
saving Grace — sixty-eight (Bingo)
snakes alive — fifty-five (Bingo)
spire and steeple — people
staying alive — eighty-five (Bingo)
straight on through — eighty-two (Bingo)
stuck in the tree — fifty-three (Bingo)
thee and me — twenty-three (Bingo)
time for fun — forty-one (Bingo)
time for tea — eighty-three (Bingo)
Tony's den — ten (Bingo)
turn on the screw — sixty-two (Bingo)
up to tricks — forty-six (Bingo)

Do a Harold Holt — Actions

This is a sizeable, if miscellaneous, category of terms for various physical actions, bodily as well as behavioural.

Botany Bay — run away, as in 'do a *Botany*'
broken mug — hug
bull and cow — row, meaning an argument
cheesy kiss — miss (miss catching a ball)
cocky's clip (2) — dip, meaning swim, as in to 'take a dip'; possibly also means 'sheep dip'
cut lunch — punch
Dan Quayle — bail, meaning flee, as in to 'bail out on' someone
dark and dim — swim
Duke of York (2) — walk
fancy sash — bash, meaning to beat someone up
Harold Holt (1) — bolt, meaning to flee; sometimes abbreviated, as in to 'do a *Harold*' or a 'do a *Harry*'
Harry Lauder — order
hit and swerve — perve
hors d'oeuvre — perve, meaning one who ogles the opposite sex
Jack Shay — stay
Jack Shea — slay
Jimmy Hix — fix, meaning mend
Johnnie Russell — hustle, meaning to hurry
Johnny Rustle — bustle, meaning to struggle, as in 'on the bustle'
Jungle Jim — swim
Mickey Finn (2) — sin
Murray cod (2) — nod (the head)
one alone — moan (complain)
optic nerve — perve, meaning one who ogles the opposite sex
Pat and Mick (1) — lick, as in defeat or best someone
pickle and pork — walk
pickled pork — walk
Roy Bull (1) — pull, as in male masturbation
stick of chalk — walk
sticky beak — peek
sway and swerve — perve, meaning one who ogles the opposite sex
swiftly flowing — going

Tiger Tim — swim
to and fro (1) — go
Tom and Dick (1) — lick
Uncle Merv — perve, meaning to ogle the opposite sex
Vickers Gin — sin

Billy Lids in the Bib and Bub — Domestic Life

Once again, in keeping with the everydayness of rhyming slang, there is
a sizeable list of terms related to domestic life.

Andy Maguire — fire (conflagration)
Anna Maria — fire (conflagration)
Barney Maguire — fire (conflagration)
Bass and Flinders — windows (pronounced 'winders')
Betty Grable — table
Bib and Bub (2) — tub, meaning bath, as in 'take a bib'
Bill and Ted — bed
billy lids — kids, meaning children
Bob Dyer — fire (conflagration)
Bobby Martin — carton
Brooklyn Bridge — fridge, refrigerator
by the light (of the silvery moon) — spoon
Cain and Abel — table
Captain — kid, meaning a child
Captain scratches — matches (firelighters)
Charlie Mason — basin
charming mottle — bottle
charming wife — knife
Clark Gable (1) — table
Darryl Patch — match (firelighter); often abbreviated to *Darryl*
David Boon — spoon
Dawn Fraser — razor
dip and chuck it — bucket
dip and duck it — bucket
do me good — (fire)wood
don't be funny — dunny, meaning toilet
Dorothy Gish — dish
down and up — cup
Duke of York (1) — fork

elephant's tool — stool (furniture)
Enoch Arden — garden
Eric Baume — home
five-eight (1) — plate
fleas and scratches — matches (firelighters)
forward passes — glasses (drinking)
fox terrier pup — cup
Fred Astaire (1) — chair
Gene Tunney (2) — dunny, meaning toilet
God strike me dead — bed
God-forbids — kids, meaning children
Harry Randle — candle
Harry Tait — plate
highland fling (2) — string
Horace Tottle — bottle
itch and scratch — match (firelighter)
jam and honey — dunny, meaning toilet
knock me silly — billy (can); sometimes abbreviated to *knock me*
Lane Cove — stove
Lillian Gish (1) — dish
Marjorie Moon — spoon
meat with rubber — cover
Michael Pate — plate
Molly Maguire — fire (conflagration)
needle and thread — bed
Neville Wran — can (usually of beer)
Oscar King — string
pig's arse — glass
purple and mauve — stove
Reg Date — plate
ridgy didge — fridge, refrigerator
Rocky Ned — bed
Ron Randle — candle
roses red — bed
Ruby Moon — spoon
saucepan lids — kids, meaning children
tin lid/s (1) — kids, meaning children
trams and trains (2) — drains

tree and sap — tap
Uncle Ned (1) — bed
white and red — bed

Around the Johnny Horner — Structures and Physical Formations

In this list of rhyming slangs dealing with physical structures, the emphasis is also on the domestic.

apples and pears — stairs
bat and ball (2) — wall
Doctor Kildares — stairs
Duncan Hall — wall
eighteen pence (1) — fence
fleas and louse — house
Georgie Moore — door
holy ghosts (3) — fence posts
Johnny Horner — corner
Mickey Mouse (2) — house
Minnie Mouse — house
Mrs Murphy's chowder — powder
pay me (the) rent — tent
Queenie Paul — wall
Rickety Kate — gate
Roger Moore — floor
Rory O'Moore — floor
shovel and broom — room; often abbreviated to *shovel*

By Airy Jane or Jam Jar? — Transport

Modes and methods of transport are many, and most seem to have been pretty well rhymed.

airy Jane — aeroplane
baa lamb — tram
ball of twine — railway line
bat and ball (1) — stall, meaning stall one's car
big and bulky — sulky (horse-drawn vehicle)
Bill Buck (1) — truck

Bing and swing — wing

Blundstone boot — ute (short for utility wagon); usually abbreviated
  to *Blundstone*

bread and jam — tram

camel's hump — pump

Chuck Berry — ferry

church bazaar — car

do as you like — bike, bicycle

Donald Duck (2) — truck

dunny door — Commodore (make of car)

Frank Buck — truck

Frankie Laine (3) — train

Geoffrey Lane (2) — train

goose and duck — truck

hail and rain — train

Hedy Lamarr — car

jam jar — car

Jimmy Pike — bike

Joe Baxi — taxi

Joe Buck (2) — truck

Joe Maxi — taxi

King of Spain (1) — (aero)plane

King of Spain (3) — train

Kirk's Bazaar — car

lah de dah (1) — car

left jab — cab, meaning taxi

Lois Lane — train

Malcolm Clift (1) — lift (in a car)

Malcolm Clift (2) — lift (elevator)

Malvern Star — car

Marie La Var — car

Mars Bar — car

Mickey Duck (2) — truck

near and far (2) — car

pouring rain — train

roaring rain — train

Sandy McNab (1) — cab, meaning taxi

shower of rain — train

slapsie maxie — taxi
smash and grab — cab, meaning taxi
swear and cuss — bus
thunder and rain — railway train
Uncle Gus — bus
virgin bride — ride, as in a lift in a car
Willy wag — swag, meaning rolled up bedding
wind and rain — train
you beaut — ute (short for utility wagon)

Now We Violet Crumble! — Communication and Comprehension

One of the largest categories of rhyming slang contains terms that deal with some aspect of communication and/or understanding, as well as the various technologies available for transmitting comprehension — both positive and negative.

Approbation
apples and rice — nice
apples and spice — nice
brass tacks — facts
Breeze(y?) — easy, as in 'It's a *breeze*'
Golden Slipper — ripper, meaning excellent
Jimmy Britt (2) — good
Mickey Mouse (1) — grouse, meaning good
plate of meat — sweet, meaning all clear, all is well
plum pud — good
ridgy-dite — all right
Robin Hood — good
sugar and spice — nice
Wee Georgie Wood — good

Condemnation
Barry Crocker — shocker, meaning very bad
George the Third — turd (faeces), meaning something or someone despicable
gone and forgotten — rotten, meaning very bad
Henry the Third — turd (faeces), meaning something or someone despicable

James Hird — turd (faeces), meaning something or someone despicable

Joe Cocker — shocker, meaning very bad

King Richard the Third — turd (faeces), meaning a despicable person

Moreton Bay Fig (2) — gig, meaning someone who is irritatingly curious; a stickybeak

Richard the Third (2) — turd, meaning despicable person; usually abbreviated to 'a *Richard*'

rinkydinks — stinks, as in something is bad

Silver Link (2) — stink, meaning trouble

WA Inc — stink, meaning trouble

Wally Prig — gig, meaning someone who is irritatingly curious; a stickybeak

Comprehension

brown Joe — know, meaning to be informed, to understand; as in to be 'in the know'

Henry Berry (1) — jerry, meaning to understand

rotary hoe — righty-o: a term of agreement and/or comprehension

Violet Crumble — to tumble, meaning to suddenly understand something

Disbelief

Cobbler's awls — balls (testicles), meaning lacking in credibility; usually abbreviated to *cobblers*

grim and gory — story

Hawkie — lie; a rhyme on *pork pie* or *porky*, another rhyming slang for lie

John Dory — story

Kidstakes! — fakes

macaroni (1) — baloney, meaning nonsense or untruth

macaroni (3) — pony (smallest glass of beer served in NSW)

Nellie Bligh or Bly (6) — lie

Pork/ie pie — lie

post and rail — *fairytale, meaning a lie*

Sargents Pie/s (2) — lie

three bags full — bull, meaning nonsense or untruth

tosh and waddle — twaddle, meaning nonsense or untruth

2KY (2) — lie

Truth
Tom Thumb (2) — drum, meaning the truth or useful information of some kind, as in 'give us the drum'

Written
Canadian caper — paper
carburettor — letter, meaning correspondence
don't forget her (2) — letter, meaning correspondence
holy ghost (1) — post, mail
never better — letter, meaning correspondence
weight for age — page

Print
bottle of booze — news
Barry Fitzgerald — *Sydney Morning Herald* (newspaper)
cattle dog — catalogue
Jim Gerald — Herald (a newspaper in Sydney and Melbourne)
Johnny Raper — newspaper
nails and screws — news

Technology
Al Capone — phone, telephone
custard and jelly — telly (short for television)
Darby and Joan (2) — phone, telephone
Davey Crockett (1) — socket (lightbulb)
dog and bone — phone, telephone; usually abbreviated to 'the *dog*'
eau de Cologne (1) — phone, telephone
King Roto — photo, photograph
Ned Kelly (2) — telly (short for television)
ozone — phone, telephone

Speech and sound
Bernie Purcell — tell, meaning to communicate
Bill Lang — slang
Bill Peach — speech
box of toys — noise
deaf and dumb (1) — drum, meaning the truth or useful information of some kind
Jack Lang — slang

Johnny Moyes — noise
lost and found (2) — sound
penny dips — lips
philharmonic — tonic
roast pork — talk
slippery dip (1) — lip, meaning cheekiness

Bird's Lime — Time

The inevitable passing of time and instruments to measure it have produced a few, often evocative rhymes.

air raid warning — morning
bird's lime (1) — time (of day)
Bluey and Curly — early
bottle of Scotch — (wrist)watch
dickory dock — clock
Eva Bartok — clock
Gordon and Gotch (1) — (wrist)watch
Gypsy's warning — morning
half mast — past
Harry Lime — time of day
hickery dickery dock — clock
hot potato (pronounced 'pertater') (1) — later
Ivy's last — past
my mother's away — (the) other day
tick tock — clock

PART 3

Don't Forget Hers — Two Rhyming Slang Letters

'Duke' Tritton's Rhyming Slang Letter

This rhyming slang letter — one of the most important examples of Australian rhyming slang known today — was written by shearer, singer, yarnspinner and folk poet Harold Percy 'Duke' Tritton. Although the letter is dated 1905, it was almost certainly written much later. It includes the term *Oscar Asche* (cash), for instance, after a renowned British actor. Given that Asche was little known in Australia before 1909–11, when he toured Australia to great acclaim, it seems unlikely that his name would have been in the Australian public consciousness in 1905. Similarly, despite his role in the relief of Mafeking during the Boer War of 1899–1902, Baden Powell is unlikely to have been an Australian household name in 1905. Although his *Aids to Scouting* text had become a bestseller in 1903, he did not found the Scouting movement until 1907, upon which rests his major claim to popular acclamation.

Tritton, who died in 1965, was — by his own account and that of others — a bit of a joker.

The letter is addressed from 'Woop Woop Beyond the Black Stump'. The italicised terms are all to be found in the A–Z listings in Part 1 (pages 25 –169).

Dear *China Plate*,
No doubt you have wondered how your old *thief and robber* has been doing since you went back to the *steak and kidney*. I know you will find it hard to believe, but I am now a married man.

I think I had better tell you the *grim and gory* right from the *horse and cart*. When I saw you off on the *thunder and rain* at Weenia, I was feeling pretty lonely being left on my *Pat Malone*. So I rambled over to the *rubbity dub* and had a pint of *oh my dear*. In fact I had several and finished up in the dead house, broke to the wide. But they left me my *Willy Wag* and gave me a bit of tucker.

So I padded the hoof along the *frog and toad*, still feeling *butcher's hook*. I saw a lot of *Joe Blakes*, but don't know if they were dinkum or just the after effects of the grog. I came to a *bullock's liver* where I reckoned I'd have a *lemon squash* and liven up a bit. So I threw off my *barrel of fat*, *dicky dirt*, *rammy rousers* and *daisy roots*, and dived into the *mother and daughter*. It was *brave and bold*, and there were plenty of *cries and screeches*, but when I rubbed the *Cape of Good Hope* over myself, they went. I felt goodoh when I came out and dried myself with the *Baden Powell*. So I gathered some *do me good*, got out the *Jack Scratches* and lit the *Barney Maguire*, put on the *knock me silly* and made a brew of *Jimmy Lee*. Then I began to live again. The *hot cross bun* was down and the *silver spoon* was rising when I spread the Wagga and turned in. Next morning I was ready to move when a *pot and pan* driving a nice high stepping *tomato sauce* in a flash *big an' bulky* pulled up and asked if I was looking for *dodge an' shirk*. Being as flat as a goanna drinking at a Billabong I replied, 'My blanky oath'. 'Well,' he said, 'I want a man that knows farm work and can shear blades or machine.' I answered, 'Mate, I know farm work backwards, and as for shearing I can blind Tom Power with wool with the Wolseleys and give Jacky Howe fifty start with the blades any day in the week. (You remember *China*, I was never backward in coming forward.)

He laughed and said 'Well I really don't want a man that good, but if twenty-five bob and tucker is any good to you, hop in.' I hopped in. We drove about ten miles to his place and he introduced me to his *cheese and kisses* and four *tin lids*, two *mother's joys* and two *twist and twirls*. When I remarked he had a nice little family, he said 'My eldest is inside. Come in and meet her.' We went in and I met her. She put out her hand and said 'How do you do?' My *grocer's cart* was racing like grandfather's clock when it slipped out of gear. After about ten seconds I managed to croak something that sounded like 'Pleased to meetcha'.

Straight wire, *China*, she is the most beautiful *ocean liner* I ever saw. Her name is Mary. Her *Dublin fair* is sort of brown, her *mince pies* are blue, her *north and south* was made for kissing and from the top of her *lump of lead* to her *plates of meat* she is perfect. And six months ago she became my *trouble an' strife*. Sometimes I wonder why she married me, and when I asked her, she just smiles and says 'It must have been because of your good looks.'

I have tossed my *cherry ripe* into the *Barney Maguire* and I have given the *mud and ooze* right away. I can go into the *rubbity dub* and have a lemonade, breasting the *near and far* with booze hounds drinking *Tom thumb*, *young and frisky*, *oh my dear*, or *Huckleberry Finn*, and no one ever laughs at me or calls me sissy because I am drinking lolly water. I hope they don't ever forget themselves, because Mary doesn't like the idea of me fighting. She thinks it is brutal. I go to *roll and lurch* every Sunday, and the *Winchcombe Carson* reckons I've got a bosker *let's rejoice*, and often gets me to sing *hers an' hims* on my *Pat Malone*. And I like meeting the *spire and steeple*. They are all nice blokes and sheilas.

And I can come home now after a hard day's yakka, change into clean duds, shove my *Dutch pegs* under the *Cain and Abel*, wade through half a dozen dishes of scran that we used to dream of when we were on the track, then finish up with *Uncle Ned and roll me in the gutter*. No doubt about it, my Mary is a bottling *babbling brook*.

And I am popular with the family, and the neighbours. So everything is jakalorum. I'm teaching Mary and all the *tin lids* in the district to *dark an'dim*, and they reckon I'm the bees knees, ants pants and nits tits all rolled into one. If I speak of Barney Keiran, Alick Wickham or the Cavells, they reckon I could give any one of them ten yards in a hundred.

My father-in-law built a nice cottage for Mary and me, so we are as snug as bugs in a rug, and it seems that the only troubles we are likely to have are little ones.

It is hard to believe that two years ago I was humpin' the drum with you, spending all my *Oscar Asche* on *mud and ooze*, and two-up, fighting and brawling, stoushing *John Hops*, getting run in and spending a few days in the cooler, pinching the squatter's lambs when we were out of meat, jumping the rattler and acting all round like a pair of half-witted clowns.

I told Mary it would be nice to have you up here for a holiday, but she is not real keen on the idea because she thinks you have been a bad influence in my life, and you might lead me astray again. Which just goes to show how innocent she is.

Well *China*, this *don't forget her* is getting long and I am out of *nails and screws*, and I have to catch the *Holy Ghost*, so will end off with all the best from,

Your old *thief and robber*,
Duke

A Rhyming Slang Letter from the Trenches

The following rhyming slang letter appeared in July 1917 in the British soldiers' newspaper *The Direct Hit*. Apparently penned by Lance-Corporal A. J. Lilliman, Royal Fusiliers, it provides an insight into the popularity of rhyming slang among World War I troops. Couched in the form of a letter to the writer's sister, it provides some news of training camp activity and expected departure to the Front, as well as an impending visit home during an upcoming period of leave. It is doubtful that this letter was ever sent, or that it was ever meant to be. Like Tritton's effort, it seems more likely to have been a manifestation of the fascination for rhyming slang at the time and place — something the editor of *The Direct Hit* also mentions in his introduction to the letter.

Many of the terms are not recorded elsewhere — meaning other publications and dictionaries of rhyming slang — or have other meanings, and so can either be considered personal inventions of the writer and/or terms that had a brief and perhaps restricted currency among those with whom he socialised.

My Dear *Just-Missed-'Er*,
Many thanks for the *all-the-better* and the *Windsor Castle* received the last *pip-squeak*. I am glad to hear mother and the *old pot-and-pan* are still keeping fit, and that the *Giddy-Gaby* is doing well. The contents of the parcel were highly appreciated by the *Sain-Foys* in my *water-butt*; the *piper's knees* went down well for supper with a piece of *mine-host* made in front of the *old-cove*, and a drop of *pig's ear*. The *you-can-bets* smoked like small *American bars*. Keep on sending the *bones-and-rags*. The *give-and-take* was one of the best, whilst the *small-kits* came in very handy on the *stiff-as-starch*.

We are still hiding in the *rob-and-pillage* and expect to be here until the *lager beer*. I suppose we shall be going *on-our-knees* early in the *wedding ring*; it is quite time we put some of the Germans' *Hampstead Heath* down their ugly *nanny-goats*. I am fed-up with cleaning my *small-trifle* to satisfy the Sergeant's *mince pie*, and with firing nothing but *muddy-banks*.

I went sick the other day with a *saucy-goat*, but the *oh-*

dear-oh! only gave me a *darling-mine* with *Sleeping Beauty*, so I went on *first-aid* the following day. I am pleased to say I am quite *William-Tell* again now, although the *tough-as-leather* has left me with a bit of a *up-the-hill* and a slight *old-toff*.

I had a *double-mine* from Jimmy last week. He has been in the *iron-wrenches* for three weeks now, and so far has come through all *John-Bright*. He says he is going back to the *fried-fillets* in a day or two for a *give-and-be-blest*. I am glad he is safe and *baker's-round*, for Jimmy was always a good *world's-end* to me.

Now I must hurry up with my *you-and-me*, get a *wave-after-wave* and a shine up, just call into the *always-mean* to get a *broom-handle* to light me to my *white-and-red* tonight, and then I'm off to the *knock-me-down* to see the pictures at the new *near-and-far*.

I am hoping to see you shortly, for I believe we are to get four day's *Adam-and-Eve*. So keep you're eye on *six o'clock*, and be sure to meet me at the *Birth-of-a-Nation* when I let you know the *only-way* I am coming, and the time the *might-and-main* will arrive.

Write soon, and don't forget the *old-nags*
Your loving Brother, SAM
Lce-Corp. A. J. Lilliman, RF

The rhyming slang terms used in this letter translate as:
just-missed-her — sister
all-the-better — letter
Windsor-Castle — parcel
last pip-squeak — last week
old pot-and-pan — old man (father)
Giddy-Gaby — baby
the Sain-Foys — the boys
water-butt — hut
piper's knees — cheese
mine-host — toast
old-cove — stove

pig's ear — beer
you-can-bets — cigarettes
bones and rags — fags (cigarettes)
American bars — cigars
give-and-take — cake
small-kits — biscuits
stiff-as-starch — march
rob-and-pillage — village
lager-beer — (new) year
on-our-knees — overseas
wedding ring — spring
Hampstead Heath — teeth
nanny-goats — throats
small-trifle — rifle
mince pie — eye
muddy-banks — blanks
saucy-goat — sore throat
oh-dear-oh! — MO (medical officer)
darling-mine — number nine (pill) (a laxative)
Sleeping Beauty — duty
first-aid — parade
William-Tell — well
tough-as-leather — weather
up-the-hill — chill
old-toff — cough
double-mine — line (letter)
iron-wrenches — trenches
all John-Bright — all right
fried-fillets — billets
give-and-be-blest — rest
safe and baker's-round — safe and sound
world's-end — friend
you-and-me — tea
wave-after-wave — shave
always-mean — canteen
broom-handle — candle
white-and-red — bed
knock-me-down — town

near-and-far — cinema
Adam-and-Eve — leave
six o'clock — clock
Birth-of-a-Nation — station (from the title of D. W. Griffith movie just released at this time)
only-way — day
might-and-main — train
old-nags — fags (cigarettes)

SOURCES AND SELECT REFERENCES

The earliest reference to rhyming slang as a sizeable body of folk speech is contained in *The Vulgar Tongue* by 'Ducange Anglicus', published in London in 1857, with an extended edition released two years later. John Camden Hotten also noted the form in his 1859 work *The Slang Dictionary*, claiming an informant told him that rhyming slang had been around for perhaps fifteen years, which places its origins to at least the 1840s in England. Eric Partridge, in his *Slang Today and Tomorrow*, produces some not very convincing 17th- and 18th-century possibilities that he thinks might be the progenitors of the form — as do one or two other slang collectors, though none of these is known to turn up in Australian folk speech. Julian Franklyn, himself a Cockney, theorises that rhyming slang arose from a collision of Cockney tongueplay and Irish exuberance. While this appears to be a sensible suggestion — that also accommodates the existence of rhyming slang in Irish vernacular — no one else has taken it seriously, possibly because it depends to some extent on stereotyping.

Early collections of Australian speech include no rhyming slang, and the first records of the form here seem to be in newspaper and magazine articles of the late 19th and early 20th century, as outlined in the Introduction. There has been, among earlier lexicographers at least, a certain disdain for rhyming slang. Partridge did not think much of it and neither did Sidney Baker, compiler of the classic *The Australian Language*. Determined research into periodicals and other primary sources might fill in the patchy picture we do have of the history of the form in Britain, Australia and elsewhere, particularly in its regional and occupational variations.

The sources for the rhyming slang that appears in this book and the history of the form in this country are various. The entries have been derived, in part, from previous published collections, from appearances in more general collections of Australian speech, as well as the work of lexicographers. The author has also collected rhyming slang since the late 1960s, either through direct conversation and questioning, through radio and other media outlets, including the worldwide web and has also benefited from the input of other folklorists using similar approaches.

Alderson, W., 'Carnie Talk from the West Coast', *American Speech* 28: 2, May 1953.

All Downunder website, available at www.alldownunder.com (5 July 2007).

Anon., *Instructions for American Servicemen in Australia 1942*, War and Navy Departments, Washington DC, 1942.

Australian War Memorial, 'Glossary of Slang and Peculiar Terms in Use in the AIF', compiled *c*.1922 by AWM staff, mainly under A. G. Pretty, then Chief Librarian, available at the Australian National Dictionary Centre website www.anu.edu.au/ANDC/index.php (May 2008).

Ayto, J., *The Oxford Dictionary of Rhyming Slang*, Oxford University Press, 2002.

Baker, S., *The Australian Language*, first published in 1945, 2nd edn, Currawong Publishing, Sydney, 1966, Sun Books 1970, 1976.

Businessballs website, available at www.businessballs.com/cockney.htm (May 2008).

Downing, W., *Digger Dialects*, Lothian, Sydney, 1919.

Factor, J., Kidspeak: *A Dictionary of Australian Children's Words, Expressions and Games*, Melbourne University Press, Melbourne, 2000 ('children' defined here as being from four to 18 years of age).

Franklyn, J., *A Dictionary of Rhyming Slang*, Routledge & Kegan Paul, London (1960), 2nd edition with additions 1961.

Garth, John H., 'Some Australian Slang', *Australian Magazine*, 1908 9:2, pp.1249–52.

Green, J., *Cassell's Dictionary of Rhyming Slang*, Cassell, London, 2000.

Gunn, J., 'Twentieth Century Australian Idiom' in Ramson, W. (ed), *English Transported: Essays on Australian English*, ANU Press, Canberra, 1970.

Hughes, J., *Australian Words and Their Origins*, Oxford University Press, Melbourne, 1989.

Johansen, J., *The Dinkum Dictionary*, Penguin, 1988 and in subsequent editions.

Lambert, James, 'Additions to the Australian Lexicographical Record', Australian National Dictionary Centre website, available at www.anu.edu.au/ANDC/index.php (September 2008).

Lambert, James, *Macquarie Australian Slang Dictionary*, Macquarie Dictionary, Sydney, 2004.

Laugeson, A., Diggerspeak: *The Language of Australians at War*, Oxford University Press, Melbourne, 2005.

Lillo, A., 'From Alsatian Dog to Wooden Shoe: Linguistic Xenophobia in Rhyming Slang', *English Studies* 82:4, 2001.

Lind, L., *Sea Jargon: A Dictionary of the Unwritten Language of the Sea*, Kangaroo Press, Kenthurst, 1982.

Little Bitch Down Under website, available at www.jendi.bowmeow. com.au (5 July 2007).

McAndrew, A., 'Hosties and Garbos: A Look Behind Diminutives and Pejoratives in Australian English', in Blank, C. (ed), *Language and Civilization*, Vol. 2, Frankfurt am Main, 1992.

Mathews, William, *Cockney Past and Present: A Short History of the Dialect of London*, George Routledge & Sons, London, 1938.

Maurer, D., 'The Australian Element in American Criminal Argots', *American Speech*, October 1944.

Meredith, J., *Learn to Talk Old Jack Lang*, Kangaroo Press, Sydney, 1984 (includes 'Duke' Tritton's rhyming slang letter dated 1905).

Meredith, J., *Learn to Talk Old Jack Lang*, titled *Dinkum Aussie Slang: A Handbook of Australian Rhyming Slang*, 2nd expanded edn, Kangaroo Press, Kenthurst, 1991.

Ozwords, Australian National Dictionary Centre, Australian National University, Canberra (various editions).

Partridge, E., *Slang Today and Yesterday*, Routledge & Kegan Paul, London (1933), 4th edn, 1972.

Ramsay, J., *Cop It Sweet*! Allegheney News Service, Sydney, 1977. (Ramsay was a founder of the *King's Cross Whisper* newspaper, in which was published a good deal of 1960s and '70s rhyming slang.)

Seal Collection — mostly unpublished slang collated since the late 1960s from predominantly oral sources, mainly in NSW and WA, as well as from print and from the worldwide web. Some included in Seal, G., *Soundings: A Collection of Australian Folk Speech*, Antipodes Press, Perth, 1990 and *The Lingo: Listening to Australian English*, University of NSW Press, Sydney, 1999.

Simes, G., *A Dictionary of Australian Underworld Slang*, Oxford University Press, Melbourne, 1993.

Spilsted E., typescript, 'The Bloody Near Definitive Book of Aussie Rhyming (and other) Slang', nd. (*c*. early–mid 1990s), in possession of Warren Fahey. Subsequently published in various editions of

The Great Aussie Slang Book, 3rd edn, Eric Spilsted Publishing, Sydney 2001, though there are differences between the published and unpublished versions.

St Leon, M., 'Australian Circus Language', *English Today*, 10, 1, 1994.

The White Hat website, available at www.whitehat.com.au (March 2008).

Troubridge, Sir St Vincent, 'Some Notes on Rhyming Argot, *American Speech*, Vol. 21, No. 1, Feb 1946, pp. 45–47.

Wilde, W., 'Notes on Thief Talk', *The Journal of American Folklore*, Vol. 13, No. 11, Oct–Dec 1890, pp. 303–10 (reviewing and correcting George Matsell's *Vocabulum, or the Rogue's Lexicon*, published in 1859).

Wilkes, G. A., *Stunned Mullets and Two-Pot Screamers: A Dictionary of Australian Colloquialisms*, Oxford University Press, Melbourne, 2008 [5th edn; 1st edition 1978].

Wright, Peter, *Cockney Dialect and Slang*, Batsford, London, 1981.